D1597043

ARCHITECTURE AND SOCIAL REFORM IN LATE-VICTORIAN LONDON

FOR STEVE

DEBORAH E. B. WEINER

Architecture and social reform in late-Victorian London

MANCHESTER UNIVERSITY PRESS
Manchester and New York

distributed exclusively in the USA and Canada by St. Martin's Press

Copyright © Deborah E. B. Weiner 1994

Published by Manchester University Press
Oxford Road, Manchester M13 9NR, UK
and Room 400, 175 Fifth Avenue, New York, NY 10010, USA

Distributed exclusively in the USA and Canada
by St. Martin's Press, Inc., 175 Fifth Avenue, New York, NY 10010, USA

British Library Cataloguing-in-Publication Data
A catalogue record for this book is available from the British Library

Library of Congress Cataloguing-in-Publication Data
Weiner, Deborah E. B.
  Architecture and social reform in late-Victorian London / Deborah E. B. Weiner.
    p.   cm.
  Includes bibliographical references.
  ISBN 0–7190–3914–2
    1. Public architecture – England – London.   2. Architecture and society –
England – London – History – 19th century.   3. Architecture, Victorian – England
– London.   4. London (England) – Buildings, structures, etc.   I. Title.
NA9050.5.W45   1994
720′.1′030942109034 – dc20   93–15941
ISBN 0 7190 3914 2 *hardback*

720.103
W42a

m.r.
Printed in Great Britain
by Biddles Limited, Guildford and King's Lynn

CONTENTS

University Libraries
Carnegie Mellon University
Pittsburgh PA 15213-3890

ILLUSTRATIONS

Credits

[1] by permission of *Architectural Review*

[3, 5, 21, 58, 62, 63, 65, 67, 69, 73, 76, 80, 81] by permission of the British Library

[7, 9, 11, 30, 38, 40] by permission of Corporation of London, Greater London Record Office

[12, 19, 20, 34, 36, 41–48, 60, 68, 91] by permission of Greater London Photography Library

[17] by permission of Chiswick Public Library, Hounslow

[49] by permission of RIBA

[53–55] by permission of Southwark Local History Library

[56] by permission of City Parochial Foundation

[57, 72] by permission of the Tower Hamlets Local History Library and Archives

[59, 70, 71] by permission of the British Architectural Library/RIBA

[61] courtesy of J. Mordaunt Crook

[78, 79] by permission of the Horniman Museum and Library

[82, 87, 88, 89] by permission of the photographer, Martin Charles

ACKNOWLEDGEMENTS

My debts are many, and I cannot possibly thank everyone who has, at different times, helped me with this project. I would like, however, to express my particular gratitude to Thomas Crow whose support and inspiring clarity of thought was of immense assistance, to Adrian Forty who gave the manuscript a careful reading at a critical stage and offered invaluable suggestions, and to Joan Weinstein who offered friendship and moral support throughout. I owe a special debt to Timothy J. Clark from whom I learned a great deal about ways to think about the relationship of art and society.

Many other friends and colleagues have assisted and I would like to acknowledge the help of Robert Gutman, Catherine Phillips, Chester Rapkin, Ruth Richardson, Andrew Saint, Stephanie Shields, Mark Swenarton, James Winter, and Anthony Vidler. Anna Davin generously shared her own unpublished work on the childhood of working class girls in the nineteenth century, and Seth Koven kindly permitted me to read his unpublished doctoral dissertation on the Settlement movement. My sister-in-law, Debra Weiner, offered invaluable assistance in preparing this manuscript for publication.

I would like to gratefully acknowledge financial support received while working on this project from a Postdoctoral Research in Art History and the Humanities Award from the J. Paul Getty Foundation, the University of California at Davis Commmittee on Research and Humanities Institute, and the University of British Columbia.

The conception of this book owes much to my parents, Ethel H. Blacker, and the late Irwin R. Blacker, who first taught me crucial lessons about struggles for social justice. My greatest debt is to Steven Weiner who was with me from beginning to end and to whom this book is dedicated.

ABBREVIATIONS

COS   Charity Organisation Society
GLRO Greater London Record Office
LCC   London County Council
PRO   Public Record Office
SBL   School Board for London

INTRODUCTION

The subject of this book is the architecture of institutions of reform and philanthropy built in late nineteenth century London. Amidst the squalid sea of brick tenements and working class two-up, two-down houses, huge buildings were erected which contrasted dramatically in both their scale and style with all else in these neighborhoods: public elementary schools, free public libraries, Settlement houses, the art gallery and the museum. In Whitechapel, for example, in the heart of London's East End, public elementary schools were built in the 1870s, imposing brick buildings two or three storeys high that accommodated over twelve hundred children and towered over the adjacent cottages. Above the costermongers and lodging houses of Commercial Road rose buildings in the 1880s which looked more like Elizabethan manor houses than the urban centers of social work which they were, buildings of red brick with stone dressings, replete with diamond-paned windows and heavy chimney stacks. Nearby on Mile End Road a grand neo-Byzantine pleasure palace with a cupola, towering minarets, a great hall, social rooms and winter garden was planned, funding to come from a public subscription in wealthier London. On Whitechapel High Street a library and a museum, both of red brick with terracotta ornament and Flemish gables in the picturesque Queen Anne style, were opened in the early 1890s. They were soon followed by a picture gallery displaying the best of the contemporary British painters; with wide and welcoming door, the gallery was built in the most fashionable style of the Arts and Crafts movement, the façade decorated with a tree of life motif in terracotta, awaiting a mosaic by one of the best known of the Arts and Crafts decorators.

Today many of these curious specimens of Victorian philanthropy and educational reform remain standing. They are the architecture of everyday life, part of the familiar background of the city, used by large numbers of people, though in many cases their initial functions have changed over time. When these buildings were first opened, however, they were understood as signs of change in a movement of social reform and education; their erection was, in fact, often the subject of debate and dissension – or intense enthusiasms. Some perceived them as representing the redemptive benefits of middle class values extended to the working classes; others, especially the residents in whose midst they were built, saw them as invading the traditional and familiar patterns of daily life. The buildings were understood by both the giver and recipient as representing change, and the nature of that change spoke of what was at stake in late nineteenth century England.

These buildings remain largely ignored by architectural historians. Their designers for the most part do not belong to the canon of great architects, nor are these building types – schools, Settlement houses, philanthropic experiments of various kinds – seen as major works of art. This study examines these buildings, not in an attempt to add new monuments or new architects to the canon, but rather in order to understand the ways in which architecture carried meaning as one of the tools by which the newly emergent institutions defined their goals and were, in turn, understood by their public. Rather than examining these buildings as primarily the achievement of particular architects, or as examples of the development of, or reaction to, a particular style, the design of these buildings is examined in terms of the social relations which informed their production and use. It is for this reason that architectural production is examined here within the context of the social history of the period.

Focusing upon the social relations involved in the production and use of buildings, E. P. Thompson's metaphor of 'theatre' suggests the way in which buildings can serve as the site of class negotiations and offers a particularly useful way of understanding how architecture functioned within education and philanthropy in the late nineteenth century, a period of profound change. In his description of eighteenth century aristocratic culture, Thompson characterises the ways in which the eighteenth century gentry presented itself to its social inferiors

> just as their formidable mansions imposed their presence, apart from, but guarding over, the village or town. Their appearance has much the same studied, self-consciousness of public theatre[1]

The buildings which were designed to play a part in the educational and cultural transformation of working class London in the late nineteenth century can similarly be understood as providing a stage on which social relations were to be recast; and they were sets for productions designed and paid for by outsiders for the communities in which they were built.

Within the metaphor of public theatre, style can be understood as one of the means by which the newly emergent institutions conveyed their meanings to their publics. Reference to past styles, whether to the Classical tradition, to Gothic or to Queen Anne is, therefore, understood as a means of expression bounded within a given moment in history.

The notion of a stage also makes clear a formal issue which is found in architectural production and discourse today. The public elementary school, the Board School, for example, was a large building self-consciously decorated with the Flemish gables and white sash windows of the Queen Anne Revival, which itself borrowed from seventeenth and eighteenth century English vernacular architecture. But unlike the middle class domestic architecture most closely associated with the Queen Anne Revival, the schools were a simplified version with just enough historicist detail to suggest the relationship to the more elaborate versions of the style. The street façade of the schools, with their carefully selected, minimal ornament provided a symbolic wrapping for these buildings, the 'decorated shed', in effect. On entering these buildings one would have found the huge, stark halls devoid of any of the decorative features associated with the cosy domestic Revival. The visitor to these early schools encountered quite a different story about the nature of education imparted to working class children from that suggested by the public face of these schools. On the inside one would have found a curriculum also stripped to the basics, a no frills education on which – like the school buildings – as little money as possible was spent.

The architecture of the institutions examined here suggests ways in which a symbolic architecture was generated, an architecture with a readable, indeed didactic, vocabulary which was intended to be comprehensible to both ratepaying public and the public which daily used the buildings. Indeed, the architect of the London School Board referred to his buildings as 'sermons in brick':

> The lessons sought to be taught in such buildings as these – the sermons in brick, so to speak – are intentionally simple, never recondite or too complex. . . . We do not expect a costermonger to understand or appreciate the sonatas of Beethoven, the operas of Mozart, or the subtle perfections of Greek Art in the time of Pericles. We do expect him to comprehend a piece of practical advice about building[2]

The desire to produce an architecture accessible to a wide public, to ordinary men and women, one which conjures up English traditions through the use of explicit historical references, and which emphasises elevation over plan, is similar indeed to some of the demands heard for architecture in Britain today. Architecture – particularly as expressed in the revival of Classical architecture – is again called upon to evoke nostalgia for a world understood as more coherent and harmonious as once more there are fears of cultural erosion and the loss of traditional expressions of social cohesion and deference.

In a way profoundly reminiscent of the late Victorian experience, in the United States as well as in Britain throughout the 1980s, the public was enjoined to bridge the growing gulf between rich and poor in urban centers through private philanthropy as the state withdrew support in the field of social welfare. Even in education, where government intervention was acknowledged as essential since the early nineteenth century, free market forces were invited to engender competition and lower costs – payment by results, school league tables, a return to the three Rs, vouchers for private schools – that is, Victorian market solutions, were promoted in discussions regarding educational provision for the poor.

Not only do the buildings examined here provide the background architecture of cities today, but the social crises which gave rise to the late Victorian institutions remain with us. Indeed, an examination of nineteenth century educational practice and social welfare suggests how little has changed. The difficulties which late nineteenth century architects faced in giving meaning to their buildings at a time when profound changes threatened traditional social relationships foreshadowed, in significant ways, the architectural solutions proffered today.

Notes

1 E. P. Thompson, 'Patrician society, plebian culture', *Journal of Social History* (1974), p. 389.
2 E. R. Robson, 'Art as applied to town schools', *Art Journal* (1881), p. 140.

CHAPTER ONE

London, Liberals and social reform

'Look at those big, isolated clumps of buildings rising above the slates, like brick islands in a lead coloured sea.'
'The Board Schools.'
'Lighthouses, my boy! Beacons of the future! Capsules with hundreds of bright little seeds in each, out of which will spring the wiser, better England of the future.'[1]

In 1892 Arthur Conan Doyle's hero praised the new elementary schools built in London following the Education Act. The schools were 'lighthouses', they were 'beacons of the future'. The schools, easily recognisable by their great size and distinctive style, wrapped as they were in the dress of the Queen Anne Revival, could be read by enlightened middle class ratepayers as symbols of a wise and prudent beneficence which had extended the advantages of education and civilisation to the working classes. Yet contemporary with these assumptions was an alternative interpretation, one which likened the construction of these schools to 'planting a fort in an enemy's country. The building was the symbol of tyranny and oppression'[2] [1].

How did these two conflicting interpretations of the hundreds of new elementary schools emerge? How was their message read and understood by both the ratepayers who paid for them as well as the parents and children who used them? In what ways were these and other buildings of philanthropy and social reform expressive of the ambitions of their founders? In what ways did they play a part in the struggle for social reform in the period? In what ways did architectural traditions play a part in determining the design of these newly emergent institutions? Above all, in what ways was and is architecture expressive of the social relations involved in its production?

1] Board School in south London, seen in situ

i   London divided

In the final decades of the nineteenth century a variety of institutions, both public and private, secular and religious, were designed to produce a harmonious society by transforming the working class into industrious, responsive citizens as so deemed by their social betters. In the heart of the most populated neighborhoods of late Victorian London buildings were demolished, often dispersing local residents, in order to raise centers of educational and philanthropic work: the public elementary school, the free public library, the Settlement house, the mission, the free public art gallery. Indeed, the largest secular building campaign in the Victorian period was the erection of nearly five hundred elementary schools in London alone in the decades following the passage of the Education Act of 1870. Although these new institutions were built in cities throughout the nation, in every locality specific conditions shaped the nature of these institutions.

The institutions that emerged in London were not unique to England, but London's role as capital city, as well as its sheer size and wealth, meant that activities there were closely watched elsewhere. Since the 1840s London had surpassed other regions in its rate of growth; between 1841 and 1911 over half the new jobs created were in London and the south-east. In the Victorian period, at the height of the nation's industrial might, London accounted for a greater concentration of wealth than did the industrial centers of the north.[3]

But by the 1860s the geographical separation of classes in London existed on an unprecedented scale. Central and East London, with its docks, markets, railway terminals, and many gasworks, remained the source of employment for unskilled labor, a casual labor force dependent upon easy access to employment. The East End was also the center of the 'sweated' trades, including tailoring, bootmaking and furniture making, and of the specialised trades that survived with apprenticeship systems – bookbinding, printing and coopering.[4] The movement of professionals and the propertied, as well as the ordinary middle class, out of Central and East London had occurred gradually over the preceding forty years, but it was given new impetus by street clearance projects and the construction of railways.[5] Whereas London in the eighteenth century had been a city in which rich and poor lived in close proximity to one another, poor housing adjacent to fashionable squares, the discovery of unsatisfactory sanitary conditions – polluted water and insanitary drainage – which affected not only the poor but their equally susceptible neighbors, hastened the transformation of the city. The campaign for healthier conditions was one factor which drove the frightened middle classes to seek refuge in the suburbs. Property developers, in turn, discovered that social segregation was advantageous in promoting residential developments.[6] The census of 1861 indicated that the division of London was virtually complete.[7] London was a city characterised by a dramatic geographic division of wealth: West End and East End, rich and poor.

The separation of rich and poor was not unique to London and had, in fact, been noted as a feature of manufacturing towns since the beginning of the industrial revolution. In 1845 Disraeli had already written of the

> Two nations between whom there is no intercourse and no sympathy; who are as ignorant of each other's habits, thoughts, and feelings, as if they were dwellers in different zones, or inhabitants of different planets; who are formed by a different breeding, are fed by a different food, are ordered by different manners, and are not governed by the same laws . . . THE RICH AND THE POOR.[8]

But nowhere was the process as complete as in London.[9] In London in the final decades of the nineteenth century the division of the population into 'two nations' was recognised increasingly as a threat to the very fabric of English society.

The differences among poor neighborhoods were lost in a pervasive single image of the East End.[10] The East End and the area south of the river were perceived by middle class Londoners as a world separate and distant from the West End and the suburbs. It was not merely distance, however, which separated the inhabitants, but the gulf of experience between them. It was a frequent refrain among writers and journalists to refer to the East End as a foreign land, 'beset with danger for the inexperienced explorer.'[11] It was

> a dark continent that is within easy walking distance of the General Post Office. This continent will . . . be found as interesting as any of the newly-explored lands which engage the attention of the Royal Geographical Society – the wild races who inhabit it will, I trust, gain public sympathy as easily as those savage tribes for whose benefit the Missionary Societies never cease to appeal for funds.[12]

In setting a story in the East End, the popular novelist Walter Besant reminded his readers of

> that region of London which is less known to Englishmen than if it were situated in the wildest part of Colorado, or amongst the pine forests of British Columbia. . . . Two millions of people, or there-abouts, live in the East End of London. That seems a good-sized population for an utterly unknown town. . . . If anything happens in the east, people at the other end have to stop and think before they can remember where the place may be.[13]

Mrs Henrietta Barnett, wife of Canon Samuel Barnett, with whom she devoted most of her life to working with the people of the East End, wrote,

> One lady, after a visit to St. George's-in-the-East and Stepney, expressed great astonishment to find that the people lived in *houses*. She had expected that they abode, not exactly in tents, but in huts, old railway carriages, caravans, or squatted against a wall[14]

The perception of the East as a separate world, unknown to the average resident in the West, persisted for decades. In drawing a picture of a street in the East End, the novelist Arthur Morrison, mimicking the middle class vantage point, wrote in 1891:

> The East-end is a vast city, as famous in its way as any city men have built. But who knows the East-end? It is down through Cornhill and out beyond Leadenhall Street and Aldgate pump, one will say, a shocking place, where he once went with a curate. An evil growth of slums which hide human creeping things; where foul men and women live on penn'orths of gin, where collars and clean shirts are not yet invented, where every citizen wears a black eye, and no man combs his hair[15]

In 1901 Charles Masterman, later Liberal MP, having worked among the poor, wrote as if from the vantage point of a local inhabitant of the 'abyss':

No intercourse or traffic takes place across the border line of the Abyss. The suburban race is hurried through our territory high on embankments or buried deep in tubes . . . an armed neutrality ranges along the limits of our region, guarded by jealous spies. Occasionally a suburban dweller gazing around in an attitude of discomfort is found pilgrimaging through our territory; occasionally the forlorn sight of a child of the Abyss, trailing behind it a line of youthful companions, inflames with disordered visions of small pox and virulent fevers the respectabilities of some quiet suburban avenue. But on the whole the tacit agreement has been faithfully maintained on both sides; the frontier being recognised as the southern limit for the wandering of our children and the boundary north of which suburbandom cannot penetrate without peril to its soul.[16]

The middle class residents of the West End were able in their rhetoric to relegate the population of the East End to the status of foreigner, even a wild race. The East End remained for decades the 'abyss' in the consciousness of outsiders, explored by those with the courage to trespass into the unknown. As one literary historian has phrased it, writers 'seem never to walk or ride into a slum, they "penetrate" it.'[17]

But the existence of poverty of such magnitude in the city was impossible to dismiss entirely. In England as in no other country was the extent of poverty as carefully documented in the late nineteenth century, an effort that one historian has called the 'pursuit of certainty'.[18] From Henry Mayhew's *London Labour and the London Poor* of 1851 to Charles Booth's massive seventeen volume, door-to-door study, *Life and Labour in London*, at the turn of the century, the nature and measure of poverty in London was available to all. Social surveys in the 1890s documented the poverty and characteristics of the inhabitants. Journalists ventured into the unknown to report their findings; Jack London went disguised as a 'seafaring-man-who-had-lost-his-clothes and money' to see for himself 'the people of the abyss'.[19]

In the popular press the East End stood for all that was sordid and frightening in the Victorian city, though London south of the Thames was also known as a place of extreme poverty. Charles Booth recorded the conditions of south London where 'Poverty in its darkest form reigns supreme'; where, 'A miasma seems to float over the long sordid street fatal to the living of anything worth calling life'.[20] Readers of West London and the northern suburbs were offered journalistic accounts of a population, which, like that of the East End, was separate and distinct:

> In South London there are two millions of people. It is therefore one of the great cities of the world. It stands upon an area about twelve

miles long and five or six broad. . . . It is a city without a municipality, without a centre, without a civic history; it has no newspapers, magazines, or journals; it has no university; it has no colleges apart from medicine; it has no intellectual, artistic, scientific, musical, literary centre . . . it has no theatres, except of a very popular or humble kind; it has no clubs, it has no public buildings, it has no West End.

They were given accounts of a 'teeming multitudinous life; these armies of men, women, and children living in the slums and in the huge, unlovely barracks.'[21]

ii   'Worthy' and 'unworthy' poor

It was the geographic separation of rich and poor in cities that was increasingly blamed for the class tensions of British society. It was argued that in earlier times rich and poor had lived beside one another, even in the city. In the country, the myth went, the landed gentry had known the peasant who worked their land, but the new separation of rich and poor who no longer associated produced an entirely new relationship. Lack of knowledge of each other, it was believed, bred suspicion and distrust. According to Masterman, 'In the old days all classes lived together in small towns and villages, the employee boarding sometimes with, always near, his master. To-day we have East and West Ends, business quarters, manufacturing quarters, residential quarters, endless vistas of villadom, acres of Lambeth and Whitechapel.'[22]

Traditional forms of charity, in which the relationships between rich and poor were defined, were no longer possible.[23] In the city, segregation by neighborhood necessitated a complex and often anonymous network. There was no bond which developed between giver and recipient when the West End gentleman made his contribution. The historian Gareth Stedman Jones has pointed to this change as critical to class perceptions in late nineteenth century London.[24] Charity had been a means of confirming class relationships: to accept without repaying had meant subordination and subservience.[25] But in Victorian London the status-maintaining function of charity, it was argued, was no longer effective. 'In London,' as one contemporary stated, 'the hand which has given and the hand that has received never felt the warm electricity of each other's touch.'[26] It was increasingly suggested that the real reason for class tensions was that the geographical gulf between classes had made the old status-maintaining functions inoperative.

Middle and upper class responses to this situation varied but all were characterised by a sense of urgency. 'Bridging the gulf' was seen as one means of restoring harmony. Penetrating the 'terra incognita', as the East End was sometimes called, and establishing relationships with the populace, were seen as the hope of the future. In many ways this foreign land was to be colonised, and the attitude was that of securing strongholds in these neighborhoods. A variety of institutions were established from which, it was hoped, association would breed a renewed and warmer relationship between classes. These institutions would provide a salutory influence on the poorer classes, re-establishing the old ties.

Critical to an understanding of the new institutions is the genealogy of the debates on poverty in nineteenth century Britain. What to do with the growing number of urban poor had been a problem debated early in the century, solutions to which found tangible form in the passage of the New Poor Law in 1834. Fundamental to the new law was the workhouse system, which established the principle that an individual must *earn* assistance. The 'workhouse test' became a central feature in the administration of assistance in England. The workhouse was to be the only form of relief offered to indigent men and women. Once inside, husbands and wives and children were separated; work entailed breaking stones, for 'the monotony, the restraint, the want of stimulants, the regularity of hours, are irksome to the pretended pauper.'[27] No one would, therefore, turn to the workhouse if any alternative presented itself. In the words of Disraeli, 'It announced to the world that in England poverty is a crime.'[28]

The underlying principle, that poverty was due to weakness of human character, meant that nineteenth century charity workers were ever looking for the 'clever pauper', the 'idle vagabond', or 'sturdy rogue' who would abuse outdoor relief, that is, relief given outside the workhouse. This assumption remained central to the debates on poverty throughout the later Victorian Period. But with growing numbers of urban poor there emerged private and public philanthropy, both secular and religious, which also tried to grapple with the problems of poverty. Some Boards of Guardians had understood the punitive nature of the workhouse, particularly when it meant the disruption of families, and therefore had not adhered to the letter of the Poor Law. The Poor Law Report of 1869, however, found that outdoor relief undermined the workhouse system, and further, when it was combined with unrestricted charity, the 'clever pauper' was able to take advantage of the generally uncoordinated state of relief offered by the Poor Law, charities and the Church.[29]

The most influential body to articulate concern about 'indiscriminate charity' was the Society for Organising Charitable Relief and

Repressing Mendicity (the Charity Organisation Society, or COS), founded in 1869 to avoid duplication of charitable efforts. A leading figure in the organisation was Octavia Hill. The 'worst result' of the uncontrolled dispersal of free boots, bread tickets, coal, soup, and shelters, she argued, 'was its evil influence on the poor, who were taught to beg, to prevaricate and to lie about their circumstances, to avoid work as less profitable than cadging.'[30] This 'demoralisation of the poor', she argued, was the real root of the social problem. The virtues of thrift, regularity, and hard work had to be reintroduced into the charitable relationship. Relief, according to the COS, should be conditional upon the behavior of the recipients, and a system was instituted whereby applicants were interviewed by a home visitor who inquired into the cause of their distress.[31]

The hey-day of the COS was the 1870s, although it continued to have its advocates into the twentieth century. Whereas the 1860s had been a time of crisis for middle class London, the 1880s was a period of more profound questioning after six to seven years of indifferent trade, the structural decline of certain older industries, chronic housing shortages for the working classes, and the emergence of socialism as a challenge to the liberal ideology of the COS.[32] The efforts of the COS to deal with widespread deprivation were recognised by many as inadequate, and by the 1880s other schemes were put forward.

In order to understand the development of Liberal thought, which is critical to understanding the attempts to alleviate urban poverty, it is also necessary to look to developments in the intellectual life of Oxford in the 1860s and onward. Benjamin Jowett, the Master of Balliol College, appealed for a 'Broad Church', rather than the elitist High Church, and worked to instill in his students a social conscience. Central to the dissenting Evangelical movement was a commitment to duty, to service as the very definition of Christianity. Balliol became known for its 'cautious radicalism, its liberal conscience which usually stopped short of social democracy.'[33] Implicit in Jowett's teachings was a commitment to social reform for the benefit of the disadvantaged.

Jowett's most influential pupil was T. H. Green, who came to Oxford from Rugby and who became the first lay tutor at the College. In the words of Jowett, 'Between 1870 and 1880 Green was undoubtedly the greatest personal force in the real life of Oxford. . . . It is not too much to say that by the time of his premature death . . . he had transformed both the atmosphere and methods of philosophical thought and study at Oxford.'[34]

Drawing on German Idealism derived from Hegel and Kant,

Green stressed the moral dignity of the individual and the perfectability of the individual through citizenship; from this he moved to a denunciation of poverty and slum conditions. He became the moral conscience of the 'new Liberalism' in late nineteenth century England. Allied to a tradition of Evangelical philanthropy he aroused his students by a plea for a Christianity not based on a belief in miracles but one grounded in good works, a Christianity in which individuals realised themselves through social service. Henry Scott Holland, who departed from Green to enter the High Church and who later became active in work among the London poor, explained that what Green had meant to his generation was that he had wedded theology to service in the world. Further, Holland explained,

> He gave us back the language of self-sacrifice and taught us how we belonged to one another in the one life of organic humanity. He filled us again with the breath of high idealism.[35]

Green did not advocate a radical restructuring of society: he was in favor of private property, family life, local government, and the non-interventionist role of the state. He believed that change could come about gradually through altruism. Green also worked actively outside the University, setting an example of citizenship, working for the Reform League to extend suffrage, for the National Education League for education reform, and for the United Kingdom Alliance for Temperance Legislation. He served on the School Board for Oxford and the Town Council and in parliamentary campaigns as a Liberal speaker. His greatest influence, however, was as a teacher.

The other figure at Balliol around whom issues of social reform and Liberalism were formulated was Arnold Toynbee, who came to Oxford as a student in 1873. Influenced by Green above all, Toynbee, too, sought a synthesis of the Liberal notions of the individual and the new demands for collective action. His academic work in economic history was bound up with his ideas of social reform. His search has been characterised as 'an almost frantic attempt to salvage the crumbling alliance of the working classes and liberalism'.[36] From Green Toynbee found direction for his deeply felt religious convictions by turning his energies to a close encounter with the poor.

In 1875, after spending two years in the heart of London's East End, where they were to remain for three decades, the Revd and Mrs Samuel (Henrietta) Barnett of St Jude's, Whitechapel, visited Oxford at the invitation of Gertrude Toynbee, sister of Arnold and a school friend of Mrs Barnett.[37] Samuel Barnett gave an address at Balliol which so moved Toynbee that he joined their efforts as best he could in the East End, taking two rooms above the COS offices on Commercial Street in Whitechapel.[38] The link between Balliol and the Barnetts' work in the East End became a lasting one, as later generations of students followed Toynbee's example. Although Toynbee, chronically unwell, did not remain long in the East End, seeing poverty first-hand had a deep effect on him.

Many, like T. H. Green, Arnold Toynbee and Green's other distinguished students, supported the activities of the COS. The Barnetts, too, supported the COS and its policies until the mid 1880s, when their experience among the poor brought them to the realisation 'that there was a deeper and more continuous evil than unrestricted and unregulated charity, namely unrestricted and unregulated capitalism and landlordism.'[39]

But, like Green and Toynbee, the Barnetts did not become socialists. One finds them involved instead in a series of social experiments designed to assuage what Beatrice Webb called the 'new consciousness of sin',

> a collective or class consciousness; a growing uneasiness, amounting to conviction, that the industrial organisation, which had yielded rent, interest and profits on a stupendous scale, had failed to provide a decent livelihood and tolerable conditions for a majority of the inhabitants of Great Britain.[40]

It was with a similar voice that Toynbee had pleaded to an audience during a lecture on Henry George shortly before his premature death at the age of thirty in 1883:

> We – the middle classes I mean, not merely the very rich – we have neglected you; instead of justice we have offered you charity, and instead of sympathy we have offered you hard and unreal advice. . . . You have to forgive us, for we have wronged you grievously – not knowingly always, but still we have sinned, and let us confess it; but if you forgive us, – nay whether you will forgive us or not – we will serve you, we will devote our lives to your service, and we cannot do more. . . . We are willing to give up the life we care for, the life with books and with those we love. We will do this and only ask you to remember one thing in return . . . if you get a better life, you will really lead a better life.[41]

Emerging from the privileged air of Oxford, this poignant plea also fell short of a radical reordering of the social structure.

Specific to the English situation was the context in which many intellectuals debated the social issues: the Oxford Union or Commons Rooms. This goes some way toward explaining the paternalism which colored social reform.[42] In a survey of the most popular reading among newly elected Labour MPs, taken as late as 1906, the works which were cited most frequently were, significantly, the Bible and the writings of Thomas Carlyle, Charles Dickens, and John Ruskin.[43] Engels' work on the British working class, written in 1844, was not published in English until 1887; Marx's *Communist Manifesto* was not widely circulated until the 1870s.[44] One can argue, therefore, that the terms of the debate – the limits of the debate within certain circles – explains in some measure why so little changed on a national level. In the 1880s a younger generation sought to reinterpret Liberal thought in England for a modern, industrialised society, resulting in the 'new Liberalism' and support for the social legislation of the 1905–14 Governments,[45] but it was not until 1909 that the passage of the 'People's Budget' institutionalised the redistribution of wealth through taxation as a means of social reform.[46]

There was, however, one area of reform in which Liberalism accepted state intervention, and that was education, although even here they first assured the continued security of the English Public Schools by the passage of the Education Act of 1869. The Liberal ethos was sympathetic to progress, individualism, rationality and nationalism,[47] all of which were called upon in a movement for universal public schooling. In particular, a belief that the middle classes could transform and lead the working classes was central to its creed. Support was, therefore, forthcoming for universal education as well as other schemes to bring the fruits of West End culture to the inhabitants of the East End.

Liberal commitment to universal education, however, was to struggle against a wide variety of interests opposed to a system of public education. It would be necessary to negotiate a complex compromise among a panoply of interests around which middle class opinion could unite in redefining the experience of the working class child.

Notes

1 A. Conan Doyle, 'The Naval Treaty', in *Sherlock Holmes: The Complete Short Stories* (1892; rpt. London: John Murray, 1928), p. 515.
2 H. B. Philpott, *London at School: The Story of the School Board 1870–1904* (London: T. Fisher Unwin, 1904), p. 40.
3 D. Feldman and G. Stedman Jones (eds), 'Introduction', *Metropolis, London: Histories and Representations Since 1800* (London: Routledge, 1989), p. 4.
4 G. Stedman Jones, *Outcast London: A Study in the Relationship between Classes in Victorian Society* (Oxford: Oxford University Press, 1971), pp. 19–32.
5 *Ibid.*, p. 247.
6 Charles Booth described the exodus of the middle class in his exhaustive series

documenting the extent of poverty in London: 'The drifting away of the better-to-do leaves a general impression of increasing poverty, and in some parts the population has become distinctly poorer', 3:1, *Religious Influences*, p. 16.

7 Stedman Jones, *Outcast London*, p. 247.

8 B. Disraeli, *Sybil: or, the Two Nations* (1845; rpt. London: Hughendon Edition, 1881), pp. 76–7.

9 Stedman Jones, *Outcast London*, p. 247.

10 J. Davis, *Reforming London: the London Government Problem, 1855–1900* (Oxford: Clarendon Press, 1988), p. 8.

11 D. L. Woolmer, 'Caring for London's children', in G. Sims (ed.), *Living London* (London: Cassell, 1901), p. 374.

12 G. Sims, *How the Poor Live* (London: Chatto and Windus, 1883), p. 1. These sketches of London life first appeared in *The Pictorial World* in the same year.

13 W. Besant, *All Sorts and Conditions of Men* (London: Chatto and Windus, 1882; 1883 2nd edn), p. 110.

14 H. Barnett, 'Passionless reformers' (rpt. from *The Fortnightly Review*, August 1882) in S. and H. Barnett (eds), *Practicable Socialism: Essays on Social Reform* (London: Longmans, Green and Co., 1888), pp. 48–61.

15 A. Morrison, 'A Street', *Macmillan's Magazine* (October 1891), p. 460.

16 C. F. G. Masterman, *From the Abyss: Of its Inhabitants by One of Them* (London: R. Brimley Johnson, 1902), p. 40.

17 P. Keating (ed.), introduction, *Into Unknown England, 1866–1913: Selections from the Social Explorers* (Glasgow: Fontana, 1976), p. 16.

18 S. Letwin, *The Pursuit of Certainty* (Cambridge: Cambridge University Press, 1965).

19 J. London, *The People of the Abyss*, introduction J. Lindsay (1903; rpt. London: Journeyman Press, 1977).

20 Charles Booth writing in 1889 as quoted in the journal of the Cambridge Settlement movement, *The Cambridge House Magazine*, 4 (August 1897), p. 4.

21 W. Besant, *South London* (New York: Frederick A. Stokes Company, 1898), p. 320.

22 C. F. G. Masterman (ed.), preface, *The Heart of the Empire: Discussions of Problems of Modern City Life in England with an Essay on Imperialism* (London: T. Fisher Unwin, 1901), p. vi.

23 For a discussion of the bonds of charity and deference in the eighteenth century, see E. P. Thompson, 'Patrician society, plebian culture', *Journal of Social History* (1974), pp. 382–405.

24 Drawing upon the work of anthropologists, particularly on the work of Marcel Mauss, Stedman Jones, in *Outcast London*, describes the ways in which philanthropy in traditional societies functioned as a means of control. Stedman Jones describes the conditions in London which altered the gift giving relationship, depersonalising the process and thereby resulting in what he calls 'the deformation of the gift'. Without the personal relationships whereby receipt of the gift was accompanied by the elements of voluntary sacrifice, subordination and obligation, the old process could no longer function, pp. 241–62.

25 B. Harrison in 'Philanthropy and the Victorians', *Victorian Studies*, 9, No. 4 (June 1966), suggests that some working people were well aware of the status-maintaining role of charity and quotes a Chartist, writing in 1840, who wanted to rid his class of 'dependent habits, selfish feelings; a crawling, slavish disposition' because 'When a man receives charity he is at once degraded', p. 371.

26 As quoted by Stedman Jones from *The Quarterly Review* (1876, p. 379) in *Outcast London*, p. 253.

27 *Extracts from the Information Received by His Majesty's Commission as to the Administration and Operation of the Poor Law*, published by Authority, 1833, and quoted by K. de Schweinitz in *England's Road to Social Security: From the Statutes of Labourers in 1349 to the Beveridge Report of 1942* (1943; rpt. New York: A. S. Barnes, 1961), p. 122.

28 De Schweinitz, *England's Road to Social Security*, p. 124. The passage of the New Poor Law has been explained as primarily a response to the growing cost of poor relief as the rural poor migrated to the city. In 1834 the landed gentry still controlled England, and they had no desire to pay relief to the rural poor or recent immigrant to the city; the 'workhouse test' was a means of controlling expenditure. The Act has been called not only a rigid and unimaginative system for an industrialising nation to use to tackle widespread distress, requiring the erection of ever more and more workhouses, but an eighteenth century solution to a nineteenth century problem, see D. Ashford, *The Emergence of the Welfare State* (Oxford: Basil Blackwell, 1986), pp. 67–9.

29 Stedman Jones, *Outcast London*, p. 256.

30 As quoted by Henrietta Barnett in *Canon Barnett: His Life, His Work, and Friends by His Wife* (London: John Murray, 1918), 1, p. 21.

31 H. Barnett, *Canon Barnett*, p. 35.

32 Stedman Jones, *Outcast London*, p. 281.

33 M. Richter, *The Politics of Conscience: T. H. Green and His Age* (London: Weidenfeld and Nicolson, 1964), p. 52.

34 As quoted in Richter, *The Politics of Conscience*, p. 158. Richter notes that after the late 1860s, with the possible exception of John Ruskin, no one rivalled Green in his 'power to stir men from the inherited allegiances and make them aware of how much remained to be done by way of reform', p. 293.

35 H. Scott Holland as quoted by Richter, *The Politics of Conscience*, p. 35.

36 A. Kadish, *Apostle Arnold: the Life and Death of Arnold Toynbee 1852–1883* (Durham: Duke University Press, 1986), p. ix.

37 J. A. R. Pimlott, *Toynbee Hall: Fifty Years of Social Progress 1884–1934* (London: J. M. Dent and Sons, 1935), p. 21.

38 Kadish, *Apostle Arnold*, p. 45.

39 B. Webb, *My Apprenticeship* (London: Longmans, Green & Co., 1926), p. 155. Beatrice Webb had worked closely with both Octavia Hill and the Barnetts.

40 *Ibid.*, pp. 178–9.

41 As quoted by P. d'A. Jones, *The Christian Socialist Revival: 1877–1914. Religion, Class and Social Conscience in Late-Victorian England* (Princeton: Princeton University Press, 1968), pp. 85–6 fn.

42 Ashford, *The Emergence of the Welfare State*, p. 35.

43 *Ibid.*, p. 47 fn.

44 *Ibid.*, p. 47.

45 For an examination of the 'new Liberalism' see M. Freeden, *The New Liberalism: An Ideology of Social Reform* (Oxford: Clarendon Press, 1978); for discussions of its chief proponents see P. Clarke, *Liberals and Social Democrats* (Cambridge: Cambridge University Press, 1978), S. Collini, *Liberalism and Sociology: L. T. Hobhouse and Political Argument in England, 1880–1914* (Cambridge: Cambridge University Press, 1979) and M. Freeden, ed., *Reappraising J. A. Hobson: Humanism and Social Welfare* (London: Unwin Hyman, 1990).

46 S. Hynes, *The Edwardian Turn of Mind* (Princeton: Princeton University Press, 1968), p. 55.

47 T. J. Lowi, *The End of Liberalism: Ideology, Policy, and the Crisis of Public Authority* (New York: W. W. Norton, 1969), p. 3.

CHAPTER TWO

The 'discovery' of working class childhood

The improvement in the scientific, artistic, and advanced education of the community is important; but time, labour and money will be expended in producing unsatisfactory results as long as a million infants continue to waste the time which might be the most valuable part of their educational career. It is leaving a delicate and plastic clay to harden before any attempt is made to mould or prepare it for the purposes for which it will ultimately be required.[1]

I freely confess that the great chance of bringing about a new and better order of things lies among the children who are to be the mothers and fathers of the future.[2]

This is the age of child worship. . . . If ever we were called to stand by the children, surely it is to-day . . . let our little slum children share in the children's Kingdom that is coming[3]

The children's hour came . . . Goth and Greek ignored them. Christian England, for all her Child-Christs, had not learned humility. But their hour came[4]

The most consistent and energetic program to reach and transform the working classes was the unrelenting effort made to alter their childhood experience. The sentiments expressed by social commentators, whether Settlement House worker, School Board member or journalist, represented a major shift in attitudes toward childhood in late nineteenth century Britain. The concept of childhood itself became something to be fought for and legislated for, and converged with broader political, economic and social debates. Whereas a period of passive dependency characterised the childhood of the middle class nursery, children's *rights* to childhood were extended to the 'street arab' and 'gutter child' and coalesced in a program of child protection laws and educational measures.[5]

In order to understand the newly emergent perception of the childhood of the poor it is necessary to examine the rhetoric and imagery of the cause, with its sense of alarm and its near missionary zeal and, more deeply, to examine what lay behind the new anxiety. In this way its ideological role, serving to unite diverse and often conflicting interests, becomes apparent.

Although the design of books, nursery furnishings and clothing for children – items which made the distinction between the world of the very young and that of the adult visually clear – dated in Britain to the late eighteenth century,[6] these distinctions remained the preserve of the middle and upper classes. The world of the protected nursery remained outside the experience of the working classes. There was no living space and there were no servants to make the separate world of the nursery possible. Childhood as a period of passive growth and nurturing was a luxury which could not be afforded. For the working class family the realities of the day to day struggle for survival required the contribution of all members. Older children helped with the care of the younger ones so that the mother might be free to attend to her household chores or, if necessary, go out to work; boys old enough to contribute to the family income did so either through odd jobs or by helping the father. As late as 1911 Alexander Paterson, in writing about the poorer population of London noted, 'The difference between a child and an adult is everywhere regarded as one of degree rather than kind.'[7]

In the last third of the nineteenth century diverse factions merged in a growing concern for the working class child, as the instrument, the 'portal to the future',[8] by which to secure England's peaceful and prosperous future. Such a notion of childhood for the working class can be traced from the late 1860s onward when a redefinition of the state's obligation toward education was part of a broader movement which redefined the experience of the working class child. Child labor in many industries was no longer needed as mechanisation replaced tasks that children had performed, alleviating significant opposition to child protection laws and compulsory school attendance.[9] The final decades of the nineteenth century also saw an increase in real wages which made it possible for an increasing number of families to do without the contribution of the youngest members. Improved wages, resulting from organised labor, as well as cheaper food, home-grown and imported, it would seem, made an extension of childhood possible.[10]

By the end of the century one finds all children of the nation referred to as a 'natural resource' to be nurtured; children, it was said, did not belong '"merely to the parents but to the community as a whole"; they were a "national asset", the "capital of a country", . . . "the citizens of tomorrow"',[11] and their welfare was a matter of national concern: 'The purely material aspect must awake every Englishman. . . . No bank or company can allow assets to lie fallow, its property undeveloped. No country that has joined the struggle for supremacy can allow the finest human material to grow stiff or die for lack of help and understanding.'[12]

Victorians were well aware of the changing status of the child. Writing on the changed role of the state in relation to its child population, Percy Alden, a social reformer, Settlement House worker and Labour MP, wrote:

> At the time of the accession of Queen Victoria not one single act of Parliament represented the parental interest which the state ought to take in the welfare of the young. The child was a chattel; it had no rights and liberties. . . . The last thirty or forty years, however, has witnessed a great improvement both in theory and in practice. We have grown more humane and more thoughtful. We are no longer prepared or at least not to the same extent – to sacrifice all the future life of our country for the sake of some present gain. . . . Looking back upon the history of those days with eyes that see more clearly now that the blurs and blots have been removed, we discern how greatly parental responsibility has been strengthened, and how completely the action of the State has been justified in its attempts to safeguard the interests of the child against inhuman and criminally careless treatment.[13]

In 1897, on the occasion of Queen Victoria's sixtieth year on the throne, one commentator, also looking back over the previous decades, singled out the growing interest in the plight of her youngest subjects: 'the shout of the children [has become] more loud and glad . . . where once the ground was barren with the salt of children's tears, now flourishes the sweet blossom of their joy.' On this occasion Revd Benjamin Waugh, a former member of the first School Board for London for Greenwich from 1870 until 1876, whose campaign slogan had been 'education for Neglected Children', and a founding member and first Secretary in 1884 of the National Society for the Prevention of Cruelty to Children and a founder of day nurseries, pointed to the legislative changes that marked the preceding decades:

> It is important to note that every Statute upon the Statute Book for the protection of the helpless subjects of the Crown has been passed

during the reign of Queen Victoria. They include Protection to
Children in Factories, in Mines, in Brickfields, in Chimneys, in
Canals, and in Agricultural Gangs; Children of Paupers; Apprentices
on the High Seas; Street Beggars and Hawkers; Child Acrobats;
Children in Pantomimes, and Children in Dangerous Performances;
Criminal and Semi-Criminal Children; Children ill-treated and starved
in the Houses of the Drunkard, or the Idle, or the Vicious, and of the
Tyrannical Parent[14]

i   The Education Act of 1870

In 1870 the Liberal government under Gladstone committed itself and
its successors to the provision of a national system of elementary
schools, that is, schools for working class children. Of all of the
attempts to transform the experience of working class children, the
Education Act of 1870 was the most systematic and far-reaching:
elementary education in England and Wales was guaranteed by law;
elementary schooling for children between the ages of five and thirteen
was no longer to be left to parental discretion and the 'voluntary' system
of religious schools which were aided by state grants. By 1876 school
attendance was defined as a parental obligation, noncompliance
punishable by law. Although government grants for elementary education dated from the 1830s, the obligation to provide education as called
for in the Act of 1870 for all children not already attending an 'efficient'
school, represented a far greater commitment and bears witness to a
significant shift in attitudes.[15]

The potential significance of the Education Act was clearly
understood by contemporaries: on the occasion of the first meeting of
the School Board for London, the body empowered to carry out the
terms of the Act for the metropolis, *The Times* wrote that, 'No equally
powerful body will exist in England outside Parliament, if power be
measured by influence for good or evil over masses of human beings.'[16]

It is perhaps useful to remember E. P. Thompson's observation
on the 'discovery' of child labor in an earlier period, the 1830s and
1840s: 'We forget,' he wrote, 'how long abuses can continue "unknown"
until they are articulated. . . . In the eyes of the rich between 1790
and 1830 factory children were "busy", "industrious", "useful"'.[17]
Similarly one must search for the reasons for the 'discovery' of the
neglected child in the period around 1870.

A sense of urgency, near panic, characterised the demands of
some leaders for a system of elementary schooling in 1870. The
Minister in charge of the Education Department under Gladstone,

W. E. Forster, a Radical and a former Quaker, declared before the House of Commons that the nation was threatened by 'invading armies of ignorance, misery, and destitution [which] swarm in upon us like insects and feed on the trees of our commercial prosperity.'[18] Although the subject of government grants in support of education had been discussed intermittently in Parliament since the 1830s, the pressure to secure a system of universal education grew dramatically after the passage of the Reform Act of 1867. With the extension of the franchise in 1867 had come an immediate demand to educate the working classes: Robert Lowe, a former Vice-President of the Education Committee of the Privy Council and a longstanding opponent of a national scheme of elementary schooling, rose in the House of Commons after the passage of the Reform Act and declared,

> Sir, it appears to me that before we had intrusted [sic] the masses – the great bulk of whom are uneducated – with the whole power of this country we should have taught them a little more how to use it, and not having done so, this rash and abrupt measure having been forced upon them, the only thing we can do is as far as possible to remedy the evil by the most universal measures of education that can be devised. I believe it will be absolutely necessary that you should prevail on our future masters to learn their letters . . . I was opposed to centralisation, I am ready now to accept centralisation; I was opposed to an education rate, I am ready now to accept it; I objected to inspection, I am now willing to create crowds of inspectors.[19]

In numerical terms, the Reform Act of 1867 increased the electorate of 1,430,000 to 2,470,000. As the Act lowered the house-holder qualification for the franchise, the new electors belonged largely to the urban working class.[20] In London the winter of 1867 was particularly severe, with bread riots in East London, a situation made all the worse by trade depression, a collapse in the Thames ship-building industry, cholera and a bad harvest.[21] Although historians debate the impact of agitation and the fear of unrest on the passage of the Reform Act, it is generally conceded that the terms of the measure were far more sweeping as passed in August, following massive demonstrations in Hyde Park, than when it was proposed in February.[22]

The immediate impact of the Reform Act must be considered cautiously. Although it altered the conditions of British politics, there were crucial factors that softened its impact. The working classes possessed no independent political organisation and could not, therefore, invade Parliament or enforce its will. Furthermore, there was no substantial redistribution of seats in Parliament: the industrial north and Midlands remained considerably under-represented in proportion to the rural and agricultural south and east.

If the immediate impact of the Reform Act was in reality diffused, the fear of a potentially powerful working class electorate was real. In the first post-Reform session education was the central social issue discussed.[23] In the end, however, succumbing to Church and agricultural opposition to compulsory school attendance, Parliament merely proposed to aid the existing system of voluntary schools; the only new feature was the establishment of an Education Minister.[24] When the new electorate returned a Liberal government in 1868, however, Gladstone placed W. E. Forster in charge of the Education Committee of the Privy Council, and it was Forster's program that laid the foundation for the system of state-supported elementary schools established in 1870.

The extension of the franchise not only made the question of working class education an urgent one, it made the particular nature of that education a crucial concern. When Disraeli had submitted the Reform Bill to Parliament in 1867, he had insisted that 'this country is a country of classes and a country of classes it will ever remain.'[25] He had tried to assure an assembly of Merchant Tailors that

> the elements of democracy do not exist in England. England is a country of classes, and the change that is impending in this country will only make those classes more united, more complete, and more cordial.[26]

The potential influence of the educational measure on the 'classes which they are all striving to elevate' was recognised by all Members of Parliament: the measure 'touches the homelife of every cottage in the land, and that not indirectly and insensibly, but directly and palpably'.[27] The question for many, after all, was not merely one of increasing literacy in England because 'the power of making the laws by which all have to abide is going to the class that cannot read a newspaper.'[28] Rather, the education to be instituted 'was not so much the imparting of knowledge as the training that would fit a child for the work to which his station would probably call him.'[29]

Earlier, in the 1860s, there had been fear that an *educated* working class might be a threat to the social order, a fear that persisted and shaped the educational system, preventing, for example, any grants of rate aid to secondary schools until after the turn of the century. By contrast was the hope that a properly organised educational system would, in fact, have the potential to strengthen the system of class relationships by instilling in the working class a sense of duty and respect for the social system: in 1862 Disraeli had described popular education as 'the best guarantee for public order'.[30] Robert Lowe, advocating universal elementary schooling as a matter of great urgency, described the nature of the education which he deemed appropriate:

> The lower classes ought to be educated to discharge the duties cast upon them. They should also be educated that they may appreciate and defer to a higher cultivation when they meet it[31]

While concern over social unrest and the franchise were critical factors in focusing attention upon the education of the nation's young, the parliamentary debate also revealed growing fears of losing England's military and commercial position abroad. The education of working class children was offered as a means of making the future workmen and soldiers competitive with those of rival nations. The Liberal MP, A. J. Mundella, pleaded that England should heed the German example:

> At the commencement of the present century, when North Germany lay dismembered and prostrate at the feet of Napoleon, a few philosophers at Berlin raised the standard of compulsory education, and Fichte, in words which now read like prophecy, described its probable results. . . . Its influence would be felt for good in every way; by national education the expense of the State would be diminished, and the cost of maintaining standing armies would be done away with, because education would produce a nation of patriots, and an army of intelligent men better fitted to defend the country than the ignorant boors who were usually drawn in the conscription; the principle of political economy would come to be understood by the working population, and industry would flourish and wealth increase.[32]

Mundella went on to warn of the technical superiority of Britain's rivals, quoting an Austrian inspector who had confessed, 'We were vanquished not by the needle-gun, but by the higher education of the Prussians.'[33] And he insisted that in his German travels he 'had gone the length and breadth of the country and had tried in vain to find an ignorant man or child.'[34]

The chief obstacle facing Forster in passing the Education Bill was the fierce controversy over religious education. It was necessary for the government to steer a course between two opposed lobbies in Parliament. The National Education League was a Radical body which had started in Birmingham and which aimed at the establishment of a national system of education that would be free, compulsory and non-sectarian. Whereas the League did not propose to exclude general religious teaching from schools, it opposed all denominational teaching in state-aided schools. In opposition to this stand, the National Education Union, which emanated from Manchester, avowedly formed to fight the League, was supported by Conservatives and Anglicans and sought to protect the voluntary system of religious schools as far as possible.

In addition to the opposition of the National Education Union, there was opposition from ratepayers who fought to limit public expenditure. In fact, the Union and the ratepayers' opposition united in a partnership which lasted through the following decades, seeking at all turns to curb expenditure on rate-supported education for the working classes. Forster was sensitive to these pressures and in introducing the measure promised that 'there must be, consistently with the attainment of our object, the least possible expenditure of public money.'[35] And he argued in favor of school fees, providing waivers only in instances of extreme poverty. He advocated the financing of schools on a proportion of one-third raised from parents, one-third from public taxes, and one-third out of local funds.[36]

The working classes, who were most profoundly affected by the passage of the Education Act, had no single, organised voice in the parliamentary debates. And, in any case, as Thomas Wright, a London School Board Visitor who described himself as a 'journeyman Engineer', wrote in 1873, they were not unified in their support:

> The working classes are not a single-acting, single-idea'd body. They are practically and plurally *classes*, distinct classes, classes between which there are as decisively marked differences as there are between any one of them and the upper or middle class[37]

Robert Applegarth, Secretary of the Amalgamated Society of Carpenters and Joiners, distinguished two primary divisions within the working class on the subject of education: 'the careless and indifferent man, who has been so long neglected and degraded that he does not understand the value of education', and 'the better class of working men'.[38] A School Board Visitor confirmed the divisions nearly twenty years later, reporting that trade unionists were too 'self respectful' to keep their children away from school, that the opposition came from 'among the very poor and unlearned'.[39] It was the very poor, the unskilled casual laborer, dependent upon his child's help at home or in work, who resisted the demands of the Education Act. These parents were rarely vocal; rather, 'they demonstrated their opposition with their feet, as it were, sending their children to work instead of to school'.[40]

Trade union leaders did work with the National Education League in support of a national, compulsory, free and non-sectarian educational system.[41] Applegarth was the leading union figure involved in this effort and the author of a pamphlet supporting compulsory education which sold half a million copies.[42] There were, however, differences of opinion within the trade union movement. Some members feared that rate-supported education would place an unfair burden upon the artisan family.[43] In opposition to Applegarth, Robert Last, General Secretary of the General Union of Carpenters and Joiners, a rival to Applegarth's union, warned that compulsion threatened 'personal parental control which the heads of families are naturally jealous of retaining in their own hands.'[44] The Trades Union Congress, founded in 1868, supported most of the slogans of the National Education League but did not develop a clearly defined education policy until the 1880s.[45]

In the end the Education Act of 1870 was a delicately framed compromise, affording concessions to both the League and Union, but leaving Radicals, Nonconformists, and the Church dissatisfied. Forster acknowledged that the voluntary system had failed to educate the nation's children, but he permitted the voluntary system a 'year of grace' in order to 'fill the gaps'. If, after a year, school provision remained inadequate, locally elected School Boards, with the power to finance schools out of rates and government grants, would provide elementary schools. The Boards would charge fees; it would be left up to each Board whether or not to enforce attendance.

On the volatile issue of religious instruction, however, Forster left the nature and extent of religious instruction up to the discretion of the local School Boards. The final version of the Bill included a conscience clause, permitting parents the right to withdraw their children from religious instruction. Radicals were angered by what they considered to be the needless period of grace granted to the voluntary schools. Bending to Nonconformist pressures, the final draft reduced the period of grace to six months and added the Cowper-Temple amendment, which stated that no catechism or formulary distinctive of any particular denomination be taught. The Church remained fearful that denominational schools would not be able to compete with rate-supported schools, yet felt that the measure offered them more than they had hoped for.[46] State grants to Church schools were increased, including building grants, though assistance out of the rates was forbidden.

ii   The School Board for London

The School Board for London emerged as a new and powerful institution in the metropolis, and its first elections were in the autumn of 1870. Because its primary concern was the provision of elementary schooling for the city's poorer children, the London Board had the authority to enter the neighborhoods of London and formulate ways in which wealthier London could transform 'the abyss'. The Board embodied the full spectrum of sentiments regarding the means to relieve distress, and over the thirty-four years of the Board's existence it represented the changing attitudes regarding education and the 'rescue' of the city's child population.

The power and influence afforded the new body was a crucial issue: should the new institution provide free meals in poor neighborhoods or assist with boots and clothing? Should children whose parents depended upon their earnings be permitted to work half-time, or should they be exempt from school attendance on grounds of poverty? Should children who came to school without the mandatory school fee be sent home? Were parents who did not send their children to school to be prosecuted, fined or possibly imprisoned? Implicit in these discussions was the old debate between those who argued that assistance would lead to the 'demoralisation of the poor' and those who believed that problems of poverty lay beyond the power of individual parents to resolve and who, therefore, advocated the short-term assistance and compassion of local authorities. The whole range of debate revolving around the 'social question' was articulated within the Board as well as in the press and in national government, particularly during the formulation of Education Department policy concerning the London Board.

As a body elected every three years, the School Board was obliged to convince the public that its money was being wisely spent. A largely middle class membership sought to assure the voting public that, through its educational policies, the social situation in London, which had so alarmed the middle classes in the 1860s and which was to emerge as an even more pressing issue in the 1880s, could somehow be ameliorated by reaching and training the working class child. It was necessary for the Board to be seen by the ratepayers as working to ensure a more peaceful and prosperous future. There was no consensus as to how this was to be achieved, and the activities of the Board and the decisions it reached were made by means of a process of continual debate and compromise.

The London School Board in 1870 consisted of forty-nine seats from ten divisions: the City, Chelsea, Finsbury, Greenwich, Hackney, Lambeth, Marylebone, Southwark, Tower Hamlets, and Westminster [2]. As the divisions were based upon the existing parliamentary divisions, they were not equal in either population or rateable value

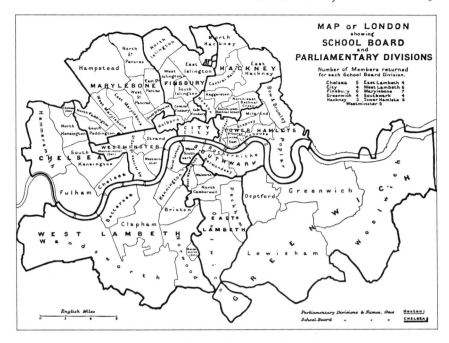

2] Map of the divisions of the School Board for London

and were, therefore, assigned varying numbers of elected members; the City, Southwark, Chelsea, and Greenwich each had four, Lambeth, Tower Hamlets, Hackney, and Westminster five, and Finsbury six.[47]

The political complexion of the Board was to vary over the thirty-four years of its existence, but it was at all times dominated by the wealthier classes who did not send their own children to Board Schools. In the first election only one working class candidate, Benjamin Lucraft, standing for Finsbury, succeeded out of a field of thirteen trade union candidates.[48] This was a national pattern. In 1873 Lucraft was joined by one more working class candidate, George Potter, standing for Chelsea.

The franchise for the School Board elections was wider than that for any other election in England in the period: all ratepaying householders, male or female, were eligible to vote, but lodgers were excluded.[49] Unlike the Board of Guardians and Town Councils, there was no property qualification for membership on the School Board.[50] Similar to the Board itself, however, of those who voted, a high percentage were members of the middle class whose own children did not attend Board Schools.[51] Board decisions were made from without. Neither the meeting time for the School Board itself nor the hours of voting on election day were conducive to working class participation. As late as 1894 representations were made to the School Board urging it to change the election day from Thursday to Saturday, enabling the many people who worked half day on Saturday to vote.[52] In 1889 Annie Besant, a Socialist member for Tower Hamlets, moved that the School Board meetings 'commence at 6 p.m. instead of at 3, on the grounds that the latter hour excluded from candidature for the Board men and women in receipt of wage.' Her motion was defeated.[53] The Board was always dominated by men; of the 326 members during the Board's life, only twenty-eight were women. Although a far higher percentage than has ever sat in the House of Commons, it was less than 10 per cent of the Board members.[54] Of the twenty-eight women, only half served for more than a single term.[55] The clergy, on the other hand, were well represented on the Board. At the peak of their influence in 1888, sixteen of the fifty-five School Board members were Anglican clergymen.[56] Only twelve ex-school teachers ever served on the Board. Teachers in the Board's employment were forbidden from serving.[57]

The School Board fell more or less into two major political camps: the Conservatives, or 'Moderates', and the Liberals, particularly the Radical Liberals, who in alliance with Socialist members, called themselves 'Progressives'. Church interests allied with Conservatives to promote, as always, economy. Moderates, Liberals and Nonconformists controlled the School Board from 1870 until 1885 when, by one vote, the Liberal Chairman, Edmund North Buxton, lost to Revd Joseph R. Diggle, an Anglican clergyman, who remained Chairman until 1894.

Throughout the life of the Board the critical election issues remained the amount of money spent by the Board and the place of religion in the curriculum. It was sometimes suggested, not surprisingly by the richer divisions with fewer Board Schools, that London should be divided into school districts, each separately rated. The election of 1891 became known as the 'Piano Election' because there had been a public outcry following a motion by the Board's School Management Committee to purchase pianos for school assembly halls, one to a school, on a trial basis. There were accusations that soon working class children would be playing the 'Moonlight Sonata' for their fathers on their return home from work. The order for pianos was subsequently reduced from 150 to 53, but Conservatives levied accusations of extravagance throughout the election campaign.[58]

The issues of compulsory school attendance and school fees also provoked intense debate. The Education Act had called for both fees and compulsion but allowed each Board to formulate the ways in which these principles were to be carried out. The new educational system was to be financed approximately one-third by the parent, one-third by public taxes, and one-third by local funds, which for all practical purposes meant the rates. The Education Act permitted school boards 'from time to time, with approval of the Education Department . . . [to remit] the whole or part of the fees of any child where the parent satisfies the school board that he is unable from poverty to pay the same'.[59] The issue of school fees had been raised before 1870 and continued to be debated until they were abolished by the Free Education Act of 1891, when it was finally decided that the cost of keeping track of the school pence outweighed the revenue.[60]

The Education Act empowered school boards to enforce compulsory school attendance but did not compel them to enact by-laws 'requiring the parents of children of such age, not less than five nor more than thirteen years . . . to attend school.'[61] It was not until 1876 that Parliament enacted further legislation to enforce school attendance, defining it as a parental duty. But in London, soon after the first School Board election, the Board decided to enact its own attendance by-laws. A Special Committee submitted its recommendations to 'provide against the evil, widely felt, of habitual irregularity, as well as of total non-attendance'.[62]

The London School Board created a system of District Visitors – school attendance officers – who were to be in charge of keeping the children on the books in their district, investigating instances of non-attendance, issuing warnings to parents called 'A' notices, and if unheeded, 'B' notices, calling parents to appear before a magistrate. Non-compliance by parents was punishable by a fine or imprisonment. It was at first hoped that these School Visitors would 'be women who have had experience in similar work',[63] to follow in the manner of Octavia Hill's rent collectors, efficient and persuasive. The Board sought middle class women, able to convince working class mothers of the wisdom of compliance. In reality the job of Visitor often proved to be a far cry from that of genteel women administering advice. The position was almost entirely filled by men, a large number of whom had been policemen or soldiers.[64] [3]. The 'School Board man',[65] as Visitors came to be known, was seen as a particularly threatening figure from outside the community. Visitors collected extensive records on the residents in their districts. In fact, it was to these records with their unprecedented amount of information that Charles Booth turned when compiling his vast study on East London; without their help, Booth wrote, 'nothing could be done'.

3] 'A London School Board Capture, 2:40 A.M.', *The Illustrated London News*, 9 September 1871

every house in every street is in their books, and details are given of every family with children of school age. . . . They are in daily contact with the people and have a very considerable knowledge of the parents of school children, especially of the poorer among them[66]

The Royal Commission on Housing of 1884–85 likewise used information gleaned from the Visitors' books.[67]

The image of the Visitor as intruder characterised for many among the poor the new educational system being instituted in their midst, and it also came to represent the tension between school and home life in the poorer neighborhoods. Whereas the Board Schools were hailed by the middle classes as an important civilising and humanising influence in the capital, resistance to school attendance, which conflicted with the needs and patterns of home life, persisted among the poor.

In 1879 the Board's efforts were described by its Chairman, Charles Reed, as doing 'more to elevate the masses of the people than all other benevolent agencies put together',[68] and the following year he reported that 'There is a general testimony that the schools have lifted up the population.'[69] But evidence suggests that the Board's efforts continued to be resisted in the city's poorer neighborhoods. The memoirs of one attendance officer, John Reeves, who worked in Shoreditch, recalled that Forster had once remarked that each Visitor should be granted the letters, MP, after his name, standing for 'Moral Policeman'.[70] The Visitor described the context in which he worked from day to day and the way in which residents of his district viewed him:

> the parents would stand at the street door and threaten and abuse me in the most dreadful language, and nearly all the people in the street would come out and see what was the matter and sympathise in their view. All this was very unpleasant, and what I found was the best way to act was to go on quietly with the visiting and take no notice, as if I was not at all interested in this display of fireworks. To attempt to reason with them was to add fuel to fire and therefore it was best to let it burn itself out.[71]

Reeves recalled the most difficult part of his job:

> One of the most unpleasant duties laid upon us at first when a man was fined and did not appear or pay the fine, a warrant would be issued, and we had to go with the officer mostly at night to identify the defendant. The reader may well understand what this meant in a district like the one we are now considering.

He went on, 'The opposition to our work at this time, was often violent and threatening, but it also took the form of cunning.'[72] Charles Morley in his vignettes of Board School life, originally published in the *Pall Mall Magazine*, recalled that Visitors were at one time greeted 'with a whirling axe; even to-day [1897] a flower-pot sometimes drops by accident',[73] and Thomas Gautrey, a former Progressive on the School Board, remembered a dead cat landing on the head of a Visitor in his district.[74] Another contemporary recalled:

> the School Board visitor who drove the children to school was a fit target for abusive witticisms, if not for still more offensive missiles. The headmaster of a Walworth school told me that he remembers seeing the school corridor thronged with men and women who had come up

to demand their children at the stroke of 12 or 4:30. 'You have had him for your two and a half hours,' they would argue. 'Now I want him to do a turn for me. He has been putting money into your pocket, now I want him to put some into mine.' And the unfortunate child would be sent off laden with a basket of fish or oranges, or perhaps dragged away home to turn the mangle.[75]

A Visitor from Tower Hamlets was asked how he carried out his work and which cases he chose to press, forcing the parent to appear before a magistrate:[76]

> 'You make a selection, and take those that appear to be the worst cases?'
> 'Yes.'
> 'You take into consideration the poverty, etc., of the parent?'
> 'No, I do not.'
> 'But you would not select very poor parents?'
> 'I would not exercise any discretion of that kind at all, because I do not consider that I have anything to do with poverty.'
> 'Suppose a parent, who usually earns 20s or 22s a-week, out of work, with four or five children not to School, would you consider that a reason for not summoning?'
> 'Certainly not.'

The Visitor explained that he took a more kindly view towards parents who were ill as the child's assistance might be required at home. The interviewer then inquired as to what the Visitor thought was the primary cause of non-attendance:

> 'Do you think poverty has anything to do with it?'
> 'I do not think that is so much poverty as the debased habits of the parents.'
> 'But if out of work for five or six weeks would the want of money induce them to keep the children from school?'
> 'I find very few cases where the want of work is not attributable to the conduct of the parent.'

The hardship imposed by school fees and compulsory attendance was dramatically related in a short story written by a school teacher, James Runciman; it appeared in the *Pall Mall Gazette*, and was later reprinted in a collection of stories by the author on Board School life, *School Board Idylls*.[77] In the story a poor widow, dependent upon the earnings of her son to feed a family of six, is ordered to send her son to school. When she ignores the School Board notices, she is duly summoned to appear before a criminal court and is given stern warnings. As the story unfolds, her daughter is forced to take to the streets to pay the school fees and feed the younger children. The story concludes with the suicide of the destitute widow. Although the story is melodramatic, an article in the *East London Observer* in 1874 recounts an attempted suicide by a laborer residing in Islington, charged with attempting to jump off Blackfriars Bridge:

> inquiries about the prisoner . . . found that he bore a good character for honesty, sobriety, and industry, but he had been out of work for three months, and the son who was under fourteen years of age, the School Board had compelled to go to school and give up his situation by which he earned a trifle for the family. They had sold all their furniture, and their home was miserably poor.[78]

Albeit extreme cases, the School Board placed a burden upon the poor and it was the very poor who found the Education Act most disruptive to their lives. London artisans had already sent their children to voluntary schools before 1870, but the sheer size of the casual labor force in London meant that a significant portion of working London felt the pressure of compulsory schooling and school fees.

That children played a crucial role in the division of labor within the family, often contributing directly to the family purse, was a fact well known to contemporary commentators. While boys might be employed outside the home, young girls were frequently needed in the home to provide child care or to help with the laundry and other weekly chores. School attendance for girls always lagged behind that of boys. The Board made provision for a time for older girls to bring the babies with them to school.[79] It was not uncommon for children to be registered for school at three years of age although the compulsory age was five. Since, as one historian has remarked, 'Even the poorest women in the riverside districts, once encumbered with children, generally took in home work, garment making, matchbox making, envelope making, etc.',[80] the disruption of traditional methods of child care made it increasingly difficult for mothers to go out to work.

Aggravating these problems were the additional difficulties of providing for school meals and boots. Parliament never granted the Board the power to feed the masses of hungry children congregated in its classrooms, as feeding and supplying warm clothing was deemed a familial obligation. Charities working in conjunction with school authorities did, however, make arrangements for hot meals and the provision of boots to the very poor, but it was a contentious issue throughout the life of the Board. Those opposed to 'indiscriminate feeding', as in old debates on outdoor relief, argued that when the poor realised that their offspring would be taken care of, they would become more improvident: 'free meals would increase the number of rash marriages, and the mischief would thereby be increased.'[81]

A common excuse for non-attendance was the lack of boots. George Sims, in his widely read *How the Poor Live* of 1883, described mothers trying to explain that their children had no boots:

> How to get the boots for Tommy and Sarah to go their daily journey to the Board School is a problem which one or two unhappy fathers have settled by hanging themselves behind the domestic door . . .
>
> Few persons who have not actual experience of the lives of the poorest classes have any conception of the serious import to them of the Education Act. Compulsory education is a national benefit . . . but it is idle to deny that it is an Act which has gravely increased the burdens of the poor earning precarious livelihoods; and as self-preservation is the first law of nature, there is small wonder that every dodge that craft and cunning can suggest is practiced [sic] to evade it.[82]

Sims gave poignant accounts of cases where school fees meant destitution, 'where the difference between the weekly income and the rent is only a couple of shillings.'

The schools did little in the way of establishing rapport with the parents. The discipline of the school, it has been suggested, extended to the parents as well as the children: they were fined for children's poor attendance and were not welcomed at school. The parents depicted in the school readers were worthy cottagers or undefined middle class, not the urban working class families of the children.[83] Annie Besant wrote of the adversarial relationship between parents and school authorities:

> At present we drive the children into school, bully the parents when they don't pay, instigate magistrates to issue distress warrants for arrears of fees and to imprison unlucky parents for non-payment of fines, and so make ourselves justly hated, when we ought to be on the best possible terms with our youngsters' legal owners.

And she concluded,

> When education is free, we can enforce attendance with a light heart, but I for one, shirk compulsion by way of the police courts so long as 'pay here' is written over school boards.[84]

The displacement of families in poor and heavily overcrowded neighborhoods, without responsibility for compensation, increased the suspicions of an already hostile community regarding the new institution. By 1872 the Board had secured from the Education Department the authority to acquire sites by compulsory powers of purchase.[85] It was, however, not until 1899 that the Board was required to rehouse tenants, and then only in special cases.[86]

The sheer size and height of the triple-decker Board Schools not only required the acquisition of large sites, but the buildings themselves often blocked the light and air of neighboring homes.[87] One commentator recalled at the end of the Board's life that building a Board School in some neighborhoods was

> like planting a fort in an enemy's country. The building was the symbol of tyranny and oppression, and often the school keeper had difficulty in protecting it from malicious damage. The School Board was the public enemy, depriving honest citizens of the services of their children, taking the children from profitable employment in shop and factory and setting them to the profitless tasks of learning to read and write. The teacher was a base creature who exploited the labour of the children for his own gain, and whom it was a meritorious act to thwart and trick in any possible way[88]

But the supporters of the educational system had on their side the School Board armed not only with the strength of the legal system and the conviction that the nation's future depended in large part upon the new system of universal compulsory education, but with a potent language of rescue and salvation. Children were no longer to be mistreated by ignorant and selfish parents. The School Visitor, John Reeves, who had suffered constant abuse in the course of his work, wrote of the transformation occurring among the child population:

> The darkness is passing away, the glimmering light of a new era is lighting up the ridges of thought, the sky is becoming radiant with the glad hope of a new day. The child life of the land, the inception of citizenship, must no longer be moulded in the slums. . . . A broader outlook will remove the suspicion which separates the classes and bring into the life of England a noble unity which will give a new meaning to patriotism and prepare us as a people to labour more consistently in the cause of peace and good will among the nations of the earth.[89]

iii   The rescue mission

The language of rescue and reclamation united proponents of all forms of child protection. This language was to become increasingly potent in the final decades of the nineteenth century, promoting not only education as a tool of social regeneration, but also many other schemes of child reclamation: the offspring of the nation were being deprived of their childhood; they were prematurely old, having been denied proper care and nurturing; they were lacking in a sense of innocence appropriate to a *natural* childhood. As one teacher recalled his impressions on entering a Board School classroom in the 1870s,

> Many of the faces had lines of care, sorrow, and crime marked on them, which would have done honour to a 'lifer'. Others seemed old, as if heads had by some mistake been misplaced and put on too youthful a body. . . . Every face seemed to say in the most desperate manner that his cup of misery had long been full[90]

A London School Visitor, whose job it was to ensure school attendance, described the children's lives as

> a constant round of sunless drudgery – they never seemed to think; they were prematurely old, and the victims of an awful cruelty. They worked at matchbox making many hours, and at other times assisted their parents in disposing of their wares in the streets. The mortality among the young was appalling.[91]

Workers at the Bermondsey Settlement 'were pained by the utter unchildlikeness' of street children there, 'little men and women at twelve years of age'.[92] A Chelsea Division School Visitor, giving evidence of his work in Hammersmith during a hearing on child labor, bemoaned, 'Children! Are they children? Go and see for oneself. There is no childhood for them; this is all labour commencing in earnest at eight years of age.'[93]

Other writers noted that the expressions of the children of the poor possessed an 'unnatural wisdom'.[94] As one commentator in an educational journal put it, 'The children never seemed young, . . . bearing terrible witness by their bodies and their minds that the sins of the fathers are visited upon the children.'[95]

The concern for the care-worn child entered the language of literature and journalism. In Arthur Morrison's novel, *The Child of the Jago*, a novel which is one of the most vivid and unrelenting in its description of the plight of the child in one of London's poorest neighborhoods, Shoreditch in the East End, the central character, a waif, is portrayed as

> a slight child, by whose size you might have judged his age at five. But his face was of serious and troubled age. One who knew the children of the Jago, and could tell, might have held him eight, or from that to nine.

And his young infant sister had a 'tiny face . . . piteously flea-bitten and strangely old.'[96] While Morrison was cynical of middle class responses, here seen in his parody of the language, he is pointing to the common rhetoric of the period.

In setting the scene for a novel which takes place in the East End of London, Walter Besant wrote in 1882, 'It is difficult, certainly, for anyone to go on laughing at Stepney; the children who begin by laughing, like children everywhere, have to give up the practice before they are eight'.[97] And Charles Morley, in his journalistic account of Board School life in London south of the river, expressed similar sentiments when he wrote of visiting schools in Walworth: 'But is anyone *ever* young in the Borough?' he asked, and went on to answer, 'Is not carking care their birthright?'[98] In a similar vein he described the features of a young child he had seen being carried in another's arms,

> It has a terribly grown-up appearance. Though less than a year old, I suppose . . . he regards you with an awful look of resignation, as if he had always known all the ills mortal flesh is heir to, and is perfectly aware that he is one of the lowest amongst the masses. It is a sort of weird, woeful, hopeless glance which makes you shudder.[99]

Mrs Helen Bosanquet (née Dendy), an active philanthropist and commentator on East End poverty and a leading supporter of the efforts of the Charity Organisation Society in promoting child study, graphically compared 'the lowest class of children' to 'rats and mice and blackbeetles [which] . . . shun the open ways'.[100]

Likewise, the findings of Thomas Wright, a School Visitor in a Thames-side district, contrasted sharply with middle class assumptions of childhood as a protected period. He appealed to his readers:

> I have heard of our 'Gutter Children' spoken of as Arabs [and wondered] whether there really could be any Arabs so hopelessly situated as to justify the comparison, and I came to the conclusion that there could not, that if there had been any such tribe of misery, travellers would have found them, and made known their hapless story.[101]

Andrew Mearns, in his highly publicised exposé, *The Bitter Cry of Outcast London*, detailed the evils which grew out of slum conditions in London:

> The child-misery that one beholds is the most heart-rending and appalling element in these discoveries; and of this not the least is the misery inherited from the vice of drunken and dissolute parents, and manifest in the stunted, misshapen, and often loathesome objects that we constantly meet in these localities. From the beginning of their lives they are utterly neglected; their bodies and rags are alive with vermin; they are subjected to the most cruel treatment; many of them have never seen a green field, and do not know what it is to go beyond the

streets immediately around them, and often pass the whole day without a morsel of food. [102]

While the plight of all poor children was a subject of growing concern, the situation of the city child was considered to be particularly painful. Rural life, with its fresh air and green fields, was thought to be a compensation even in the midst of grinding poverty; but the urban child was deprived of even this. [103] Family life in the country, even when it included child labor, was assumed by reformers to be healthier and more wholesome than home life in the urban slum. It was a life, it was believed, rooted in traditions. The campaign to assist the city child included schemes that would provide for visits to the country. When the Children's Country Holiday fund was established in 1884, amalgamating a number of private charities which provided country visits for city children, the society set down among its aims the placement of children in private homes in the country, if only for a few weeks, so that they might get a glimpse of 'more real homelife'. [104] In the country, even on a brief visit, the child would be brought in touch with a better way of life:

'God is love' is almost unthinkable in a slum, so we shall want to take everyone of our children away from the baking streets, with their foul smells, into the cool green country, where young life as God meant all young life to live when He gave it life, where our children will go to sleep under the starry sky with no drunken yells to rouse them till they are waked by birds. [105]

Mrs Bosanquet went so far as to declare that country visits 'might figure in social history as the initiator of a great social reformation.' [106] But some educators and politicians were more cautious and stressed the limitations of such experience. Charles Masterman warned:

Spaciousness, quiet, a large horizon, flowers by the roadside, the willow by the stream: this is the world of dream. Stepney or Camberwell, the roar of traffic, the crowded street's, hot, restless, hurried life – this is the real world. Soon even the dream itself will have vanished [107]

From the 1870s onward medical experts delivered papers to the Social Science Association, putting forward theories that ranged from a lack of oxygenisation in the blood to the inhalation of foul air as causes of physical degeneration. [108] Indeed, the city child, it was feared, might represent the beginnings of a 'new city race', [109] threatened with both physical and moral degeneration. 'London children,' wrote Mrs Bosanquet, are always tired; the dark rings under their eyes tell of the nervous strain which is breaking down their health, and their very restlessness is the restlessness of fatigue and nervous exhaustion. They begin to share the life of their parents so early that they often see no real childhood.[110]

And she posed the question,

Is it possible for children to grow up healthy and strong – mentally and physically – in large towns, or is it as inevitable as it is true that the race degenerates with town life until the third generation dies out from mere want of vitality?[111]

The real root of the problem, however, in the rhetoric of child rescue, remained parental ignorance and neglect, 'the sins of the father visited upon the children'. Such language depicted the parents as neglectful, drunken, and dissolute. The accusations were often emotional, as in an article which appeared in *The School Board Chronicle* in 1872, entitled 'The Rights of the Child', in which the author wrote,

I have stood humbled and abashed in the presence of these loathesome lepers of society. . . . Whence comes their leprosy? It is not the Will of God but the deadly fruit of human transgression. The rights of the children were denied to them by their parents. And Society that punishes vice and crime did not intervene to save the children from certain ruin[112]

The writer went on to say that it was the duty of the state to intervene to protect the children from the parents. Thomas Wright, the School Visitor, wrote, 'Home influences . . . are . . . speaking broadly evil ones.' The children, he wrote, were '"allowed to hang as they grow", and the soil in which they grow is morally rank and deadly.'[113] In writing of the 'outcasts which shun the open ways' Mrs Bosanquet pointed to parental neglect:

The responsible members of the family, the fathers and grown-up sons, are generally on guard at the public-house at the corner. . . . Down a side street and into a little court off it you will find the wives and families at home. . . . Every doorway is occupied by a more or less sturdy woman . . . with her sleeves rolled up ready for work which she never does. . . . Swarming up and down the doorsteps, or camping out in the roadways, are countless numbers of puny, dirty children[114]

The critical attitude of reformers like Mrs Bosanquet was reinforced by the experiences of School Visitors and charity workers who, in the course of their work, visited homes and reported findings that contrasted dramatically with the middle class model of family life.

In the fiery language of General William Booth, founder of the Salvation Army, readers were warned of the evil influences which prey upon city children in the absence of a proper home environment: 'it can be imagined,' he wrote in his book *In Darkest England and the Way Out*,

> what kind of a home life is possessed by the children of the tramp, the odd jobber, the thief, and the harlot. For all these people have children, although they have no homes in which to rear them. Not a bird in all the woods or fields but prepares some kind of a nest in which to hatch and rear its young, even if it be but a hole in the sand or a few crossed sticks in the bush. But how many young ones amongst our people are hatched before any nest is ready to receive them?[115]

He went on to describe the effects of overcrowding on the young, which 'compel the children to witness everything. Sexual morality often comes to have no meaning to them. Incest is so familiar as hardly to call for remark. The bitter poverty of the poor compels them to leave their children half fed'.[116] Booth's solution to the evils of city life and the 'home that has been destroyed, and with the home the homelike virtues' was the resettlement of the population in the countryside. He also proposed a vast scheme of emigration to the colonies as the only viable long-term solution to the iniquities of city life in Britain. The missionary zeal of a conviction that children must be saved from the evil influences of home and street also propelled and justified the work of Dr Barnardo in Stepney, who in 1866 began organising the resettlement of thousands of young people to the colonies, often against the wishes of their parents.[117]

The most commonly proposed solutions, however, entailed provision of alternative spaces for children in the poor districts, away from the corrupting atmosphere of their homes. Sister Grace of the Bermondsey Settlement in south London described her decision to work with children:

> if we better the conditions of the coming men and women, the children, should we not be doing much more lasting work in the long run? . . . In some cases the children come to us from homes where for the most part sin and wretchedness reign supreme . . . [the children] are born in Rotherhithe and Bermondsey, and they live there, and they grow up there, unimaginative, sordid, and dull, like their parents before them, and there they die . . . when we see the children so good and happy at the Happy Evenings and Story Hour, and then think of the future! When we think of the homes they are going back to after they leave us! When we look at their little old-fashioned faces, as they kneel round with folded hands to say 'Our Father, which are in heaven'

before we separate, I almost choke. 'Lead us not into temptation' the
children pray, and we know they are trying to be good. But what
chance is there for them with all the youth and brightness crushed out
of their lives by the misery of home?[118]

The Bermondsey Settlement organised a Children's Guild of Play 'to
make them children again, keep them little children, and fill their
minds with real child's play.'[119]

Mary Ward, like Sister Grace, organised children's activities.
She was the founder of 'Play-Centres' in London in the 1890s and was
influential in extending elementary schools in London to include
'Vacation Schools'[120] during the summer months.[121] She pleaded for
what she called 'Play-time Reform'. Even the play of the children was
understood as subject to the insidious influences of their surroundings:

> babies may be seen everyday with their arms around each other's necks,
> dancing in imitation of the drunken frolics of their parents. A little
> child comes up to me and frames with its lips the obscene expletive of
> the slums, and the two girls in charge of the infant laugh the hoarse
> laugh of mingled shame and empty wit. . . . The principal part of the
> slum child's education takes place in the streets; he is what the street
> makes him.[122]

She described seeing children playing games 'like "Father and Mother",
where a drunken father comes home and turns the mother and children
into the streets; or "Funerals"; or "Cherry-'ocks", where the stones
of rotten cherries, wetted in the mouth, are thrown in clouds at
passer-by'.[123]

A member of the Helpers Association, which provided organised
'Happy Evenings' for children in poor neighborhoods, wrote, when
pleading for more volunteers,

> there are hundreds of children who have no room to play any of
> the games which your children play, have never been taught to
> amuse themselves and to whom the enchanted realm of fairyland is
> unknown.[124]

In an effort to recruit workers a volunteer expressed the need for
outsiders to provide what poor mothers could not:

> for recreation is that part of a child's education, which a poor mother
> often overlooks, and for which she rarely feels herself responsible. As
> the Duchess of Bedford said, when she opened the Strand Branch of
> the Children's Happy Evenings Association, the work of this Associa-
> tion can almost be called the work of organised 'Motherlove'. . . . It
> must necessarily devolve on others to initiate the children of the poor

into the mysteries of 'Hunt the Slipper', and 'Round and Round the Village', and many other games wholly unknown to them.[125]

Canon Samuel Barnett wrote in 1886 of the 'Play-classes' organised at the Settlement House in London's East End for 'children from homes in which there is no room to play, and whose play-ground is the streets.' He described the 'Parties of ladies and gentlemen [who] come regularly to act as playmates, to suggest games, and to inspire, if not to dictate, order.'[126] Of children left on their own, Mary Ward asserted, 'The play-time of the poor lacks joy, discipline and protection.'[127]

The Happy Evenings, the Story Hours, the Play Centres, Magic Lantern Services, and the Country Holidays were all efforts to rescue the slum children from the depravity of home and street:

> How to deal with our gutter children, how to elevate, civilise, Christianise them, how to take them from the gutter, and make them as other children are – this is one of the most difficult problems of the day. . . . If we could but raise these unhappy children, could give them a childhood calculated to lead to a better manhood, we should be looking at the costliness of our criminal classes, be effecting a national savings . . . I am decidedly of the opinion that the gutter child is a very reclaimable subject.[128]

Child reclamation, the salvation of the young by means of a vast and urgent rescue mission, was the cry put out by educators, reformers, and politicians. The parents might be hopelessly beyond redemption, but there was yet hope that the children could be saved. In *How the Poor Live*, George Sims wrote:

> I am not of the school which says that the regeneration of the masses is hopeless, but I freely confess that the great chance of bringing about a new and better order of things lies among the children who are to be the mothers and fathers of the future. In the old Biblical times water and fire were the elements which solved the knotty problem of regenerating a seething mass of humanity sunk in the lowest abysses of vice and degradation. The deluge that shall do the work now must come of the opening of the floodgates of knowledge. . . . It is this river of knowledge which modern wanderers in the wilderness must ford to reach the Canaan which the philanthropist sees waiting for them in his dreams[129]

The concept of a childhood for the poor as a category of experience to be protected and carefully groomed within a framework of nationally supported institutions emerged with the commitment to the notion that the transformation of the working classes, and thereby the future stability of the nation, lay in the rescue of its children. The language of child rescue was one of the ways in which the importance of the Education Act of 1870 was conveyed to reluctant ratepayers and to those fearful of an educated working class; it likewise served in succeeding years to justify and explain further intrusions of the state into patterns of working class home life. In visual terms, the language of rescue and reclamation found its architectural analogue in the style chosen for the new elementary schools built in every poor neighborhood of London.

Notes

1 G. C. T. Bartley, 'The alpha of universal education', *School Board Chronicle* (18 March 1871), p. 181.
2 G. R. Sims, *How the Poor Live* (London: Chatto and Windus, 1883), p. 48.
3 Sister Grace, 'Our children's work', *Bermondsey Settlement: The Monthly Record*, 2:2 (February 1896) p. 22.
4 M. MacMillan, *Child Labour and the Half-Time System*, Clarion Pamphlet, No. 15 (London: 'Clarion' Newspaper Company, 1896), p. 1. Margaret MacMillan, Socialist member of the Bradford School Board, was an outspoken advocate of child welfare, particularly as it related to primary education.
5 Education for the poor in the 1830s and 1840s is examined in R. Johnson's 'Educational policy and social control in early Victorian England', *Past and Present*, No. 49 (1970), pp. 96–119.
    See D. Vincent, chapters on 'Family economy' and 'Childhood' in *Bread, Knowledge and Freedom: A Study of Nineteenth-Century Working Class Autobiography* (London: Europa Publications, 1981), pp. 62–108, for the place of the child within the domestic economy of working class families.
    In the field of English nineteenth century social history, the work of Anna Davin, to date largely unpublished, represents the most far-reaching attempt to examine the experience of working class children, in particular the lives of girls. Her doctoral thesis, in progress, University of London, 'The childhood of working class girls in late nineteenth century London', looks specifically at the relationship of schooling after 1870 to the experience of working class home life in London; she has also done research in the areas of both children's work and children's play. I am indebted to her generosity in sharing this work with me.
6 See for example, J. H. Plumb, 'The new world of children in eighteenth-century England', *Past and Present*, No. 67 (1975), pp. 64–95. Also reprinted in N. McKendrick, J. Brewer, and J. H. Plumb, *The Birth of a Consumer Society: The Commercialization of Eighteenth-Century England* (London: Europa Publications, 1982), pp. 286–315.
7 A. Paterson, *Across the Bridges or Life by the South London River-side* (London: Edward Arnold, 1911), p. 38.
8 The Association of Helpers, *Are We Making the Most of Our Board School Building? The Wealth of King Demos* (London: Mowbray House, 1893), n. pag.; rpt. *Review of Reviews*, March 1893, p. 3.
9 G. Best, *Mid-Victorian Britain, 1851–1870* (1971; rpt. Fontana, 1979), pp. 129–33. In agricultural communities, where child labor continued to play a significant role, one finds employers uniting in opposition to compulsory school attendance.

Anna Davin in 'Imperialism and motherhood', *History Workshop Journal*, 5 (spring 1978), p. 10, notes that from the 1870s onward there was a declining birthrate: the concern for the welfare of children coincided, she suggests, with their diminishing supply.

10 See for example E. J. Hobsbawn, *Industry and Empire: An Economic History of Britain since 1750* (London: Weidenfeld and Nicolson, 1968), pp. 128–43, on the rise in the standard of living in the late nineteenth century.

11 Davin, 'Imperialism and motherhood', p. 10.

12 Paterson, *Across the Bridges*, p. 170.

13 P. Alden, *Democratic England*, see 'The child and the state' (London: Macmillan, 1912), pp. 31–2.

14 Revd Benjamin Waugh, introduction, *Queen's Reign for Children* by William Clarke Hall (London: T. Fisher Unwin, 1897), p. vi.

15 The text of the Education Act states 'There shall be provided for every district a sufficient amount of accommodation in public elementary schools . . . available for all the children resident in such district for whose elementary education efficient and suitable provision is not otherwise made'. Forster defined what he meant: 'by efficient I mean schools which give a reasonable amount of secular instruction' as quoted in J. Murphy, *The Education Act 1870: Text and Commentary* (Newton Abbot: David and Charles, 1972), p. 39.

16 *The Times*, 29 November 1870, p. 1.

17 E. P. Thompson, *The Making of the English Working Class* (1963; rpt. Pelican Books, 1977), p. 377.

18 W. E. Forster, Third Reading of the Education Act, House of Commons, 25 July 1870. *A Verbatim Report with Indexes of the Debates in Parliament During the Progress of the Elementary Education Bill, 1870, together with a Report of the Act* (London: National Education Union, 1870), p. 515.

19 As quoted by D. W. Sylvester, *Robert Lowe and Education* (London: Cambridge University Press, 1974), p. 118).

20 F. B. Smith, *The Making of the Second Reform Bill* (Cambridge: Cambridge University Press, 1966), p. 2.

21 G. Stedman Jones, *Outcast London: A Study in the Relationship between Classes in Victorian Society* (Oxford: Oxford University Press, 1971), pp. 241–2.

22 Stedman Jones (*ibid.*) argues that the extension of the franchise was a means of forestalling 'an incipient alliance between the casual "residuum" and the "respectable working class", as fear grew on a national level of a possible coalition between reformers, trade unions and the Irish', pp. 241–2. Smith in *The Making of the Second Reform Bill*, on the other hand, explains that 'the Riots were a protest against class isolation, not a symptom of class war', p. 132. R. Shannon, *The Crisis of Imperialism, 1865–1915* (London: Paladin Books, 1976), while summarising the positions concludes that 'a series of massive demonstrations in the major cities through-out 1866–67 added weight to the argument that expediency pointed to a prompt settlement', p. 64.

23 Smith, *The Making of the Second Reform Bill*, p. 105.

24 *Ibid.*, pp. 105–12.

25 Disraeli introducing the Reform Bill on 18 March 1867, as quoted by Smith, *The Making of the Second Reform Bill*, p. 102.

26 Disraeli as reported in *The Times*, 12 June 1867, as quoted by Smith, *The Making of the Second Reform Bill*, p. 102.

27 Winterbotham, in *Verbatim Report* (see note 18), p. 54.

28 J. Morley, *The Struggle for National Education* (1873; rpt. Brighton: Harvester Press, 1972), p. 109.

29 Sir C. Adderley, North Staffordshire, Second Reading, House of Commons, *Verbatim Report*, p. 114.

30 As quoted by Smith, *The Making of the Second Reform Bill*, p. 75.

31 Lowe from a pamphlet of 1867, *Primary and Classical Education*, quoted by D. Rubenstein, *School Attendance in London 1870–1904: A Social History* (Hull: University of Hull, 1969), p. 5.

32 A. J. Mundella, Sheffield, Second Reading, House of Commons, *Verbatim Report*, p. 115.

33 *Ibid.*, p. 117.

34 *Ibid.*, p. 118.

35 W. E. Forster, introducing the Education Bill, 17 February 1870, in J. Stuart Maclure (ed.), *Educational Documents England and Wales, 1816 to the present day* (1965; rpt. London: Methuen, 1973), p. 100.

36 Forster, *ibid.*, p. 103.

37 T. Wright, *Our New Masters* (London: Straham, 1873), p. 2.

38 As quoted by D. Rubinstein, 'Socialisation and the London School Board 1870–1904: aims, methods and public opinion', in P. McCann (ed.), *Popular Education and Socialization in the Nineteenth Century* (London: Methuen, 1977), p. 234.

39 As quoted by Rubinstein, 'Socialisation and the London School Board', p. 235. According to R. McKibbin, *The Ideologies of Class: social relations in Britain 1880–1950* (Oxford: Clarendon Press, 1990), about 80 per cent of the male work-force was non-unionised and the female work-force outside the cotton industry was almost entirely non-union, p. 2. In exploring the lack of a collective consciousness among the British working class, McKibbin suggests that the very nature of casual labor and its dependence on self-reliance placed such workers outside any collective activity and common goals and strategies.

40 G. Sutherland, *Policy-Making in Elementary Education 1870–1895* (London: Oxford University Press, 1973), p. 118.

41 P. McCann, 'Trade unionist, co-operative and socialist organisations in relations to popular education 1870–1902', dissertation, University of Manchester 1960, p. 40.
   McCann notes that Trade Union support for the League's policies 'represented the electoral force of the newly enfranchised artisans. Without this backing the League would have had a rather narrow social basis in the Radical and Nonconformist middle class. The alliance suited both sides. The middle class Radicals gained powerful allies; the unions gained what was important to them at the time, the cachet of respectability attaching to an alliance with middle class men of good standing in furtherance of the eminently respectable aim of the provision of a system of national education', p. 39.

42 B. Simon, *Studies in the History of Education: Education and the Labour Movement, 1870–1920* (London: Lawrence and Wishart, 1965), p. 121.

43 McCann, 'Trade unionist, co-operative and socialist organisations', p. 40.

44 As quoted by McCann in 'Trade unionist, co-operative and socialist organisations', from the 43rd Annual Report of the General Union of Friendly Operative Carpenters and Joiners' Society of Great Britain and Ireland, p. 40.

45 Even by the end of the century, trade union membership was only 15 per cent of the employed work-force; see McKibbin, *The Ideologies of Class*, p. 2.

46 Smith, *The Making of the Second Reform Bill*, p. 53.

47 T. A. Spalding and T. S. Canney, with a preface by Lord Reay, Chairman of the Board, *The Work of the London School Board Presented at the Paris Exhibition, 1900* (London: P. S. King and Son, 1900), p. 27.

48 McCann, 'Trade unionist, co-operative and socialist organisations', p. 71. Lucraft was to hold his seat for twenty years.

49 *The Times*, 29 November 1870, p. 9.

50 M. Sturt, *The Education of the People: A History of Primary Education in England and Wales in the Nineteenth Century* (London: Thames and Hudson, 1973), p. 313.

51 D. Rubinstein, 'Annie Besant and Stewart Headlam: The London School Board Election of 1888', *East London Papers*, 13, summer 1970.

52 J. S. Hurt, *Elementary Schooling and the Working Classes 1860–1918* (London: Routledge and Kegan Paul, 1979), pp. 83–6.

53 *National Reformer*, 17 February 1889, p. 101. Annie Besant wrote a regular column for the *National Reformer* during her term on the School Board, 1888–91. She was one of the few women and Socialists, representing one of the poorest divisions; her column provides a valuable insight into the key issues raised on behalf of working London. She was an outspoken advocate of free school meals, secular education, the abolition of school fees, and fair wages paid for all work commissioned by the School Board for London; the latter was an issue she pursued as a member of the Works Committee.

54 Rubinstein, 'Socialisation and the London School Board', p. 239.

55 T. Gautrey, *Lux Miki Laus: School Board Memories* (London: Link House Publications, 1937), p. 27. For a discussion of women seeking Board election and their service, see P. Hollis, *Ladies Elect: Women in English Local Government 1865–1914* (Oxford: Clarendon Press, 1987), pp. 71–131.

56 Rubinstein, 'Socialisation and the London School Board', p. 240.

57 Gautrey, *Lux Miki Laus*, p. 28.

58 Gautrey, *Lux Miki Laus*, pp. 108–9.

59 Elementary Education Act 1870, Section 74, part 3.

60 Rubinstein, *School Attendance*, pp. 86–7.

61 Education Act of 1870, Section 74, part 1.

62 *Final Report of the School Board for London 1870–1904* (London: P. S. King and Son, 1904), pp. 193–4. The committee submitted its recommendations in June 1871.

63 *Final Report*, p. 194.

64 Rubinstein, *School Attendance*, p. 44.

65 Gautrey, *Lux Miki Laus*, p. 35.

66 Charles Booth, as quoted by Rubinstein, *School Attendance*, p. 53.

67 Rubinstein, *School Attendance*, p. 52.

68 School Board for London (SBL) 1331, 1879 report, p. 7. The SBL records are held by the Greater London Record Office (GLRO).

69 SBL 1331, 1880 report, p. 3.

70 J. Reeves, *Recollections of a School Attendance Officer* (London: Arthur H. Stockwell, c. 1915?), pp. 12–13.

71 *Ibid.*, pp. 34–5.

72 *Ibid.*, p. 37.

73 C. Morley, *Studies in Board Schools* (London: Smith and Elder, 1897), p. 224.

74 Gautrey, *Lux Miki Laus*, p. 35.

75 H. B. Philpott, *London at School: The Story of the School Board 1870–1904* (London: T. Fisher Unwin, 1904), pp. 40–1.

76 The testimony is taken from SBL 129: The Minutes of Evidence taken before the Committee with Reference to the uniform enforcement of the by-laws in the metropolis 26 March 1874, pp. 8–32.

77 J. Runciman, *School Board Idylls* (London: Longmans, Green and Co., 1885).

78 'School Board Cruelty to the Poor', *The East London Observer* (17 January 1874), p. 7.

79 J. Greenwood, *Low-Lifes Deeps: An Account of the Strange Fish to be Found There* (London: Chatto and Windus, 1876), p. 140.

80 G. Stedman Jones, 'Working-class culture and working-class politics in London, 1870–1900; notes on the remaking of a working class', *Journal of Social History*, 7:4 (summer 1974), p. 486.

81 Annie Besant quoting her opposition in *National Reformer*, 3 February 1889.

82 Sims, *How the Poor Live*, pp. 26–9.

83 A. Davin, 'The childhood of working class girls', n. pag. The anger of mothers who felt mistreated resulted not infrequently in physical assault upon teachers, a fact recorded in school log books.

84 A. Besant, 'The London School Board: what we do, and what we don't do', *National Reformer* (12 May 1889), p. 293.

85 SBL 1413: Letters from the Education Department, 13 May 1872, Provisional Order for putting in force the Land Clauses Consolidation Act of 1845.

86 '[A]ny Parish in the Metropolis where twenty or more houses occupied by persons of the labouring classes had been or were about to be scheduled and acquired in that and the preceding four sessions'. SBL 1534: Report of the Works Committee for the year Ended at Lady-Day, 1901, p. xiii.

87 SBL 927D: Works and General Purposes Committee, Record of complaints lodged against the School Board for London.

88 Philpott, *London at School*, pp. 40–1.

89 Reeves, *Recollections*, p. 67.

90 P. Dane, *Mad By Act of Parliament; or, Groan from Helpless Victims* (London: Brighton: privately printed, 1887), p. 42.

91 Reeves, *Recollections*, p. 15.

92 As quoted by Davin, 'The childhood of working class girls'.

93 As quoted by Rubinstein, *School Attendance*, p. 73.

94 D. L. Woolmer, 'Caring for London's children', in G. Sims (ed.) *Living London* (London: Cassell, 1901), p. 374.

95 J. B. Hopkins, 'The Rights of the Child', *The School Board Chronicle* (30 March 1872), p. 213.

96 A. Morrison, *The Child of the Jago* (London: Methuen, 1896), pp. 8–11.

97 W. Beasant, *All Sorts and Conditions of Men* (London: Chatto and Windus, 1882; 1883 2nd edn), p. 110.

98 Morley, *Studies in Board Schools*, p. 52. Charles Morley had been editor of the *Pall Mall Gazette*. These sketches of Board School life first appeared serialised in that periodical.

99 *Ibid.*, p. 43.

100 H. Bosanquet, 'The children of working London', in B. Bosanquet (ed.), *Aspects of the Social Problem* (London: 1895; rpt. New York: Kraus Reprint, 1968), p. 40.

101 T. Wright, *The Great Army: Sketches of Life and Character in a Thames-Side District by the River-Side Visitor* (London: Daldy, Isbiter and Co., 1875), 2, p. 2.

102 A. Mearns (W. C. Preston), *The Bitter Cry of Outcast London: An Inquiry into the Condition of the Abject Poor*, introduction Anthony S. Wohl (1883; rpt. Leicester: Leicester University Press, 1970), p. 67.

103 The case for the country v. the city is stated in a particularly vivid fashion by R. Bray, 'The Children of the Town', in C. F. G. Masterman (ed.), *The Heart of the Empire: Discussions of Problems of Modern City Life in England with an Essay on Imperialism* (London: T. Fisher Unwin, 1901), pp. 111–64.

104 'Children's Country Holiday Fund', *Bermondsey Settlement Magazine* (May 1897), p. 74.
105 'A Guild of Play Holiday', *Bermondsey Monthly Record* (February 1896), p. 22.
106 Bosanquet, 'The children of working London', p. 33.
107 C. F. G. Masterman, *From the Abyss: of its Inhabitants by One of Them* (London: R. Brimley Johnson, 1902), p. 80.
108 D. H. Reeder, 'Predicaments of city children: a late Victorian and Edwardian perspective on education and urban society', in D. H. Reeder (ed.), *Urban Education in the Nineteenth Century*, Proceedings of the 1979 Annual Conference of the History of Education Society of Great Britain (London: Taylor and Francis, 1977), p. 77.
109 Bray, 'The children of the town', p. 111.
110 Bosanquet, 'The children of working London', p. 36.
111 *Ibid.*, p. 29.
112 Hopkins, 'Rights of the child', p. 213.
113 Wright, *Great Army*, p. 20.
114 Bosanquet, 'The children of working London', p. 40.
115 W. Booth, *In Darkest England and the Way Out* (London: International Headquaters of the Salvation Army, 1890), pp. 64–5.
   Booth regarded the city as particularly unsuited to child-rearing: 'The town-bred child is at a thousand disadvantages compared with his cousin in the country . . . if he has nothing but skim milk, and only little of that, has at least plenty of exercise in the fresh air. He has healthy human relationships with his neighbours. He is looked after, and in some sort of fashion brought into contact with the life of the hall, the vicarage and the farm', pp. 62–3.
116 Booth, *In Darkest England*, p. 65.
117 G. Wagner, *Barnardo* (London: Weidenfeld and Nicolson, 1979), pp. 216–55.
   According to Wagner, nearly 100,000 children were sent to Canada between 1870 and 1924; others were relocated in Australia, New Zealand and South Africa. Wagner has also written of the charity movements to resettle children in 'Education and the destitute child after 1870', in J. Hurt (ed.), *Childhood, Youth and Ecuation in the Nineteenth Century*. Proceedings of the 1980 Annual Conference of the History of Education Society of Great Britain (Leicester: History of Ecucation Society, 1981), pp. 58–9.
   Revd A. Osborn Jay of Shoreditch wrote in *The Social Problem: Its Possible Solution* (London: Simpkin, Marshall, Hamilton, Kent, 1893) of establishing 'penal colonies' for those of the poor who appeared to be beyond redemption so that their influence upon the rest of the population would be removed. They should be 'comfortably bed and fairly housed, and never allowed to return to the outside life for which their very nature enirely unfit them.' Arrangements should be made 'preventing wretches of the most abandoned type from propagating continually fresh examples and likenesses of themselves', pp. 92–103. Revd Jay was the figure upon whom Arthur Morrison based his hero in *The Child of the Jago*, the selfless Clergyman working for the public good.
118 Sister Grace in the *Bermondsey Monthly Record*, p. 22.
119 Davin, 'The childhood of working class girls', n. pag.
120 Mrs Humphry Ward (Mary Ward), *Play-Time of the Poor* (London: Smith, Elder and Company, 1906), p. 14.
121 SBL 795: Special Sub-committee of the School Management Committee, signed minutes, vol. 7, to consider the Desirability of Establishing Vacation Schools, 1902, pp. 361–2.
122 Ward, *Play-Time of the Poor*, p. 8.

123 *Ibid.*, p. 5
124 Association of Helpers, *Are We Making the Most of Our Board School Building?*,
    p. 3 (see note 8).
125 'The children's happy evenings', *Child Life*, 2, No. 10 (1892), p. 154.
126 H. Barnett, *Canon Barnett*, 1, p. 288.
127 Ward, *Play-Time of the Poor*, p. 6.
128 Wright, *Great Army*, p. 23.
129 Sims, *How the Poor Live*, p. 48.

CHAPTER THREE

The public face of the London Board School

With the passage of the Education Act there came the immediate and daunting task of supplying the capital with school accommodation.[1] It would not only be necessary to calculate need, but, further, to determine what a public elementary school – an institution without precedent in English history – would look like. However difficult such a problem appeared, within a few years the London Board School was a well-known feature of the metropolis, easily recognisable by its brick triple-decker buildings with their large white sash windows and Flemish gables. How did the Board arrive at a public face for its new schools? How was the appearance of the new schools to play a part in portraying the role of this new institution? What was intended by the choice of style and location of these buildings, repeated nearly five hundred times in the city, concentrated in the poorest neighborhoods? How were the commanding structures intended to be viewed by local residents and the ratepaying public at large? In what ways was the architecture of the elementary school to speak of the intentions of the new institution? Or in what ways was the public face of the new institution designed to mediate – or obfuscate – the conflicting perceptions of this new school system?

i   The institution and its public

That the School Board for London, aware of its unique position in the capital and the potential of architecture to express this position, self-consciously sought a new form, is evident from contemporary commentators, including the Board's own Chief Architect, Edward Robert Robson: 'The design of a building should clearly express its purpose',[2] he explained to an audience at the Architectural Association in 1872. Yet the

> Public Elementary School – the school for the rudimentary education of the poor – has, in the nature of things, no remote history as an English institution, neither has the scientific, constructional, or artistic aspect of its buildings any annals.[3]

And a school inspector of the period recalled the general sense that it was necessary to devise a new form for an utterly new building type:

> There was no model building upon which the new structure might be planned; no type of school architecture which has received enlightened recognition. To fall back on tradition was useless.[4]

Robson also acknowledged the role of design for the place in which children learn

> manners, morals, habits of order, cleanliness, and punctuality, temper, love of study and of the school, [which] cannot fail to be in no considerable degree affected by the attractive or repulsive situation, appearance, out-door convenience and in-door comfort of the place where they . . . spend a large part of the impressionable period of their lives.[5]

It was not only the schoolchildren themselves who would be affected by the new architecture. Robson cited as a major source for his own ideas on school architecture the 'excellent and well illustrated work' on school plans[6] written by an American, Henry Barnard, which stated that

> The style of the exterior should exhibit good, architectural proportion, and be calculated to inspire children and the community generally with respect for the object to which it is devoted. . . . Every school-house should be a temple, consecrated in prayer to the physical, intellectual, and moral culture of every child in the community, and be associated in every heart with the earliest and strongest impressions of truth, justice, patriotism, and religion. . . . No public edifice more deserves, or will better repay, the skill, labour, and expense which may be necessary to attain this object, for here the health, tastes, manners, minds and morals of each successive generation of children will be, in a great measure, determined for time and eternity.[7]

The buildings, Robson wrote, were in fact 'sermons in brick'.[8] And the sermon was directed to the parents as well as the children. Robson wrote,

> We have seen how abject are the homes of the countless thousands. If we can make the homes of these poor persons brighter, more interesting,

nobler, by so treating the necessary Board Schools planted in their midst as to make each building undertake a more leavening influence, we have set on foot a permanent and everlasting good. It is in the nature of things, purely an external influence, but a glimpse of nobler things will have been brought under the daily ken, and to the very door, of the working man.[9]

There was another audience as well to view these new buildings: the London ratepayers who voted in elections, and who, although usually sending their own children to voluntary schools, nevertheless saw the future of the capital and the nation bound up with the newly emergent educational system. It was in these 'oases in the desert of drab two-storied cottages',[10] that London's child population, rescued from the evil influences of home and street, was to be educated and civilised.

Although the internal planning of the school was slow to evolve, drawing in its early development on the precedents of English charity schools, the main features of the façade, which would be retained for over thirty years, easily recognisable to 'Every railway traveller in London',[11] were firmly established by the mid-1870s; indeed, their uniform appearance was cause for comment in the building journals by the mid-1870s.[12]

In Charles Booth's study of London poverty the significance of the large school buildings looming over London's poorer neighborhoods was described:

> In every quarter the eye is arrested by their distinctive architecture, as they stand closest where the need is greatest, and each one 'like a tall sentinel at his post', keeping watch over the interests of the generation that is to replace our own. . . . Taken as a whole they may be said fairly to represent the highwater mark of the public conscience in this country in its relation to the education of the children of the people.[13]

As an institution emerging at the center of debate, every decision of the School Board regarding its buildings was subject to public scrutiny. But what decision-making process led to the form of the London Board School? Before examining the complex of meanings associated with the new building type, it is important to understand the sheer enormity of the job which the London School Board faced. Even as the School Board set about to determine the number of children who were not attending school and the state of existing voluntary schools, there was little comprehension of the scale of the task that lay ahead.

Equipped with the 1871 census, which listed the name of every child of school age who slept in London on the night of 2 April 1871, house to house investigators determined what schooling children were receiving. Basing the computation on a calculation of child population used by the Education Department before 1870, an estimate of one-sixth of the total population, the Board would have arrived at a figure of some 560,000 children of school age in London; subtracting existing school places, which were estimated at 308,000, the balance would have been 252,000. The need for school places, computed as 112,000, was to fall far short of the real need.[14] The overwhelming cost of providing for over a quarter of a million school places appears to have motivated the initial incorrect figure. Inherent in the initial calculations, it would seem, was the unresolved conflict which would shape Board policies and public opinion in the years to follow: on the one hand, the desire to alleviate the tensions that were thought to result from the general ignorance and squalor in which many young Londoners grew up, and, on the other hand, the resistance to paying for the institutions which were to bring about their transformation.

Although the Education Act provided for the means of transferring existing schools to the Board's jurisdiction – the first was transferred in February 1871[15] – most of the schools were in disrepair and were closed as soon as more acceptable school accommodation could be provided. Nonconformist bodies as a whole surrendered their schools, but there was no general willingness on the part of the Church to transfer its schools; only those in the worst condition were given up.[16] By March 1872 twenty-three schools had been transferred to the Board and sanctioned for use by the Education Department, with an additional thirty-three awaiting Department approval; in addition, thirteen hired buildings were in use with an additional forty-one hired with tenancy to begin shortly.[17]

As early as 1855 Matthew Arnold, an Inspector for the Department of Education, had described the state in which he found London schools:

> In no school premises anywhere, so far as my observation goes, is want
> of space, want of cleanliness, want of ventilation, want of playground,
> so much felt as in the school premises of London.[18]

The London School Board was to discover that Arnold's verdict was not unfounded. Difficulty in enforcing the by-laws concerning school attendance due to a shortage of school accommodation resulted in such stop-gap measures as making use of temporary quarters, including old hospitals, assembly halls, mission halls, even warehouses.

The decision to construct a Board School in a particular location could prove to be contentious. Although the construction of public elementary schools was necessarily concentrated in the poorest districts

4] Locality of the first Board School erected in London from
E. R. Robson's *School Architecture*, 1874

of the city [4] – the number of schools built in the 1870s in the three
poorest London districts was larger than the number built in the
remaining six – schools were also built in predominantly middle class
areas that had a sufficiently large population of artisans and workers in
service occupations to warrant a Board School. But the proposal to
build a Board School could engender the fury of local residents in a
'locality, inhabited . . . by persons whose social position in life is far
above the wants or requirements of such an institution.'[19]

The anxieties of a proprietor of a voluntary school were spelled
out in a letter to the Education Department which set forth the reasons

why a Board School in South Kensington should not be constructed near his school: the proposed school 'seriously threatened' adjoining property; 'parents of his pupils will absolutely refuse to allow their sons to mingle or associate with the pupils of the Board School.' Preventing such association would be very costly and, finally, 'besides this evil of comingling of the pupils of the two Schools which must ultimately prove ruinous to your Petitioner, the noise and tumultuous uproar connected with the assembling of several hundred School Board pupils . . . must, of necessity render the work to be done practically impossible.' And the letter concluded that

> for the above and other reasons, and more especially considering that your Petitioner's School is a large and old established Middle Class One, some of the pupils belonging to which pay an annual fee of eight guineas, your Most Honourable Board may take all the premises laid down into your most favourable consideration, and prevent the completion of the purchase of the ground[20]

If, however, the School Board had evidence from the Statistical Committee that school accommodation was needed in a particular location, and if no alternative sites were available, a temporary iron building or a rented premise would be used to test the number of children likely to attend a Board School.[21]

ii   Finding an architect

In the summer of 1871 the Board decided to proceed with the design of its first twenty new schools in neighborhoods with the greatest need rather than to wait for the complete return of statistics.[22] The Board was empowered to borrow money, with the approval of the Education Department, from the Public Works Loan Commission or from the Metropolitan Board of Works in order to purchase land and erect the buildings. In order to permit the Board to proceed quickly the Education Department waived the need for statistical results on receipt of the first application for a loan,[23] requiring instead a site plan, statement of cost of the site, an estimate for the building and furniture, a description of the schoolhouse and numbers, ages, and sex of the children to be accommodated.[24] The Finance Committee predicted the opening of fifty new schools to accommodate seven hundred children each by January 1873; the predicted figures proved to be overly optimistic, as only sixteen new schools were opened in 1873, followed, however, by forty-nine in 1874.[25]

The means by which architects should be chosen to design the first twenty schools fell to the Works Committee to decide, some Committee members 'suggesting that the design of the first schools should be open to the whole profession.'[26] In the end, however, a motion was carried whereby twenty architects were invited to participate in a competition for the first school.[27] By the following year, 1872, the procedure usually allowed for a closed competition in which six architects were selected to compete for each new site for the first thirty schools. It was left to the Works Committee to select the six architects.

In July 1871 the Works Committee appointed as part-time architect Edward R. Robson to co-ordinate the building activities of the Board at a salary of £500 a year.[28] This initial appointment entailed overseeing the Board's existing properties – those transferred to the Board and often in need of repair – as well as the critical job of site acquisition.[29] The process by which the very first schools were planned, selected, and built appears to have been characterised by a series of experiments, representing a variety of styles and approaches.

The basic brief handed to competing architects was extremely simple, designed primarily to accommodate the Teaching Code of 1872. Essentially that meant that all entries should conform to a few basic rules: there were to be six standards (grades), plus the infants' schools for children from three to five years old. For every sixty children there was to be one certificated teacher and one 'pupil-teacher' – an assistant of not less than thirteen years of age – and for every additional eighty children either one certificated teacher or two pupil-teachers were required. As far as was practical, separate classrooms were to be provided for each standard, 'But, as each School is under the general supervision of one master or mistress, this principle must, in some degree, be subordinate to the necessity for such supervision.' The final requirement was the use of sturdy building materials and construction, with a view to the cost of annual maintenance.[30] The architects were given additional particulars regarding the size of rooms, the amount of space to be allotted per child – the rules set by the Education Department – as well as details concerning each site and the projected requirements of the particular school.

The Battersea Road competition in the Lambeth Division in 1872 was typical, requiring three departments (boys, girls, and infants) of equal number, 9 sq. ft (0.83 sq. m) per child, schoolrooms for both the boys' and girls' schools in which all could also assemble, with 4 sq. ft (0.37 sq. m) per child, a caretaker's residence, rooms for the head-master and headmistress, a stipulated distance from the road, an indication of the method of warming and ventilating, and an estimate of total cost. There was no stipulation as to the style to be used, although brick or stone was required for reasons of fire prevention.[31] The architect was to receive a commission of 5 per cent. There was no honorarium for unsuccessful entries in closed competition.[32]

Architectural journals were quick to criticise the Board's practice, although it was noted with some relief, considering the history of Victorian competitions, that the London School Board did, at least, intend to let the winner design the building. But the journals predicted that a system that offered nothing to competing architects who did not win was doomed to failure:

> No limited competition worth having can be just unless each unsuccessful competitor be paid sufficiently to cover his working expenses. And in the case of an open field, the first half-dozen should be regarded in the same light as the select half-dozen of a limited fight[33]

A reviewer of an exhibition of school designs at the Old Bailey likewise pointed to the fact that the Board's procedures did not offer architects of quality enough inducement to compete: 'few architects of ability or experience care to waste their time and thought on the remote chance of obtaining a commission for a very moderate-sized building.'[34] The writer went on to state that with a system of competition in which school designs were selected two at a time, with 'Three hundred new schools . . . wanted at once . . . we may confidently predict that the educational scheme will result in a complete failure.' On behalf of the profession, *The Architect* proposed that the vast work of the Board be shared among its members, fifty or one hundred architects to be employed. Warning against the tendency toward corruption which closed competitions seemed to invite – the final selection going to 'personal friends or *bon vivants*' – the writer concluded that if the Board was committed to a system of competitions, competitions should be open to all.[35]

There was no immediate consensus as to what a public elementary school in the nation's capital should look like. The result of the early competitions was a variety of styles, but versions of Gothic predominated [5–8, 27] as architects fell back on religious schools as their model. [9] Critics varied, although the notion that the form of the schools should 'bear evidence in their external appearance of the purposes to which they are devoted'[36] was a sentiment often repeated. How this was to be translated into school design was less clear.

Though unclear as to what this new public institution should look like, critics were often harsh in their verdicts on what was selected. There was a general recognition that economic restrictions

5] London Board School, Forest Hill, architect H. Saxon Snell,
from *The Builder*, 14 March 1874

limited the possibilities for elaborate façades and internal planning, but
the architectural press was often highly critical nonetheless. The
architect E. W. Godwin, reviewing an exhibition of Board School
designs for *The Architect*, wrote,

> To ignore the question of art; to count as nothing pleasing grouping,
> elegant proportion, refined detail, and at the same time to provide a
> room for drawing class [a provision in many schools], would be like

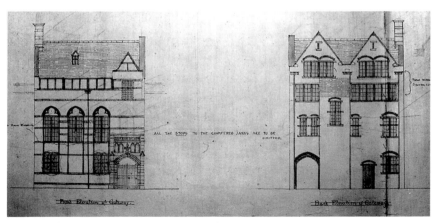

6] London Board School, Turin Road, Bethnal Green, 1873?, architects
G. F. Bodley and T. Garner

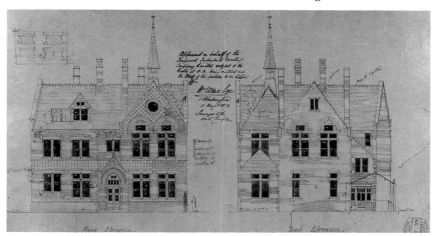

7] London Board School,
Brewhouse Lane,
Wapping, opened in 1874,
architect E. R. Robson

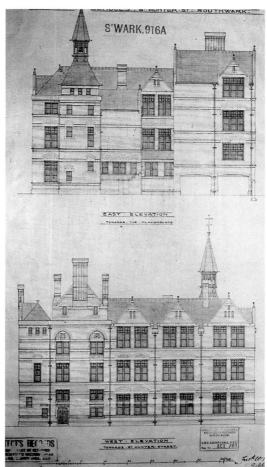

8] London Board School,
Great Hunter Street,
Southwark, 1873?,
architect Frederick Roper

robbing with one hand and calling a policeman's attention to it with the other – a piece of inconsistency scarcely to be conceived outside a competition.[37]

In May 1872 Basil Champneys competed for a school to be built in Stepney, East London. Although he did not succeed his entry was singled out for praise in *The Architect*:

> The rival merits of the arrangements or planning we cannot now attempt to analyse, but as to architectural merit there need be no hesitation in saying that Mr. Champneyes [*sic*] design is more pleasing, more English, and more school-like than any other.[38]

T. Roger Smith won the competition based on his use of the Prussian system of separate classroom planning – a singular experiment in these early years, to be discussed in greater detail later – but Champneys was

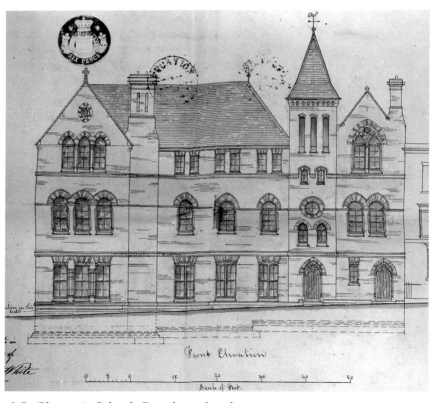

Front Elevation

Scale of Feet.

9] St Clement's School, Barnsbury, London, 1865, architect Lacy W. Ridge

invited to compete again for a Board School in Fulham, Harwood Road
School. His design [10], worked out in June and July of 1872,[39] was
characterised by the use of red brick and white sash windows, large
chimney stacks, and Flemish gables – features that became the
hallmarks of the 'LSB style', a style which was noted as the 'pervading
character' of Board Schools in London by 1874, displaying 'the semi-
Classical features of the style known as Queen Anne.'[40]

To speed up the process whereby schools were designed and
built, as well as for reasons of greater economy – it would no longer be
required to allot 5 per cent to each architect – the Board extended
Robson's duties in August of 1872 and raised his salary from £500 to
£1,000 per annum, 'With a view, amongst his other duties, to his
designing and building the Schools of the Board.'[41] In assuming the
position of Chief Architect in 1872 Robson was to oversee the buildings

10] London Board School, Harwood Road, Fulham, 1872, from
E. R. Robson's *School Architecture*, 1874

in progress designed by other architects, but further competitions which had been planned were cancelled. With few exceptions, Robson became the designer of the London Board Schools.

Details surrounding the selection of Robson as chief 'architect and surveyor', and the decision to entrust him with the design of the schools, are not recorded in the School Board Minutes.[42] But Robson came to the position in London with considerable experience in architecture and building as well as property management and site acquisition. Edward Robert Robson was born in 1835 in Durham where his father had served three terms as mayor of the city. He served an apprenticeship in the building trades, followed by three years in the office of the prominent Newcastle architect John Dobson. In 1857 he joined the London office of Sir Gilbert Scott where he worked on restorations for three years. During this time he also travelled extensively to study Continental architecture. In 1859 he went into partnership with J. Walton-Wilson, whom he had met in Dobson's office, jointly opening offices in London and Durham. For six years he was Architect to Durham Cathedral, working on its restoration. In 1864 he was appointed Architect and Surveyor to the Corporation of Liverpool. His son recalled that for this position he had been supported by such eminent architects as Smirke, Street, Scott, Ewan Christian, William Burges and Sir J. Mowbray,[43] but on his doctor's advice Robson and his family returned to London.

At the time of his initial appointment as part-time architect and property manager for the School Board for London, Robson's experience went beyond that required by the Board. The ultimate appointment as designer of the London Board Schools, however, with its generous salary of £1,000 and the stipulation that he could maintain a private practice as well – terms he was not granted in Liverpool – was more in keeping with his background and experience. He settled his family in the Paragon, a cluster of fashionable early Georgian houses at Blackheath.

Robson's staff in the Architect's Department of the Board was extended to include a Chief Draughtsman, an Assistant Draughtsman, and a man to assist with structural drawings and specifications.[44] It was referred to the Works Committee to make arrangements for Robson to be relieved of the task of looking for and negotiating for the acquisition of sites; the tasks of finding sites and of valuation were given over to an Outdoor Assistant.[45] Although the procedures by which builders tendered for school contracts and by which the Architect oversaw the construction of the schools were flawed and in some cases resulted in the use of poor materials and substandard workmanship, as was revealed by investigations in the 1880s, a large number of elementary schools were built in an extraordinarily short period of time: nearly three hundred schools had been completed by the time Robson resigned his position in 1884.[46]

iii   The Queen Anne style

A Board School should look like a Board School, and like nothing else. . . . Some may even think that [Art] has no right to trouble herself where only ragged children are concerned, and that in doing so she is, in some way, derogating from her lofty mission. Yet there is a sense in which she may exert her influence in the highest and best manner. She may suitably mark a great social movement if invited to be present in its buildings, may show what can be done in the merest plain brickwork if her fundamental principles of truth and common sense be adhered to throughout; and, in making her mark on the schools of the people, show in some wise what the homes of these people ought to be. Although dealing broadly with schools for large towns, the text applies more directly to those of the metropolis. And in London the schools are intended to be in some sense the future homes of the poor, writ large.[47]

It was the elevation rather than the plan that concerned Board members in selecting designs in the early years: 'in the earlier history of the Board' there were schools built 'with no halls, and narrow corridors, and but little real convenience for teaching', but 'the character of the elevation led to considerable cost'. On the subject of decoration of the façade, the *Final Report* further concluded that, 'It is the policy, however, of the Board, while studying, in the first instance, suitable arrangements for teaching, not to set aside the dignity and attractiveness of buildings, which the Board have always felt should be a contrast to their poor surroundings.'[48] The *Report* estimated that the difference in cost between schools built with only the barest utility in mind and those designed 'in some sort of style and with regard for materials and colour, was rather less than 5 per cent.' Although efforts were made to economise, schools built at prominent locations, according to the report, received greater attention to ornament.[49]

Like many of their contemporaries, Robson and Champneys had been trained in the Gothic style for church architecture, Champneys in the office of J. P. Seddon and John Prichard, Robson working for Sir Gilbert Scott.[50] Robson, drawing upon his own training as well as upon the designs of about thirty schools previously commissioned by the Board, experimented with a variety of Gothic façades. Robson's

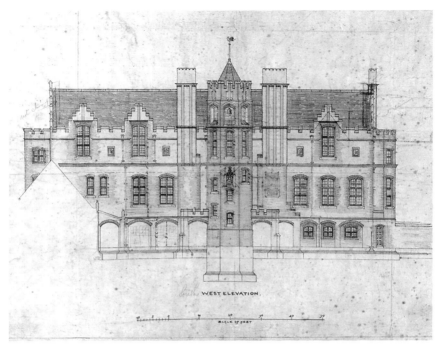

11, 12] London Board School, Winstanley Road, Lambeth, opened in 1874, architect E. R. Robson

early schools in Gothic varied in appearance with no consistent vocabulary emerging, as can be seen in the elaborate, castellated front of Winstanley Road School in the West Lambeth Division, opened in 1874, or in the Gothic form of Mansfield Place School in Camden Town or Jonson Street School, opened in the same year [11–13, 27].

There was a critical reason why the Gothic style was soon

13] London Board School, Mansfield Place, Camden Town, architect E. R. Robson from Robson's *School Architecture*, 1874

deemed inappropriate for the new school system, a reason which was far more compelling than the training or preference of any architect in the Board's employment: the place of religious instruction in the school curriculum remained a deeply contested issue for the School Board. The issue had been central to the Parliamentary debate preceding the passage of the Education Act, and in the end the Cowper-Temple clause, which had stated that 'No religious catechism or religious formulary which is distinctive of any particular denomination shall be taught in school', had been included. But the volatile question of religious instruction in the daily school curriculum remained unsolved. Forster himself had asserted that it was not a question of producing a secular educational system:

> Why do we not prescribe that there shall be no religious teaching? . . . We want, while considering the rights and feelings of the minority, to do that which the majority of parents in this country really wish: and we have no doubt whatever that an enormous majority of the parents of this country prefer that there should be a Christian training for their children – that they should be taught to read the Bible. . . . Would it not be a monstrous thing that the Bible . . . should be the only book that was not allowed to be used in our schools?[51]

Whereas the Education Act forbade denominational teaching within the Board Schools, it remained up to the School Boards to interpret the form of religious instruction permitted. The 'London Compromise', as the School Board's own interpretation was called, was passed on 8 March 1871 by a vote of 38 to 3.[52] The motion read:

> In the schools provided by the Board the Bible shall be read, and there shall be given such explanation and such instruction there from in the principle of Morality and Religion as are suited to the capacities of children, provided always – (i) That in such explanations and instruction the provisions of the Education Act, 1870 . . . be strictly observed both in the letter and spirit, and that no attempt be made in any such schools to attach children to any particular denomination. (ii) That, in regard to any particular school, the Board shall consider and determine upon any application by managers, parents or ratepayers of the district who may show special cause for exception of the school from the operation of this resolution, in whole or in part.[53]

Although religious instruction did become part of the curriculum – school prizes for knowledge of Scripture being offered in arrangement with the Religious Tract Society from 1875 onward[54] – the compromise was a significant break with traditional denominational education in the country.

The ecclesiastical associations of Gothic Revival architecture were, therefore, seen by many to be inappropriate to the spirit of the new school system. This sentiment was expressed by a number of commentators, including the Board's Architect, who wrote that 'the forms of medieval architecture run the risk . . . of being simple anachronisms.'[55] On the national level, a Report of the Committee Council on Education stated that 'The pseudo-Gothic form of school rooms should be abandoned, the high-pointed roof, the narrow lofty windows and the leaded panes are totally unsuited for school work.'[56] Perhaps more to the point, a member of the Committee noted that Gothic windows let in only 'dim religious light'.[57]

Robson expressed the view that the new school buildings should rather be an expression of the changes that had occurred in English education:

> If a church should at once be recognised as a church by the character of its architecture, and a prison as a prison, so should a school-house be immediately known as a home of education. It is clear also, that a building in which the teaching of dogma is strictly forbidden, can have no pretence for using with any point or meaning that symbolism which is so interwoven with every feature of church architecture as to be naturally regarded as its very life and soul. . . . A continuation of the semi-ecclesiastical style which has hitherto been almost exclusively followed in England for National schools would appear to be inappropriate and lacking in anything to mark the great change which is coming over the education of the country.[58]

Though the schools taught Scripture as an integral part of Board School education, their façades portrayed a departure from the traditions of voluntary schools with their denominational instruction, avoiding the religious associations which continued to divide public opinion. In its place, a style was introduced which told a different story of what the new institution had to offer. It was a style borrowed from a different building type, altered and modified, carrying with it particular associations, fitted to the needs of the public elementary school in London. In the 1870s the vocabulary of the Queen Anne Revival rendered it particularly appropriate to the new institution, and it became the style of the London Board Schools.[59]

Essential to an understanding of how this new vocabulary came to be used to create what was to be known as the 'LSB style' for the London School Board is an understanding of the ways in which Queen Anne had come to carry particular meanings and associations. Mark Girouard's *'Sweetness and Light': The 'Queen Anne' Movement 1860–1900*, is widely acknowledged as the major contribution to a social history of Queen Anne Revival architecture;[60] in it, he maintains that Queen Anne 'flourished because it satisfied all the latest aspirations of the English middle classes.'[61] Girouard examines a number of applications of the style, from Board Schools to pubs as Queen Anne moved 'down the social scale.' Girouard argues, as the title of his book suggests, that Queen Anne connoted both art and enlightenment, the 'sweetness and light' of Matthew Arnold's famous essay on culture. These, he argues, were the preoccupations of two particular circles within the middle class: broadly speaking, 'aesthetes' on the one hand, concerned with beautifying their domestic interiors, and, on the other hand, 'progressives' agitating for 'light' in the form of education and worthy causes. Girouard's description of the London Board Schools as representing 'the Architecture of Light'[62] results from a restricted view of social context. For Girouard, the context which explains the LSB style is the middle class 'progressive' circles that agitated for education and served on the School Board. However, complex and more diverse motivations and interests of the larger public were represented on the Board, which necessarily contributed to its fundamental attitudes regarding the very nature of working class education and childhood. Girouard's discussion of style ignores the ways in which the urban geography of London in the 1870s necessarily played a part in the process by which Board School architecture was read and understood in the period.

The language of Queen Anne architecture was one of the tools by which the new institution defined itself to a heterogeneous public. Style, including reference to past styles, is to be understood as a means of expression, one of the ways in which meaning is conveyed. 'Context', in which meaning emerges, is the complex of social relationships interwoven in the conception, design and construction of buildings.

An examination of the origins of the Queen Anne Revival is central to an understanding of its selection as the style of the new Board Schools. 'Queen Anne', as contemporaries noted, was a misnomer, as it did not refer specifically to the architecture during the reign of Queen Anne, but rather to the vernacular styles of the seventeenth and eighteenth centuries. Other names were put forward by its exponents, particularly 'Re-renaissance' and 'Free Classic'[63] and by its critics, 'Debased Classic'. But 'Queen Anne' was the term accepted by the public, and it came to mean an architecture of red brick and white sash windows which freely combined mid-seventeenth century gables, brick pilasters, brick pediments, and ribbed chimney stacks, wrought-iron railings, hipped roofs, wooden cupolas, external shutters, fanlights and brick aprons beneath the windows. Prominent roofs and chimney stacks were often decorated with the sunflower motif. It was an architecture of the façade, which in domestic buildings left the interior arrangement of earlier stucco terrace houses intact behind a picturesque red brick street front. The use of prominent gables, however, made the boundaries of one home distinct from those of its neighbor, in contrast to the image of the extended villa which the unity of white stucco had tried to convey.

In the 1870s a number of architects trained in the offices of prominent Gothic Revival architects designed buildings which partook of the new vocabulary. With Robson in Scott's office, for example, there had been George Frederick Bodley, George Gilbert Scott Jr, Thomas Garner, Thomas Graham Jackson, and John James Stevenson. The leader of the Revival, Richard Norman Shaw, had worked in the office of the Gothic Revival architect George Edmund Street. There were reasons that explain in part at least the departure from Gothic: the nature of architectural patronage was changing dramatically and the younger generation found itself confronted with new demands for which their earlier training in Gothic seemed to have left them unprepared.

Of the leaders of the architectural profession born between 1810 and 1830, two in three were church architects, including Pugin, Scott, Butterfield, Carpenter, Pearson, and Bodley. Church design was the primary means by which an architect made a reputation, more quickly than designing country houses, and churches were more frequently illustrated in the professional journals than any other buildings.[64] In contrast, all the future leaders of the profession who emerged in the late 1860s and 1870s produced primarily secular buildings: houses, schools and, occasionally, town halls. Norman Shaw produced domestic architecture almost exclusively until he was fifty-five years old.[65]

Queen Anne Revival architecture emerged in the 1870s above all as a domestic architecture. It became the architecture of the new middle class suburbs and the West End in the 1870s and 1880s – the architecture of Kensington, Holland Park, Bayswater, Chelsea, and Hampstead, as well as the garden suburb of Bedford Park, south-west of London. In the words of J. J. Stevenson, one of the chief exponents of the Revival, the meaning of Queen Anne was bound up with all of the 'pleasant associations of the English home'.[66] And Stevenson suggested that the emergence of the style was related to the contemporary enthusiasm for an image of eighteenth century life as depicted in the novels of Thackeray, which portrayed country gentlemen, doctors and writers, rather than the tales of medieval chivalry which had enchanted a previous generation. Stevenson illustrated his book on domestic architecture with examples of Queen Anne vernacular architecture [**14–15**].

Robson retained a private practice in partnership with J. J. Stevenson while in the Board's employment which would prove important in the development of a Board School style. The possibilities suggested by Basil Champneys' façade, 'pleasing' and 'more English, and more school-like design', were carried further by the Board's own architect in 1873 and 1874. Robson, assessing Champneys' school in 1874, described it as a 'quaint and able adaptation of old English brick architecture to modern school purposes',[67] in contrast to the large number of buildings that 'aim rather to attract the eye by startling novelties than to produce enduring impressions.'[68]

John McKean Brydon, a former assistant to Norman Shaw and William Eden Nesfield shared an office with Basil Champneys from about 1872 until 1875 around the corner from his former teachers; Brydon declared of the Queen Anne movement:

> now, at the end of the nineteenth century, we have a domestic Architecture unsurpassed for its high and artistic qualities by that of any other country in the world. The home is a peculiarly English institution, and certainly no houses, be they stately or be they humble, express the feelings of homeliness more truly than those of England.[69]

14] Drapers' Almshouse, Margate, from J. J. Stevenson's *House Architecture*, 1880

15] Kew Palace, from J. J. Stevenson's *House Architecture*, 1880

16] The Red House, architect J. J. Stevenson, 1871–3, from *The Building News*, 18 September 1874 (demolished)

That Queen Anne architecture embodied the cosy comforts of the English home was also spelled out by Stevenson:

> when we find that an Italian style is unsuited to our climate, that Greek architecture becomes in our hands cold and insipid, and gets misunderstood and vulgarised, when we find from experience that Englishmen are not Italians or Greeks in their tastes or their artistic powers, we may turn again with new pleasure to the cheery comfort of an English red-brick house.[70]

There were practical reasons as well which explain the success of the Revival in domestic architecture. In 1871 Stevenson designed a house for himself in Bayswater which he named 'The Red House', a self-conscious reference to the house that Philip Webb had designed for William Morris in 1859 [16]. Whereas Webb's house was notable for its fine workmanship, designer and patron aligning themselves with the medieval traditions of craftsmanship, Stevenson explained his design in very different terms:

> [the style] has much to be said for it in practical terms. Take the ordinary conditions of London building – stock bricks and sliding-sash windows. A flat arch of red cut bricks is the cheapest mode of forming the window head. The red colour is naturally carried down the sides of the window, forming a frame, and is used to emphasise the angles of the building. As the gables rise above the roof it costs nothing, and gives interest and character to the building, to mould them into curves and sweeps. . . . With these simple elements the style is complete, without any expenditure on ornament.[71]

Stevenson's house was built of London stock brick, with façade decoration of Flemish gables, tall chimneys, small sash windows, louvered external shutters, and scroll work reminiscent of eighteenth century buildings. In contrast to Webb's house built in rural Kent, which evoked an image of a medieval parsonage in its finely detailed workmanship, Stevenson's house in London offered an inexpensive urban housing type which the Gothic revival had never done. It could be repeated countless times with small variations in the basic vocabulary – as indeed it would be by both architects and speculative builders in the following decades.

While there are many examples of Queen Anne homes designed for well-to-do clients in London's fashionable suburbs, an examination of Queen Anne in the hands of a speculative builder at Bedford Park, who created a middle class garden suburb in the 1870s and 1880s, illustrates most clearly the features of economy and domestic connotations of the Revival spelled out by Stevenson. At Bedford Park the alliance of an economic building style with the associations of Queen Anne were particularly clear. These were trumpeted in the advertising campaign to promote the suburb: one advertisement which appeared in newspapers between 1875 and 1883 referred to the 'artistic treatment of plain brick and tiles rather than . . . meretricious ornament', to the 'placing' of 'homes varying in size and design' in order to avoid the usual dull monotony, and commented that in interior decoration, 'it has been endeavoured to obtain a general scheme of decoration which shall render them, as they have been not ineptly described, "comfortable homes".'[72]

Bedford Park was founded by Jonathan Carr, a speculative builder with connections in the art world. His brother, Joseph Comyns Carr, was an art critic, dramatist and a director of the Grosvenor Gallery. The suburb was located to the south-west of the City, thirty minutes by train from Turnham Green station which opened in 1869. It was designed to recall a country village [17] with its own church, an inn, a co-operative store, an art school, and tennis courts, the whole dominated by the squire's house occupied by Jonathan Carr. As such, a self-conscious venture intended to conjure up quaint and homey connotations, it was satirised in the press, particularly in *Punch*.[73] The strain here to recreate the homely ambience of an eighteenth century village through the use of Queen Anne architecture revealed the recognition of illusion in the contemporary perception of the style.

There was to be nothing in Bedford Park to remind commuters who worked in London that they were within a half-hour's ride from the City. Carr employed Queen Anne architects: first E. W. Godwin and then in 1877 Norman Shaw was appointed the Estate Architect. After a falling out with Carr, Shaw was replaced by the architects E. J. May and Maurice B. Adams. At Bedford Park designs by architects were repeated over and over with slight variations to prospective residents. There were both detached and semi-detached models from which to choose. The houses were simple but flexible. Carr paid Shaw for his designs, which Carr was then free to use as many times as required. In all, nearly five hundred homes were built.[74]

An enthusiastic commentator described the effect of Bedford Park as a 'little piece of an old English town which has somehow or another escaped the ravages of time.'[75] Another description referred to it as possessing 'a strong touch of Dutch homeliness, with an air of English comfort and luxuriousness'.[76] It was like walking through a 'water colour', '*en tableau*'.[77] The writer went on to describe the sense of identity that living in Bedford Park lent to its inhabitants: 'For those who dwell here the world is divided into two great classes – those who live at Bedford Park, and those who do not.'[78]

Stevenson enthusiastically described eighteenth century examples in his history of house architecture: 'Such houses are common over all England. With their cheerful red brick fronts among the green, the windows with their broad white frames and small window panes twinkling in the light, they suggest all the pleasant associations of an English home.'[79] This, then, was the meaning of Queen Anne Revival domestic architecture in Bedford Park and other middle class neighborhoods, as it provided the requisite image of a more secure and comforting past.

There was no theory upon which the Queen Anne Revival was based as there had been for the Gothic Revival. Certainly Norman Shaw felt no necessity to write a justification of his architecture. There were no diatribes like those of Pugin or of Ruskin which had espoused a moral and social purpose for their movement. As one prominent architectural historian has written, 'Queen Anne, in all its multifarious forms, meant the final end of Puginian discipline. . . . [F]unction and propriety . . . had finally been abandoned in favour of the aesthetics of hedonism.'[80] Both J. J. Stevenson and T. G. Jackson, however, attempted to justify their departure from the high ideals of the Gothic Revival, which attests to the weight of that tradition upon a younger generation. Using strained, near-Ruskinian language, they endeavored to link the current revival of Queen Anne to the 'spirit' of Gothic: 'modern Gothic architecture . . .,' Jackson wrote, 'will come simply to this – "The practice of architecture in Great Britain according to true and natural principles"';[81] 'Let us once catch the spirit of old work, let us once master the principles which made it what it was, and carry them out thoroughly in our practice, whatever we may have to do, and the revival of Gothic will have answered its purpose.'[82] Stevenson, in his two-volume work, *House Architecture*, described the conditions under which seventeenth and eighteenth century architecture had been built. Reminiscent of Ruskin, who was writing of the medieval craftsmen, Stevenson wrote of English workmen 'following their own instincts'.[83] 'English workmen,' he wrote, 'gave the style a character in accordance with their own nature and common sense.'[84] And he described the results: 'the style was a living one, understood by every workman, who worked as he had trained, in harmony with his fellows.'[85]

But William Morris lamented the departure from the high ideals advanced by the Gothic Revival, and his assessment of the Queen Anne Revival leaves no doubt that he read the meaning of the new style with abundant clarity:[86]

17] Bedford Park, from Edward Walford's *Greater London*, 1883

> as time passed and the [Gothic] revivalists began to recognise, whether
> they would or no, the impossibility of bridging the gulf between the
> fourteenth and the nineteenth centuries; so the architects began on
> the fifteenth century forms . . . we have sunk by a natural process to
> imitating something later yet, something so much nearer our own time
> and our own manners and ways of life. . . . The brick style in vogue
> in the time of William the Third and Queen Anne is surely not too
> sublime for general use; even Podsnaps might acknowledge a certain
> amount of kinship with the knee-breeched, cock-hatted bourgeois of
> that period

Morris went on to present the case, in rather bitter irony, for 'The turn
that some of our vigorous young architects . . . took towards this latest
of all domestic style.' And he wrote

> let us be humble, and begin once more with the style of well-
> constructed, fairly proportioned brick houses which stand London
> smoke well, and look snug and comfortable at some village end, or
> amidst the green trees of a squire's park. Besides our needs as architects
> are not great; we don't want to build churches any more; the nobility
> have their palaces in town and country already (I wish them joy of
> some of them!); the working man cannot afford to live in anything
> that an architect could design; moderate-sized rabbit-warrens for rich
> middle-class men, and small ditto for the hanger-on groups to which
> we belong, is all we have to think of . . . we have come down a weary
> long way from Pugin's *Contrasts*[87]

Queen Anne architecture became synonymous in London with
middle-class domestic architecture in the 1870s and 1880s. Gothic
remained the style used for churches. Lucy Crane, in a series of lectures
delivered in 1882 on the formation of taste, summed up the situation:

> Perhaps it may be said that house-architecture is the thing in which
> we are really beginning to excel; not the architecture of stucco-fronted
> terraces, or seven or eight or nine storied flats, but of those gable-
> roofed, casemented, red-brick houses that are now often to be seen in
> town and country . . . we shall have an ideal dwelling-house – a home
> of cheerfulness, comfort, hospitality, – and this is much nearer of
> attainment by people of moderate means than it seemed a few years
> ago.
> For our churches it seems we can do no better than follow the patterns
> set us in ages of more faith than the present; in public buildings, there
> is much costliness and little grandeur; but the *home*, – that, at least, it
> seems within our power to make solid and beautiful and comfortable –
> a something 'not too bright or good for human nature's daily food.'
> And with this, for the present at least, we must be satisfied.[88]

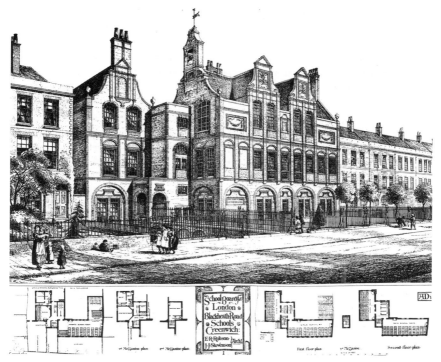

18] Blackheath Road School, architects E. R. Robson and J. J. Stevenson, *The Building News*, 19 February 1875

Stevenson was in partnership with Robson from 1870 until 1876, and there can be no doubt that Robson was well aware of the meanings and associations that the new style was intended to evoke. From the recollections of Robson's son and from Stevenson's writings, it is known that the designs of some of the early Queen Anne Board Schools were worked out in some form of collaboration between the two architects, as, for example, the design for Blackheath Road School, **[18]** although accounts differ in awarding credit for the 'London Board School style'. Stevenson claimed in *House Architecture* that 'For the architecture of a few of the earliest . . . I am responsible'.[89] In an article written by Robson's son, however, the collaboration is described in rather different terms: 'The late J. J. Stevenson joined him during the rush of work at the School Board. But he told me once that "he was occupied often in the afternoons rubbing out what John had done in the morning".'[90] Although the exact nature of the collaboration cannot be reconstructed, Robson certainly knew of the lectures that Stevenson delivered in the

1870s, in which he articulated the meanings associated with the new Revival, as well as Stevenson's two-volume work, *House Architecture*.

iv   The gift giving relationship

> In all 'good architecture' there is no vagueness, no indecision, no doing of things by accident, no drifting helplessly from one idea to another. The artist first grasped his building comprehensively as a whole with a clear definite intention of what he meant to say . . . and he conveyed his meaning and purpose on the face of his work, every moulding and member, window and door architrave, cornice and sculpture, being in his hands, so many opportunities for proclaiming his intention.[91]

The public face of the Board School was one of the means by which the architect, working on behalf of the School Board for London, presented the new institution to a heterogeneous and wary public. The Queen Anne style of the new schools, with its specific associations and meanings, was directed at both the local residents in whose midst the schools were built and the London ratepayer. The style suggested the avowed intention of Board School education as child rescue, and the relationship of the School Board to the ratepayer and to the communities in which the schools were built.

The Queen Anne Revival connoted the middle class origins of these schools for the working classes, but the schools were a simplified version of Queen Anne, bearing just enough of the features to be readable as such [19–20]. The Board School style was designed to impress and exhort but to withhold praise. How pared down this version of the style was is clear when contrasted with the Board's own headquarters on the Embankment, designed by George Frederick Bodley in 1873. [21] This can be explained only in part by the financial restraints which were ever present. In the words of the Board's architect,

> The lessons sought to be taught in such buildings as these – the sermons in brick, so to speak – are intentionally simple, never recondite or too complex. . . . They are simply common schools for the common people of the present time. We do not expect a costermonger to understand or appreciate the sonatas of Beethoven, the operas of Mozart, or the subtle perfections of Greek Art in the time of Pericles. We do expect him to comprehend a piece of practical advice about building, and to admire a lively tune, especially if well played on a good instrument for the benefit of his own children.[92]

H. G. Wells in his autobiography recalled the Education Act as a measure designed 'to educate the lower classes for employment on lower class lines.'93 In the words of R. H. Tawney it was intended 'in the main to produce an orderly, civil, obedient population, with sufficient education to understand a command.'94 The first curriculum of the London Board Schools was submitted by Thomas Huxley, Chairman of the Scheme of Education Committee of the Board in 1871. Huxley proposed to include besides the three Rs instruction in religion and morality, physical science, English history, elementary geography, elementary social economy, music and drill, and elementary drawing. Considered as far too 'literary'95 and ambitious a program for the simple wants of a Board School child, the syllabus was pared down: 'it was necessary,' as one sympathetic commentator noted, 'to breed a sturdier race before such dizzy intellectual heights could be scaled.'96

In 1873 John Morley, editor of the *Fortnightly Review* and a vehement spokesman for universal secular education, contrasted the education on offer at Board Schools to that received by

> the gentleman's son [who] at nine is barely supposed to have begun his education, yet this child at nine possesses an amount of knowledge that represents more than the whole educational stock in trade which is thought sufficient for four-fifths of the children of the workmen.97

The education of a Board School child began at an earlier age than his or her middle class contemporary but ended at a much younger age. The usual leaving-age was thirteen.98 It was not until the 1902 Education Act that secondary education was provided; previous attempts had been declared illegal, beyond the intentions of the Education Act of 1870. Middle class children received their earliest education from parents, older sisters or a governess. The education of middle class girls might take place solely within the home until the age of fifteen when they might attend a 'finishing school'. Boys generally attended a day or boarding school by the age of eight, by which time they had already had a grounding in the three Rs, the focus of a Board School child's entire education. A middle class boy would continue his education throughout his teens in school or university, or in professional training or apprenticeship.99

The limited nature of the education imparted can be seen most clearly in the description of the course in Elementary Social Economy, which was listed among the 'Essential' subjects taught by the Board Schools from 1871 to 1883. To what extent Social Economy was actually taught in Board Schools is impossible to determine, but the syllabus drawn up by the Board reveals what the Board members deemed 'essential'. The message of submission to authority and financial self-discipline was found in a less structured way throughout Board

19] London Board School, Gloucester Road, Camberwell, opened in 1875, architect E. R. Robson

20] London Board School, Tottenham Road, Hackney, opened in 1874, architect E. R. Robson

School instruction. Elementary Social Economy covered 'the production of wealth', 'the distribution of wealth', and 'the exchange of wealth'. The teacher was to explain the 'contract between employer and employed', 'the impossibility of increasing wages by law', and the 'division of labour and its advantages', along with a list of necessary character traits to be discussed: 'thrift, temperance, and economy'.[100] *The Social Economy Reading Book* included such chapters as 'What Shall We Live on When We Grow Too Old to Earn Wages', with warnings against frivolity that leads to the workhouse and a parish burial.[101]

The message that underlay much of the curriculum was adjusted to the age of the students. For example, a nature lesson in the Board's infants' schools – children from three to five years of age – was given in the belief that

21] London School Board headquarters, architect G. F. Bodley, from *The Architect*, 10 May 1873

Children can be taught to understand harmony in the relationship of their lives to the larger world about them, and it is through the recognition and development of this dim feeling of community and their innate love of order, that we get ultimately real discipline in the school, when children are obedient, orderly, and industrious because their relation to the community in which they live demands that they should be so. [102]

A Board School reader of 1878 designed for infants' schools carried this message:

Mistress: What do you come to school for, Mary?
Mary: To learn to read and write and sum.
Mistress: There is something else that you learn. What is it?
Mary: I don't know.
Mistress: Then I will tell you. You will learn to be obedient. [103]

A description given in Charles Morley's sketches of Board School life sums up the relationship the Board School child was to have to those who provided his or her schooling:

'Now what . . . do you see on the board?'
'A work-ouse.'
'A Board school.'
'A water-cart.'
'A dustman.'
'That's right. Now, who pays for all of them? You know the dustman must live; and the man who drives the water-cart, and the horses that draw it along; and hundreds of poor people have a home in the workhouse without cost to themselves; and then there's the infirmary, where we can go to if we are sick and can't afford to call in a doctor ourselves; and then there's the school here, where you are taught for nothing. Now, who can tell me where the money comes from to pay for all these?'

The teacher goes on to explain that everyone contributes but that in all likelihood those that benefit the least, pay the most:

'Now, who can tell me why Mrs Smith, although she pays more money for her shop, and is less likely to want relief from the parish, and very likely has a doctor of her own when she is not well, has to pay twice as much rates as Mrs Jones. . . . Now – why is that?' . . .
''Cos she's better off nor Mrs Jones. She can afford it better.'
'That's right. Mrs Smith is better off than her neighbour Mrs Jones, so roughly speaking she pays according to her ability. . . . So the idea is – ?'
'That she pays to help her poorer neighbours'

The teacher proceeds to explain how the Free Library is paid for in the same way, and then returns to the Board School in which the children are sitting:

> 'Well – and then we come to the place we are now in – the Board school. There again we all agree to contribute to the education of everybody's children, and whether Mrs Smith has a child of her own or not she still pays her share – say sixpence in the pound – and again befriends her poorer neighbours'[104]

In a city divided geographically, rich and poor, West and East End, a city in which the hypothetical Mrs Smith and Mrs Jones did not know one another, the use of an architectural style distinctive of the West End and the growing middle class suburbs for schools built predominantly in the city's poorest neighborhoods, put into clear visual terms the relationship of giver to recipient. In particular, the concentration of attention on the elevation attests to the emphasis placed upon the appearance of these schools against the squalor in which they were built, giving visual form to the relationship between giver and recipient.

Although the interior of the schools might tell a different story, to the London ratepayer who passed by the red brick triple-decker schools, with their Flemish gables and white sash windows, even replete with characteristic terracotta sunflowers – viewing them perhaps from a railway carriage – the schools represented to them, as Charles Booth's survey had described it, the 'high-water mark of the public conscience in this country in its relation to the education of the children of the people.'

The rescue mission – children rescued and educated in these 'homes of education', as Robson described them – was a source of pride and pleasure to the middle class ratepayer: the children who went back to the slums from the Board Schools, 'are themselves quietly accomplishing more than Acts of Parliament, missions, and philanthropic crusades can ever hope to do.'

> Already the young race of mothers, the girls who had the benefit for a year or two of the Education Act, are tidy in their person, clean in their home, and decent in their language.[105]

By 1879 the Chairman of the Board in his annual report quoted a colleague who claimed that

> wherever a Board School was set down, a transformation in the habits of the people soon followed; the child's face was polished until the parents grew ashamed of their own; habits of order and cleanliness were

formed, and in many other ways the little one became a channel of civilising influence to hitherto inaccessible courts and lanes.[106]

Within the Queen Anne schools, the 'street arab' and 'gutter child' could be rescued, humanised and civilised. The middle class values associated with the architectural style assured the London rate-payers that their will was being carried out. That Queen Anne architecture represented the complete antithesis of all that the image of the urban slum conjured up, is attested to by a description in the immensely successful novel of the early 1880s, Walter Besant's *All Sorts and Conditions of Men*. The wealthy Miss Kennedy disguises herself as a poor seamstress during her sojourn in the East End in order to see how the poor really live. Moved by the grim monotony of their surroundings and the utter hopelessness of their plight she desires to transform their dreary lives and fantasises:

> In blissful reverie she saw already the mean houses turned into red brick Queen Anne terraces and villas; the dingy streets were planted with avenues of trees; art flourished in the house as well as out of it; life was rendered gracious, sweet and lovely.[107]

It was that potent image of the schools as a palliative, an alternative home, restoring the bonds between classes and instilling in the working class habits of 'cleanliness, order, and industry',[108] that the architecture of the Board School was intended to realise.

Notes

1 Section 67 of the Education Act set down that within four months of the School Board election in the metropolis, returns were to be sent to the Education Department 'containing such particulars with respect to the elementary schools and children requiring elementary education in their districts the Education Department may from time to time require.'

2 E. R. Robson, 'Address Delivered on London Board Schools to the Architectural Association', *The Building News* (5 July 1872), p. 5.

3 E. R. Robson, *School Architecture*, introduction Malcolm Seaborne (1874; rpt. Surrey: Leicester University Press, Victorian Library edn, 1972), p. 159.

4 P. Ballard, Introduction in T. Gautrey, *Lux Miki Laus: School Board Memories* (London: Link House Publications, 1937), p. 10.

5 E. R. Robson, 'On planning and fitting of schools', *The Building News* (4 July 1873), p. 4; also reprinted in Robson's *School Architecture*, p. 6. This was one of three articles which appeared in *The Building News* in 1873 which were included the following year in Robson's larger study; see also 18 July 1873, pp. 60–2 and 1 August 1873, pp. 107–9.

6 Robson, *School Architecture*, p. 27. Robson also cited Henry Barnard's work two years earlier in his paper delivered to the Architectural Association which appeared in *The Building News*, 5 July 1872.

7   H. Barnard, *School-House Architecture* (Hartford: Case, Tiffany and Burnham, 1842?), p. 3.
8   E. R. Robson, 'Art as applied to town schools', *Art Journal* (1881), p. 140.
9   *Ibid.*
10 C. F. G. Masterman (ed.), *The Heart of the Empire: Discussions of Problems of Modern City Life in England with an Essay on Imperialism* (London: T. Fisher Unwin, 1901), p. 16.
11 J. R. Diggle, 'School boards and voluntary schools: The educational outlook for 1896', rpt. from *Fortnightly Review* (January 1896), by the Voluntary Defence Union, p. 249.
12 'The architecture of the past year', *The Building News* (2 January 1874), p. 1, and the following year, 'Architectural glance at 1874', *The Building News* (1 January 1875). Both of these articles are retrospective reviews of the previous year's architectural accomplishments.
13 M. C. Tabor, 'Elementary education' in *Blocks of Buildings, Schools, and Immigration*, 3, C. Booth (ed.), *Life and Labour of the People in London* (London: Macmillan, 1892), p. 204.
14 Robson, *School Architecture*, p. 292.
15 Gautrey, *Lux Miki Laus*, p. 21.
16 M. Sturt, *The Education of the People: A History of Primary Education in England and Wales in the Nineteenth Century* (London: Thames and Hudson, 1973), p. 19.
17 SBL 195, p. 71.
18 As quoted by T. A. Spalding and T. S. Canney, *The Work of the London School Board Presented at the Paris Exhibition*, 1900 (London: P. S. King and Son, 1900), p. 53.
19 Quoted from a Memorial from the Chelsea Division, see SBL 935: Works Committee Minutes, 17 December 1877, pp. 430, 527, 546, and SBL 936: pp. 3, 52, 173; in this instance the original site was abandoned. As late as 1904 a similar argument was made regarding the construction of a Board School: in the end the school was built, tucked behind the main streets, essentially hidden from view. SBL 1025, p. 199.
20 Letter to the Education Department, 25 November 1873, from Revd John McKechie from the 'united parishes of Lambeth and Camberwell'. Public Record Office (PRO): ED 5.
21 In *School Architecture*, Robson noted that iron buildings were too hot in summer and too cold in winter but the Metropolitan Building Act prohibited the erection of temporary buildings wholly of wood because of liability to fire; in London, therefore, the outer covering of temporary buildings was of corrugated iron, while the construction was of wood and iron combined. These buildings, Robson noted, were never in one place for long, usually sited in the playground area until the permanent school was completed. The cost of a temporary structure was almost as great as a common brick building, p. 204.
22 The detailed Report of the Board based on the inquiry into school accommodation was not placed before the Board until 27 March 1872, *Final Report of the School Board for London 1870–1904* (London: P. S. King and Son, 1904), p. 11.
23 See Letter to the School Board for London, 11 July 1871, SBL 1413: Letters from the Education Department December 1870–1 July 1881.
24 SBL 1413: Letter dated 12 August 1871 from the Education Department to the Board.
25 *Final Report*, p. 41. In July 1871, four standing committees were established

by the Board: the Statistical and Law and Parliamentary Committee, the Works and General Purposes Committee, the Finance Committee and the School Management Committee, the latter made up of the whole Board, See SBL 195: Signed Minutes of the Finance Committee, 19 July 1871, p. 71.

26 SBL 927A: Works and General Purposes Committee, 16 August 1871, p. 102.

27 SBL 927A, 23 October 1871, p. 139.

28 SBL Printed Minutes, 1, 28 June 1871, pp. 183–8. The position was advertised in professional journals. Eighty-four letters of application were received. The Works Committee selected six names from which to choose; Robson was elected by an overwhelming majority. No discussion of the selection process itself exists in the minutes.

29 *Ibid.*, p. 525.

30 SBL 927A, pp. 345–50.

31 SBL 927A, March 1872, p. 286. A list of requirements for the first seven schools appears on pp. 311–18.

  A set of Building Rules approved by the Board 24 April 1872, were published in *The Architect* (4 May 1872), pp. 226–7. They included certain fire precautions, e.g., stone staircases, and the separation of departments by sex, the general placement of waterclosets and lavatories; the appearance of the building remained the architect's domain.

32 SBL 195, p. 256.

33 'School Board and competitions', *The Architect* (6 April 1872), p. 169.

34 'Another School-Board Competition', *The Building News* (7 June 1872), p. 465. The drawings of competitors do not survive so it is difficult, except from the limited descriptions offered in the professional journals, to determine why particular designs were accepted and others rejected. No discussion of unsuccessful entries exists in the School Board Minutes.

35 'School Board and competitions', *The Architect*, (6 April 1872), pp. 169–70.

36 'School Board for London', *The Architect* (4 May 1872), pp. 226–7

37 E. W. Godwin, 'The London School Board competitions', *The Architect* (25 May 1872), p. 265.

38 'School Board for London', *The Architect* (4 May 1872), p. 226.

39 M. Girouard, *'Sweetness and Light': The 'Queen Anne' Movement 1860–1900* (Oxford: Clarendon Press, 1977), p. 66.

40 'Architectural glance at 1874', *The Building News* (1 January 1875), p. 1.

41 SBL 1115: Minutes of the Works Committee, Subcommittee on Sites, p. 30.

42 William Wigginton and Thomas Porter were eliminated on the first ballot, John Quilter on the second and Joseph James on the third. On the fourth ballot Robson was elected, eliminating J. W. Morris. Both James and Morris were experienced in school building. For discussion of Robson's appointment and career see P. A. Robson, 'Edward Robert Robson F.S.A.: A Memoir by his Son, *Journal of the Royal Institute of British Architects*, (February 1917), pp. 92–6, and M. Seaborne in the Introduction to E. R. Robson, *School Architecture*, pp. 10–13.

43 P. A. Robson, 'Edward Robert Robson', p. 93.

44 SBL 1115, p. 31.

45 SBL 1133: Minutes of the Works Committee, p. 197.

46 *Final Report*, pp. 30–1.

47 Robson, 'Art as applied to town schools', p. 137.

48 *Final Report*, p. 39. For example, one school singled out by the report to support this assertion was Blackheath Road, Greenwich, designed by Robson, opened in 1874, described as having 'no halls, narrow corridors, but ornate

elevation', p. 58. The building is in fact an early example of a Queen Anne Revival Board School, given a double page illustration in *The Building News* (19 February 1875), p. 206. **[18]**

49 *Ibid.*

50 Basil Champneys' participation may well have been made at the prodding of Robson as the two travelled in the same circles, as suggested by Girouard, 'Sweetness and Light', pp. 49–50, 65.

51 Forster, as quoted by J. Murphy, *The Education Act 1870: Text and Commentary* (Newton Abbott: David and Charles, 1972), p. 60 (H CXCIX, 457–8). Murphy notes that Cowper-Temple himself was the Chairman of the National Education Union and an important advocate of denominational instruction. He was endeavouring to counter the argument that the use of particular books and forms of words too closely linked with particular religious communion would tend to imply some form of acceptance by teachers and children of an adherence to that communion. As Forster put it, there was 'an objection in the country to catechisms and special formularies . . . not so much on account of the actual words, but because the putting of them into the hands of children appeared to be like claiming those children as belonging to a particular Church', as quoted by Murphy, p. 61.

52 *Final Report*, p. 99. The Cowper-Temple clause was included in the final version of the Education Act, along with the Conscience Clause put forward in the 'London Compromise', p. 102. In her column in the *National Reformer* of May 1889, p. 327, Annie Besant wrote of her belief that many of the parents who might have wanted to withdraw their children from religious instruction faced obstacles in doing so.

53 In 1894 the words 'Christian Religion and Morality' were substituted for 'morality and Religion', evidence of the fact that the nature of religious instruction within Board Schools remained an issue.

54 *Final Report*, p. 99.

55 Robson, *School Architecture*, p. 339.

56 From a Report of 1870–71 as quoted by M. Seaborne and R. Lowe, *The English School: Its Architecture and Organization 1870–1970*, 2 (London: Routledge and Kegan Paul, 1977), p. 8.

57 From a Report of 1876–77 as quoted by Seaborne and Lowe, *The English School*, p. 8.

58 Robson, *School Architecture*, p. 321.

59 The minutes of the School Board carry no discussion regarding the choice of a style for the new schools.

60 See, for example, M. Trachtenburg, 'Some observations on architectural history', *Art Bulletin* (June 1988), pp. 219–23, or D. Watkin, *The Rise of Architectural History* (London: Architectural Press, 1980), pp. 184–5. Watkin characterises Girouard's writings on the 'connexion between patron and architect' as 'fruitfully and fully explored' in his review of the book, 'Conservative Principle', *Apollo* (March 1978), p. 230.

But Girouard does not explore the ways in which meaning shifted, or was transformed in crucial ways, as the social context of the style changed. Rather, his concern throughout lies primarily with artistic quality and whether it is or is not sustained as Queen Anne gained in popularity. With a critical eye for detail and a keen appreciation for the individual hand of the architect, Girouard is concerned primarily with the development of the style in the hands of select architects and their imitators, tracing the style from the first 'foretaste' of the Revival through 'pioneering' works to the 'advanced' style in a variety of institutions.

Mark Girouard's is the only book to date devoted to an exploration of the Queen Anne Revival. See J. M. Crook, *The Dilemma of Style: Architectural Ideas from the Picturesque to the Post-Modern* (Chicago: Chicago University Press, 1987), for example, for a consideration of the formal characteristics of Queen Anne understood as a step between the Gothic Revival and a return to Classicism in British architecture; or A. Saint, *Richard Norman Shaw*, for an in-depth study of the major figure of the Revival.

61 Girouard, '*Sweetness and Light*' p. 1.

62 Girouard's title of the chapter devoted to Board Schools, in '*Sweetness and Light*', pp. 64–70.

63 J. J. Stevenson, 'On recent re-action of taste in English architecture', *The Builder* (27 June 1874), p. 540.

64 P. Thompson, *William Butterfield* (Cambridge, Massachusetts: M.I.T. Press, 1971), p. 27.

65 N. Pevsner, 'Richard Norman Shaw', in A. Service (ed.), *Edwardian Architecture and Its Origins* (London: Architectural Press, 1975), p. 51.

66 J. J. Stevenson, *House Architecture*, 1 (London: Macmillan, 1880), p. 336.

67 Robson, *School Architecture*, p. 296.

68 *Ibid.*, p. 298.

69 As quoted in 'William Nesfield', Service (ed.), *Edwardian Architecture*, p. 34.

70 Stevenson, *House Architecture*, 1, pp. 382–3.

71 Stevenson, 'On recent re-action of taste', p. 540.

72 As reproduced in M. Bosterli, *The Early Community at Bedford Park: 'Corporate Happiness' in the First Garden Suburb* (Columbus: Ohio University Press, 1977).

73 Bedford Park also served as the prototype for G. K. Chesterton's aesthetic suburb, Saffron Park, in *The Man Who Was Thursday: A Nightmare* (Bristol: Arrowsmith, 1908). It opens, 'The suburb of Saffron Park lay on the sunset side of London, as red and ragged as a cloud of sunset. It was built of bright brick throughout. . . . It had been the outburst of a speculative builder, faintly tinged with art, who called its architecture sometimes Elizabethan and sometimes Queen Anne . . . its pretensions to be a pleasant place were quite indisputable [to] the stranger who looked for the first time at its quant red houses. . . . The place was not only pleasant, but perfect, if once he could regard it not as a deception but rather as a dream.'

74 T. Affleck Greeves, *Bedford Park, The First Garden Suburb, A Pictorial Survey* (London: Anne Bingley, 1975), pp. 1–4.

75 W. Hamilton, *The Aesthetic Movement in England* (London: Reeves and Turner, 1882), p. 117.

76 (M. Conway) 'Bedford Park', *Harper's New Monthly Magazine*, 170: 62 (March 1881), p. 489, quoted from *Sporting and Dramatic News*, 27 September 1879.

77 *Ibid.*, p. 485.

78 *Ibid.*, p. 483.

79 Stevenson, *House Architecture*, pp. 335–6.

80 Crook, *The Dilemma of Style*, p. 179.

81 T. G. Jackson, *Modern Gothic Architecture* (London: Henry S. King and Company, 1873), p. 23.

82 *Ibid.*, p. 22.

83 Stevenson, *House Architecture*, 1, p. 331.

84 *Ibid.*, p. 337.

85 *Ibid.*, p. 344.

86 Girouard, '*Sweetness and Light*'. Girouard's unproblematic inclusion of William Morris as a central figure and supporter of Queen Anne is only possible if

one looks at visual similarities without looking at broader ambitions, intentions, and contradictions within the movement: Girouard's reference to Morris as commenting enthusiastically on Shaw houses is actually misleading, p. 99, as it is borrowed from a longer piece, quoted at length here.

87 W. Morris, 'The Revival of Architecture', *The Collected Works of William Morris*, p. 22 (London: Longmans, Green and Co., 1915), rpt. from the *Fortnightly Review*, May 1888.

88 L. Crane, *Art and the Formation of Taste: Six Lectures by Lucy Crane with illustrations by Thomas and Walter* (London: Macmillan, 1882), p. 39.

89 Stevenson, *House Architecture*, 1, p. 348.

90 P. A. Robson, 'Edward Robert Robson', p. 95.

91 Robson as quoted by D. Gregory-Jones, 'The London Board Schools of E. R. Robson', in Service (ed.), *Edwardian Architecture*, p. 89.

92 Robson, 'Art as applied to town schools', p. 140.

93 H. G. Wells, *Experiment in Autobiography: Discoveries and Conclusion of a Very Ordinary Brain (Since 1866)*, 1 (London: Victor Gollancz and Cresset Press, 1934), p. 93.

94 R. H. Tawney, *Education, The Socialist Policy* (London: Independent Labour Party, 1924), p. 22.

95 By the end of 1872 accusations of extravagance were leveled at the Board. 'It was also alleged', according to the account of Spalding and Canney, 'that the scheme of education was unnecessarily liberal, that it would tend to make fine ladies and gentlemen of the children in Board Schools, *The Work of the London School Board*, pp. 95–6.

96 H. B. Philpott, *London at School: The Story of the School Board 1870–1904* (London: T. Fisher Unwin, 1904), p. 35.

97 J. Morley, *The Struggle for National Education* (1873; rpt. Brighton: Harvester Press, 1972), p. 28. Of what the Board schools did provide Morley wrote: 'The children no doubt receive a certain amount of drill in cleanliness, order, punctuality, obedience; more than this they are made in a silent and unconscious way alive to the presence of social interest and duty around them. They are not left in that half wondering desolation, that forlorn abandonment, which stamps itself in the weird features of the gutter children of all great cities. . . . But such drill is not enough. . . . It is essential that the children of the workmen and of the poor be admitted a little further within the gates of civilization', p. 26.

98 There was a system of half-time attendance for children whose families suffered from extreme destitution which permitted children in exceptional circumstances to work; this meant that for some children the time in school was even less.

99 J. Burnett (ed.), introduction, *Destiny Obscure: autobiographies of childhood, education and family from the 1820s to the 1920s* (London: Allen Lane, 1982), p. 169. According to Burnett even in 1914 the likelihood of a child from an elementary school obtaining a free secondary education was only one in forty, although by 1902 local authorities were empowered – though not compelled – to provide secondary schools, p. 89. Sutherland offers the figure of 14 per cent as representing the number of children over twelve years old who were on the register of all inspected elementary schools: G. Sutherland, *Policy-making in Elementary Education 1870–1896* (London: Oxford University Press, 1973), p. 340.

100 Mrs Fenwick Miller, Chair, Special Subcommittee on teaching Social Economy, presented this outline of 27 February 1883 included in SBL 790: Minutes of

Special Subcommittees of the School Management Committee. According to the *Final Report* this constitutes the essence of the course from 1871 onward, p. 95. In 1893 a course entitled 'The Life and Duties of the Citizen' was introduced. This course, according to the *Final Report*, was to proceed 'from the known and familiar, such as the policeman, the rate collector, the board of guardians, and the town councillors', p. 289.

101 J. M. Goldstrum, *Education: Elementary Education 1780–1900* (Devon: David and Charles, 1972), pp. 152–3.

102 Spalding and Canney, *The Work of the London School Board*, p. 190.

103 As quoted by A. Davin, 'The childhood of working class girls', n. pag.

104 C. Morley, *Studies in Board Schools* (London: Smith and Elder, 1897), pp. 23–9.

105 From George Sims in *The Pictorial World*, 1883, as quoted by the Chairman of the School Board, Edward North Buxton, in his annual report delivered in October 1884, SBL 1331: Annual Reports, p. 7.

106 SBL 1331: Annual Report of 1879; the colleague referred to is not identified.

107 W. Besant, *All Sorts and Conditions of Men* (London: Chatto and Windus, 1882; 1883 2nd edn), p. 52.

108 SBL 1331: Annual Report of the Chairman, 1896.

CHAPTER FOUR

Inside the 'decorated shed'

On entering a Board School a visitor would have found the language of Queen Anne, with its suggestion of domesticity, left behind. Queen Anne architecture was an architecture of the façade; decoration was applied without concern for the expression of structure. It was an architecture of ornament, which 'prided itself on . . . only one Gothic legacy, its *truthful* planning.'[1] The asymmetrical school buildings expressed adjustments to often awkward urban sites; yet, in a crucial way, the façade of the London Board School revealed little of what lay on the inside. In the 1870s the characteristic Queen Anne wrapping

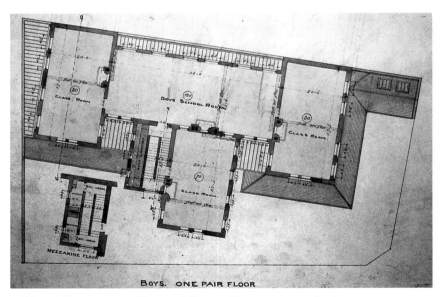

22] Boys' Department, Hamond Street, Hoxton, opened 1873, architect E. R. Robson

enclosed schools designed on the basis of extremely crude notions of school planning.

Board School planning in the early years was based on the use of large open rooms in which large numbers of children received simultaneous instruction [22], essentially one large schoolroom with an adjoining classroom on either side. This plan was replicated on three storeys: infants' school, girls' school and boys' school. The size of the school building varied, depending upon the requirements of the particular location, but Hamond Street School, Hoxton, of 1873 was fairly typical. The infants' school on the ground floor accommodated nearly 400 children between the ages of three and seven: one large schoolroom equipped with a gallery intended for 215 children, a classroom for 80 with a sliding partition [23] which could transform it into two rooms of 40 each, and a classroom with a gallery designated as a 'Babies' Room' for 80 children between the ages of three and five. The boys' and girls' schools, each reached by a separate entrance and a separate staircase, were divided on similar lines. The large schoolrooms were intended for 120 children and the two adjoining classrooms for 80 each, or twice 40 each if partitioned, with another classroom for 70, a total of 350. Children in a boys' or girls' school were seated at paired desks, five rows deep with gangways between, supervised by a single teacher, with the help of 'pupil-teachers' sometimes as young as thirteen years old, for every 40 children. The upper half of the doors to classrooms were usually of glass, enabling the Head Teacher to keep watch over the activities of children and pupil-teachers.

That visitor entering a Board School would also have been struck by the constant din of 1,000 children receiving lessons which in large measure consisted of simultaneous recitation. For infants, instruction took place with more than two hundred children in one room. Although the use of wood block on the ground floor, and felt stripping on the floors above, might have helped to keep the noise from carrying, the sound of four hundred infants marching, or the sound of nearly three hundred children reciting lessons in the girls' and boys' departments must have been formidable, the teachers straining to keep order. The sliding partitions which permitted children to be divided into two classes of forty each were sometimes merely curtains rather than wooden screens on rollers; in either case the partitions would have divided the two groups from each other's gaze but would have done little or nothing to diminish noise. Mezzanine floors might contain lavatories, a Head Teacher's room or cloakrooms. In spite of the inconvenience and the odor of damp clothing on wet days, some classrooms were lined with pegs for coats and caps where no cloakrooms were provided or when theft presented a problem.

23] Divided classroom with sliding partition, from E. R. Robson's
School Architecture, 1874

A Board School classroom might well have appeared cheerless.
No wall decoration was used in the school; a suggestion by the Board's
architect to stencil the walls was rejected.[2] A dark-painted dado ran
around the room, finished with a moulding at the window sill line,
above which was a white or buff distempered wall. Similarly, as a cost-
saving measure, paint was used for the dados instead of the Portland
cement recommended by the architect.[3] Classrooms were heated by an
open fire or by a specially designed stove. The heating and ventilation
of Board Schools were constant sources of complaint and continuing
experimentation. Rooms were lit by the large windows characteristic
of Board Schools, but, although side-lighting was recognised as superior,
it was not always achieved, and lighting was supplemented by artificial
light provided by a row of three-lamp pendants, fitted with flat-frame
burners hung along the center of the room.

The discrepancy between exterior and interior, the Queen Anne
'wrapping' for a 'shed', had its roots in English traditions of school
planning for the poor.

i   English traditions

The School Board for London drew upon earlier English traditions of
building schools for the poor. Robson stated his position:

> It will thus be seen that (so far as we treat of Public Elementary
> Schools) our object is not to start new-fangled ideas which might
> appear directed to revolutionise the system in use in this country – a
> system which differs from any other, and which has grown through
> many years of care and studious effort – but rather to present it in the
> new light which is the necessary outcome of new legislation; . . . and
> to glean from other countries, as well as from many sources of
> observation and experience in our own, such further hints as may tend
> to develop still further the principles of English school-planning.[4]

Robson asserted that the 'school's plan has always been of paramount
concern.'[5] And in answer to his own question, 'How should we build
schools in England?', he contended that 'something more is necessary
than merely to count cost. The aim and object of the enterprise should
be clearly defined, and the theory of the school determined completely.'[6]
Yet one can observe within the first few years of the Board's existence
a telling disparity between the evident sureness with which a public
face was developed for the new institution and the rudimentary
provisions for accommodation within.

In 1874 Robson published *School Architecture*, which represented
the most thorough compilation of elementary school designs published
in Britain to date. It represented the research he had carried out in
travels to the Continent – having secured a leave from the School
Board for London[7] – as well as a careful study of the most recent
examples of elementary schools in America and the British Isles. The
work stands as a testament to what was known about school buildings
in France, Germany, Austria, Switzerland, and the United States as
well as Scotland and Ireland; yet, in the end it was a book which
justified English traditions of school planning for the working classes
based on what Robson called a 'theory of English Elementary Schools'.[8]
The underlying reasons for the insistence upon English traditions would
seem to derive from Robson's keen awareness of his client's attitudes
toward the nature of working class education in England and the
concomitant reluctance to meet the expense which would have been
required to bring England's elementary schools in line with school
planning abroad. While aware of the restrictions placed before him,
and regretful, as he put it, that 'The English nation as a whole has not
yet grasped the importance of the Elementary Education Act',[9] he
nevertheless presented the case for the perpetuation of English teaching
methods and the corresponding architectural provisions derived primarily
from early nineteenth century voluntary schools for the poor:[10]

> A careful consideration of the plans of those [schools] erected in other
> countries, while affording hints on isolated features, do not furnish in

point of general scope and idea anything of the kind wanted in England. They are, one and all, un-English in spirit, and based on systems of training not in favour with us.[11]

Robson admitted that English prototypes were below the standard presently sought, but argued that 'We must think for ourselves in this matter, and, so to speak build on our own foundations.'[12]

English 'foundations' for the instruction of large numbers of working class children dated from the late eighteenth and early nineteenth century experiments of Joseph Lancaster, a Quaker who worked on behalf of the British and Foreign Schools Society founded in 1814 to promote non-sectarian education, and Andrew Bell, a clergyman working for the National Society for Promoting the Education of the Poor in the Principles of the Established Church, founded in 1811 to promote the educational program of the Church of England. These two societies played a major part in the history of voluntary schools, the National Society establishing schools in every parish in England and Wales. Both Lancaster and Bell advocated a system whereby large numbers of children could be instructed simultaneously by a single teacher assisted by selected children.[13] The monitorial system, as it was called, was modified during the nineteenth century, but its basic tenet of employing young assistants in order to provide mass instruction at a minimum cost remained an important feature of English elementary education for the working classes.

The National Society had been founded with the objective that 'the National Religion of the country should be made the foundation of national education, which should be the first and chief thing taught to the Poor, according to the excellent *Liturgy and Catechism* provided by our Church for that purpose.'[14] The Society adopted the ideas of Andrew Bell, which he had developed while working at a Male Orphan Asylum in Madras during a strike of the asylum's employees: children were set to work as assistants to the master rather than staff. Bell published an account of his system in England in 1797.[15]

Joseph Lancaster's teaching career began in London in 1798 among the poor. He offered free education by means of pledges by well-to-do supporters who paid the fees of a certain number of children at the rate of a guinea per head per year. In 1803 Lancaster introduced the monitorial system in order to accommodate the growing numbers of children.[16] A single qualified master could instruct a school of 1,000 pupils if divided into smaller groups, each aided by a monitor. A single book could serve an entire school if its contents were written in large type on a piece of paper glued to a pasteboard suspended against the wall. Using writing slates and one boy spelling a word to a whole class, five hundred boys could spell at the same time. Ciphering books could be totally eliminated as 'any child who could read might teach arithmetic with utmost certainty.' Using these techniques education could be supplied at 'a trifling sum'.[17]

Lancaster and Bell vied for the credit for the basic principle of using children to teach other children. Both men conceived of the school as essentially a large hall in which the simultaneous instruction of large numbers of children could take place. Lancaster's school was arranged with long unbroken rows of desks with wide passage-ways along the sides for lessons conducted by monitors [24]. Lancaster's system provided for smaller groups – from eight to ten pupils – arranged in semi-circles around a large printed sheet, thus eliminating the need for each pupil to have his or her own textbook. Bell's system kept the center of the great hall open with desks set along the walls and the students' backs to the center of the room, the center of the hall marked into squares for different classes, which in Bell's system contained between twenty-four and thirty-six pupils. The 'teachers' of these classes were typically between eleven and fourteen years of age, aided by even younger 'assistant teachers' between seven and eleven years old, chosen from the top of the class. The children stood – as in Lancaster's system – for all exercises except writing.[18] Further, all students were paired, the poorest with the best. Lancaster asserted that an efficient model for the design of a school, with its great space and lofty ceiling, was a barn.[19]

The confusion and noise engendered by the simultaneous activities of mass education under a single roof in an open-plan hall could be tolerated only if education was thought of in terms of drill and rote memorisation. Class lessons involving teachers in lengthy explanation could have no place. The employment of young children as monitors kept all lessons simple and mechanical. The necessary regimentation and mechanical teaching methods that were required in order for such a system to work at all were, however, lauded as a virtue. Bell compared his system to a 'regiment on a ship', as 'every boy had his place and every hour its proper business . . . and there grows up imperceptibly a sense of duty, subordination, and obedience.'[20]

A contemporary observer reported the horror of watching a well-meaning teacher attempt to give a lesson in such a hall. The schoolmaster is

> labouring to subdue the excitement which has awakened in his mind by noise and disorder, which he perceives to have been gradually increasing from the moment that his attention has been diverted from a general supervision of the school . . . the schoolroom has become to

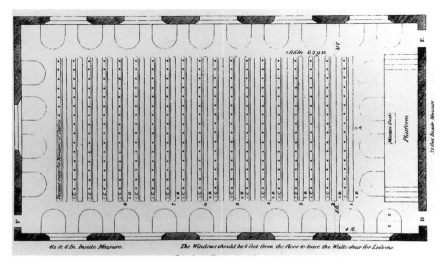

24] Lancasterian plan, school for 304 children, from the British and Foreign Society's *Manual of the System of Primary Instruction*, 1831

him a vast sensorium – that his feelers are thrown out over the whole surface of it, and his sensibilities awakened everywhere to the quick.[21]

In order to teach he is forced to assert himself with a cane, gaining once more his 'ascendancy in the school' and he finally 'gives up his task'. Robson's account of visiting an open-plan school in Dublin, however, defended the English tradition. He assured his reader that one is struck by the 'admirable discipline and system. The Lancasterian principle of large and noisy school-room may not be the visitor's *beau ideal*, but the noise is that of work, and is under the most complete control.'[22]

The English foundations upon which, Robson argued, the Board Schools should be based also drew upon the ideas of David Stow, a philanthropist influential in the provision of education for the working classes in Glasgow from the 1820s onward. Stow was concerned with the 'moral and Intellectual Elevation of Youth, especially in Large Towns and Manufacturing Villages', as the title of his treatise indicates. He devised a 'Training System', central to which was the use of a playground and a gallery **[25–26]** for instruction: 'It is as impracticable,' he wrote, 'for a teacher to train morally and intellectually without a gallery and a play-ground, as it would be for a mechanic to work without his tools.'[23] Robson used these features in designing Board Schools, employing the gallery particularly in infants' schools.

25] Uncovered playground, from David Stow's *Training System*,
11th edition, 1859

Critical to Stow's conception of education was moral training,
and this, he argued, went hand in hand with social pressure exerted by
a master over children assembled in large groups. Stow argued that
being seated in a gallery, side by side with fellow pupils, responding in
unison, enforced the learning process:

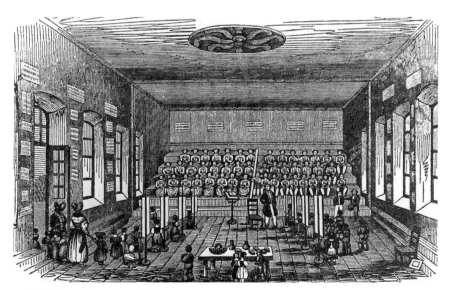

26] Gallery, from David Stow's *Training System*, 11th edition, 1859

Every word spoken is more easily heard by all – individual, but more particularly *simultaneous* answers, are more readily obtained – order is promoted, and instant obedience and fixed attention are more certainly secured, than when children are placed at desks, on level forms, in semi-circles, or in squares. Imitation and social sympathy thus also operate more powerfully with children when answering simultaneously or individually, . . . what is most important of all, breathless attention is secured while the trainer reviews any case of misconduct[24]

While the gallery secured attention and obedience, the play-ground, or 'uncovered schoolroom', as Stow called it, was the place where children expended pent-up energy and learned to get on with their fellows: there the child was 'surrounded for several hours a-day by a world of pupils.'[25] Stow saw the playground as the place in which moral training found expression. Children were to be overseen by an attentive superintendent, who 'applauds or condemns' their behavior; the stealing of a ball, for example, could then be discussed when the children reassembled in the gallery, all eyes on the guilty pupil:

Any case of oppression, or dishonesty, or particular act of generosity or disinterestedness, is, on the return to the gallery, taken up by the master, and thoroughly investigated, and condemned or applauded before the whole pupils, or rather simultaneously with the whole scholars, they sitting, in a sense, both as judges and jury.[26]

Stow's defense of simultaneous instruction and the concept of 'sympathy of numbers' were employed by Robson in defense of large classrooms and schoolrooms.[27]

The monitorial system was modified, raising the age of assistants, with the advent of state grants to schools in the 1830s. Further reforms included the introduction of galleries and subdivision of large school halls into smaller classrooms.[28] Until the advent of School Boards, however, no consistent policy emerged either widely accepted or enforced for the instruction of working class children. Rather, one finds instead variations on plans to accommodate the monitorial system and the pupil-teacher system. The changes which were made in elementary education, in fact, perpetuated education that was mechanical in nature and limited in scope as pupils continued to be taught *en masse*.

The education on offer was further restricted by the Revised Code of 1862 which had introduced the system of 'Payment by Results' and provided, it was argued, value for money, as teachers' salaries were linked to the performance of their pupils: HM Inspectors annually examined all children in schools in receipt of government grants. As the examinations were limited to the thee Rs, and needlework for girls, it was to these subjects that instruction was necessarily directed.[29] Payment by Results encouraged rote memorisation, which would ensure a pass from an Inspector with limited time to probe the comprehension level of his subjects. Payment by Results had been introduced as a means of reducing government expenditure, and in this it succeeded: whereas the Treasury grant had been £813,441 in 1861, in 1865 the government contribution was £636,806.[30]

There was opposition to the system from such distinguished spokesmen as Kay-Shuttleworth who had served for ten years as the Secretary of the Committee of Council, which administered Treasury grants, and Matthew Arnold, who objected strenuously to 'the principles of the free market . . . applied to education.'[31]

> it fosters teaching by rote; . . . The school examinations in view of *payment by results*, are . . . a game of mechanical contrivance in which the teachers will and must more and more learn how to beat us. It is found possible, by ingenious preparation, to get children through the Revised Code examination in reading, writing, and ciphering, without their really knowing how to read, write, and cipher.
>
> To take the commonest instance: a book is selected at the beginning of the year for the children of a certain standard; all the year the children read this book over and over again, and no other. When the Inspector comes they are presented to read in this book; they can read their sentence or two fluently enough, but they cannot read any other book fluently.[32]

Arnold explained how the children were prepared for the examinations in writing and arithmetic in a similar fashion. Having traveled extensively abroad, he unfavorably compared English schools to those elsewhere and concluded that 'It may be said that there are at present but three obligatory subjects in our schools, fewer, by much, than in the schools anywhere else.'[33]

Even the inspections were mechanical: one inspector in 1878 boasted of his method of examination which enabled him to inspect 41,908 children in one year.[34] Further, an Inspector's report carried great weight, as his comments on a teacher's performance remained part of a teacher's record for future employment and there was no doubt that a harsh assessment could ruin a teacher's career.[35] As one headmistress put it, 'stated flatly . . . an Inspector could wreck a teacher's career.'[36] It was, therefore, necessary to impart knowledge in such a way as to *ensure* the appropriate results.

A teacher who had been at a National School from infancy through service as a pupil-teacher recalled how inspection crippled the whole process of education:

It seemed that the main reason for a child's attendance at school was to gain sufficient ability in the three Rs to enable him to pass the examination by the Government Inspectors, and thus help him to earn the highest grant for the school. Little or no notice was taken of a child's health, comfort or well-being; that was someone else's business, certainly not the schoolmasters . . . the school stood in a district abounding with religious, historic and commercial associations. Yet we were told little or nothing about such interesting things. The teaching of the three Rs seemed to dominate everything – but possibly the cash element was really at the bottom of it[37]

And Edmond Holmes, a former Inspector, wrote in a frank and impassioned tone of the ills of the system which he had served. The teacher, wrote Holmes, aspired to dominate the child,

to leave nothing to his free activity; to repress all his natural impulses; to drill his energies into complete quiescence; . . . when severity and constraint have done their work, when the spirit of the child has been reduced to a state of mental and moral serfdom, the time has come for the system of education through obedience to be applied to him in all its rigour.

Because the teacher depended upon the child's performance,

the child is not allowed to do anything which the teacher can possibly do for him. He has to think what his teacher tells him to see, say what his teacher tells him to say, to do what his teacher tells him to do.[38]

It was, Holmes wrote, 'an ingenious instrument for arresting the mental growth of the child, and deadening all his higher faculties.' Holmes explained how he came to see himself as the 'victim of a vicious administrative system, perhaps the most vicious that has ever been devised.' The teachers, he lamented, 'had drilled themselves into automatism and their pupils into passivity and helplessness.'[39] Though modified, Payment by Results was not abolished until 1897.

Sidney Webb, writing in 1904, criticised the pupil-teacher system as a 'combination of child-labour and soul-destroying intellectual drudgery unworthy of a civilised nation.'[40] As early as the 1870s there were educators who, like Robson, travelled to the Continent to observe the European methods of education yet returned far more critical of England's elementary schools, focusing much of their criticism on the pupil-teacher system. One such educator was Joseph Payne, an Education Department Inspector and a former Professor of Education to the College of Preceptors, who visited Germany in 1874. His observations of elementary schools visited were published in 1876. He concluded of the German elementary school 'that as a rule, development and culture were aimed at and secured'. The success of the German schools he attributed to the system of teaching:

> *Every German elementary teacher has a separate class-room.* By this means the distraction arising from the juxtaposition of several classes, under different teachers in the same room is absolutely excluded. The teacher is 'monarch of all he surveys', and is therefore invested with complete responsibility for all that goes on under his administration. . . . In the second place, *there are no pupil-teachers in the German primary schools.*

The Germans recognised that teaching was

> a psychological art – the result or practical outcome of a thorough training in principles – it is justly presumed that crude children entirely ignorant of such principles, unformed in character, and for the most part destitute of well-digested knowledge, are entirely unfitted for the important business of teaching others.[41]

Condemning the English system, he wrote that 'The contrary assumption involves indeed a direct denial of the existence of a science and art of education, and strikes at the root of any radical improvement in it.'[42] He left no room for doubt about how he felt the English system measured up against that of Germany: 'Our system stands condemned by its unsatisfactory results.' And Payne had no doubt that much of the blame lay with the pupil-teacher system which, he asserted, was maintained only for reasons of economy.[43] The pupil-teacher system, like the system of Payment by Results, had its critics; though modified, it was not abandoned until the twentieth century.

ii   The Prussian system

An alternative to the large classrooms had existed even in the early years of the Board Schools. The 'Prussian-system', which entailed separate classrooms arranged along a corridor, each class supervised by a certificated teacher, was well known to English educators. In October 1871 the Board requested the School Management Committee to obtain information concerning the Prussian system and to investigate the possibility of building a school based on the system.[44] The Committee referred the matter to the Special Committee on the Scheme of Education, chaired by Thomas Huxley, and on 19 November, on a motion by Huxley, the Board resolved that in one of its new schools the boys' and girls' schools should be 'divided into classes of not

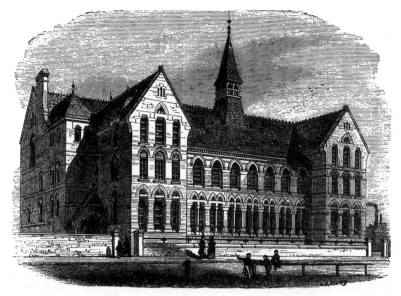

206.—JONSON STREET SCHOOL, STEPNEY.

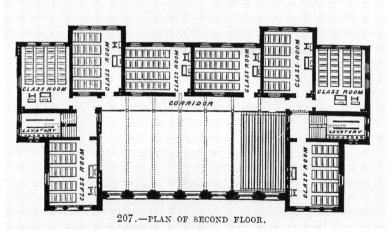

207.—PLAN OF SECOND FLOOR.

27] Jonson Street School, architect T. Roger Smith, 1871, from
E. R. Robson's *School Architecture*, 1874

more than eighty each, with a special Teacher for each class; and that
a separate room be provided for each Class.'[45]

Six architects were invited to compete for the commission.[46]
The brief presented to the architects called for separate classrooms in

the boys' and girls' schools as well as assembly rooms large enough for all girls and all boys, but which could be used as classes on a regular basis. The total accommodation was to be for 1,080 children, with equal numbers in the infants', boys' and girls' schools; provision was later increased to 1,500. The infants' school was to consist of the usual arrangement of a simple division between babies and older infants. Entries were exhibited at the Guildhall, and members of the Works Committee met there on 1 May 1872 and selected the design by T. Roger Smith[47] [**27**].

The decision to proceed with even a single school designed on the Prussian model was carried out with reluctance and even resistance. An account of the Board's work states that the recommendation to proceed with such a plan

> was not adopted without considerable searchings of the heart. Some members dreaded the expense of staffing such a school. Another feared that the supplanting of the 'schoolroom' by a series of classrooms would create a congeries of little schools that would have no effective educational co-ordination. Another thought that classrooms might 'cause invidious distinctions among the pupils'.[48]

The Board's minutes suggest that the Education Department likewise questioned the idea of building a school along these lines, requesting a special appointment between its own architect, E. R. Robson, and T. Roger Smith.[49] It has been further suggested that the Board proceeded with the groundbreaking before securing Education Department approval in order to force the issue.[50] The Education Department conceded to the plan, however, and the Jonson Street School in Stepney opened in September 1873.

In assessing the school in 1874, Robson criticised the size of it but conceded that German schools were equipped with 'appliances and provisions of all kinds, bearing on the subject of education itself . . . [which] cannot fail to strike an Englishman with astonishment',[51] and that 'the provisions lacking to English, and liberally supplied to German academical life, are those on which education itself, in its completer form, in no slight degree depends for excellence.'[52] Yet his defense of *English* traditions included harsh criticism of German practices:

> The appearance of the school is very different from that of an English model. There is no general school-room. No raised gallery where the children can receive 'simultaneous instruction'. No breaking the business to him gradually. There is a series of class-rooms entered from a wide corridor. He is placed in one of these, fitted with benches and

desks precisely similar to, but smaller than, those used by boys twice his age, and there he commences that intellectual drill which is continued till the age of fourteen. Such a system must give the dull boy a better chance, for the most awkward recruit will make a tolerable soldier if drilled regularly, and among others, for a sufficiently long time. It can hardly fail to raise the masses of a nation. On the other hand the tendency to destroy individuality of character must be ranked as a loss. [53]

Robson characterised the educational system in Germany as being un-English and military in spirit:

the system of public instruction is almost, if not quite, as military in spirit as that which governs the army, and the buildings do not escape the regime. If Berlin may be described as a vast barracks, German schools may equally be classed as a series of small barracks. [54]

The German system of separate classrooms for separate classes, each instructed by a certificated teacher, was a system with 'decidedly military objects constantly in view.' [55] The English system, Robson suggested, offered greater freedom for development.

T. Roger Smith's design contained two features that would not have been found in a Prussian school: the infants' school with a covered playground and the general assembly hall. [56] Robson criticised the very large size of the Jonson Street School as well as the most distinctive feature of its design, the separate classroom system. 'The Jonson Street school,' he wrote, 'cannot, when critically considered, be regarded in the light of a success which invites general imitation.' The luxury of an assembly hall and the staffing of separate classrooms he deemed an extravagance. In addition he criticised the relatively small accommodation for infants. [57]

Robson's criticisms represented the general consensus of Board School planning in the early years. One finds discussion in the following years of the pros and cons of expenditure on corridors, [58] but in 1874 Smith correctly predicted the ultimate success of the separate classroom system. [59] By the 1880s the central hall also became a feature of all Board Schools [60] **[28]**, as did an increasing number of classrooms organised along a corridor. Smith's design had also introduced teachers' rooms on the mezzanines, a feature which soon became standard in London Board Schools.

When the Board experimented with the Prussian system, schools for middle class children were already being built on the separate-classroom principle, although the children who attended these schools were often older than their Board School counterparts. The fears

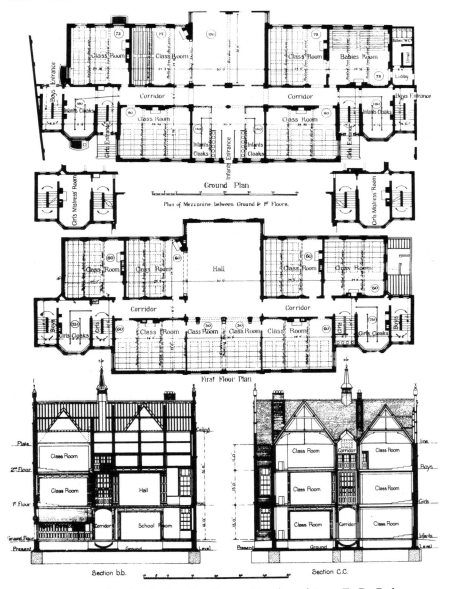

28] London Board School plan, Latchmere Road, architect E. R. Robson, from *The Builder*, 20 April 1889

expressed by Robson of the negative impact of the separate-classroom system on character or its military spirit appear to have been totally absent from discussions on the design of middle class schools. Smith had, in fact, argued that his plan was already the plan of middle class schools and would become the school of the future for all: he pointed to the 'Cowper-street Middle-class School, the magnificent new Merchant Taylor's School, and the schools proposed to be built by the Grocers' Company as examples of the class-room system.'[61]

An examination of a well-appointed middle class school designed by Alfred Waterhouse in 1880 in London illustrates that the reluctance to build smaller classrooms in London's Board Schools owed more to conceptions about the nature of education for the working class, and the very different kind of financial commitment involved, than to adherence to any educational theory. Besides separate classrooms, Waterhouse's plans for St Paul's School [29] included a library, Masters' Common Rooms, workshops, a Great Hall 125 ft (38.1 m) long, a sloping lecture hall, 88 ft by 40 ft (26.8 m by 12.19 m), which could be divided by a partition if smaller rooms were wanted, and chemistry and physics laboratories. The drawings for St Paul's were exhibited at the Royal Academy in April 1880. The façade, as viewed from Hammersmith Road [30], with its elaborate terracotta detailing, was drawn with well-dressed promenaders and spoke of an utterly different world from that in which the Board Schools were being built at the same time. The cost of Waterhouse's building was £98,250.[62] Board Schools at that time were calculated at £10 per head, or £12,000 for a school of 1,200. In order to abide by this calculation a special committee of the Board recommended in 1879 the elimination of all covered playgrounds, gymnastic apparatus, drinking fountains and filters, casing to girders and corbels under girders, extract flues for ventilation in cases where open fires were used, and all mouldings and ornament inside and out.[63]

In his private practice, Robson designed schools which represented a very different approach from that which he carried out in service for the School Board. The Blackheath High School for Girls [31] was described by *The Builder* as a 'girls' school of the middle class', built for the Girls' Public Day School Company, 'The chief feature' of which 'consists of a central lofty hall measuring 62 feet by 30 feet 9 inches (18.8 m by 9.41 m), around which are grouped eight class-rooms on the same level, lighted from the side, and connected with the hall.' Two classrooms were designed so that when opened they added to the accommodation of the central hall.[64]

By 1902 Felix Clay, in compiling his comprehensive study, *Modern School Buildings*, looked back on the Jonson Street School design and noted that 'though condemned as a failure in 1873, [it] is practically the prototype of the modern Board School.'[65] In 1888 Robson himself wrote of 'the last twenty years' which 'gradually but

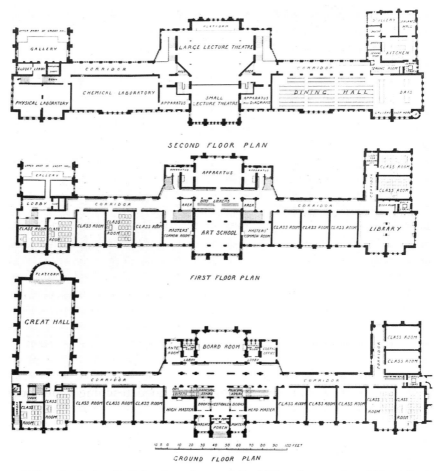

29] Plan for St Paul's School, architect Alfred Waterhouse, from Felix Clay's
Modern School Buildings, 1902

30] St Paul's School, as viewed from Hammersmith Road

31] Blackheath High School for Girls, architect E. R. Robson, from *The Builder*, 3 April 1880

completely revolutionised school planning.'[66] The features to which he drew attention were precisely the separate classrooms and the central hall. In contrast to his opinions in the 1870s, he wrote 'School-masters had found out, among other things, that good teaching could only produce satisfactory results when carried out in separate rooms.'[67]

iii   The infants' school

The history of architecture is the history not only of what was built but of those decisions as well not to build or change. The infants' school in England is the story of the decision to transform the childhood of the youngest working class children but only within narrowly defined limits. The discrepancy between avowed concern for the most vulnerable members of society and the actual provision made was striking. The infants' school, for children between the ages of three and seven, was without direct counterpart in either English middle class or Continental traditions. Though early childhood learning was widely studied among educational theorists on the Continent, the infants' school was stubbornly resistant to innovation, drawing upon the same narrow English traditions guided by parsimony.

The infants' school had been a feature of voluntary schools for the poor. The credit for the foundation of the first such establishment generally goes to Robert Owen at his cotton mills at New Lanark in the early nineteenth century. The New Lanark experiment was soon followed by a similar experiment in London in 1818, guided by the master of the New Lanark Infants' School. In 1824 the Infant School Society was founded in order to promote such schools.[68] After 1870, as children were compelled to attend school, the infants' school became an important feature of the Board School. There was a 'Babies' Room' for children as young as three, who had traditionally been cared for by older siblings, particularly girls. Although the legality of spending public money on 'Babies' Rooms' remained in some doubt, as the Education Act had not called for them, they existed on a limited scale in the city's poorest neighborhoods throughout the life of the Board.[69]

While acknowledging the ambiguity of the Education Act on the subject of nurseries, Robson, in his book of 1874, referred to the demand that made them an important feature:

> So glad are the labouring poor to provide for the care of their young children during the day at a small weekly fee of a penny or twopence, thus enabling the mother to earn wages, that, in many of the London schools, the babies' room is always crammed and numbers are refused admittance. . . . No Infant school, however small, can be regarded as complete which does not at least provide a separate room for 'babies' apart from the general room.[70]

The congregation of such young children in such large numbers was described in the evocative language of the rescue mission.

> Here the babies can be left by the mothers who have to go out to work, and the tiny mites are looked after with motherly care by a kind-hearted creature whose lot I do not envy. Fancy forty infants, some of them little over two years old, to take care of for eight hours a day![71]

The school was there to step in where home life had failed. George Sims described dinners provided by charities through the Board Schools and the beds in which

> tired babies sleep eight or ten in a row sometimes, and forget their troubles. The *crèche* is a boon and a blessing to the poor woman who going out to work has a choice of keeping an elder girl at home to nurse the baby and be summoned for it, or locking the said baby up alone in a room all day with the risk to its life and its limbs inevitable to such a course, not to mention the danger of fire and matches and fits.

Charles Morley's sketch of Board School life also depicted the infants' school as a substitute for home; the infants' teacher, he wrote, is truly their good mother, and often washes them, tidies them up, and puts them to bed in the cot yonder, when little bodies are weary of the day's labour. They are none too well nourished, I dare swear; slumbers at home may be often broken.[72]

Sims also noted a new sense of order:

The lady who manages the infant old enough to learn has no easy task, but the order is perfect, and the children drill like little soldiers.[73]

From the very outset of the School Board Huxley emphasised both the rescue of children and the new habits of order:

In a properly conducted Infant school, children are not only withdrawn from evil and corrupting influences, and disciplined in habits of order, attention, and cleanliness, but they receive such an amount of positive instruction as greatly facilitates their progress in the more advanced schools.[74]

The zeal with which very young children were encouraged to attend school was not accompanied by any serious examination or implementation of any emergent theory of early-childhood development or education. There was, however, one child-centered theory of education in particular which was available to educators in England in the 1870s, with origins on the Continent, one which in its language and its concerns might well have been expected to play a major role in the development and organisation of infants' schools. Child development had been studied by both Herbart and Pestalozzi, but it was in the work of the German Friedrich Froebel (1783–1852) that English educators found a system that corresponded to observed stages of development. In England in the 1870s the most famous name in early-childhood education was that of Froebel, who had originated the concept of *Kindergarten*, the creation of a distinct children's world, or 'garden', a place in which – pursuing Froebel's metaphor – the young seeds of humanity were to be nurtured.

Froebel's system exposed children to a series of interrelated 'games, gifts, and occupations', and encouraged them to experience nature through physical contact with certain 'objects'. Froebel's 'gifts' included a series of objects, soft balls, then larger sets of wooden spheres, cubes, and cylinders, and finally to more complicated, larger cubes divisible into smaller cubes, oblongs and prisms. His 'occupations' included drawing, modelling with clay and plaiting. Froebel contended that his graduated series of activities was derived from the careful observation of children at play.[75] The child's actions were the 'outward expression of inward development'.[76]

In his language and assumptions Froebel shared the belief espoused by many in England that childhood was a distinct and critical step in human development, as well as the conviction that only through an appreciation of childhood experience would the future of humanity be secured. He implored, 'Come, let us live for our children', and he proposed the development of institutions in which to train the young child:

> We have in mind primarily families and schools for the care of little children, but our appeal refers also to primary and elementary schools and, indeed, to every person who aims at full and complete development. Already many families in Germany, Switzerland and North America have joined in accomplishing the ideas expressed in this appeal[77]

The Kindergarten, like the public elementary school in England, was put forward as an extension of home life: the teacher was imbued with maternal qualities. Froebel even assured his audience,

> There need be no fear that individual pupils will want to improve their position and leave their own class. On the contrary, this system will produce educated men, each true to his calling, each in his own position. No creature, and certainly no man whose life is undisturbed, seeks to go beyond his powers and abilities. He wants only to perfect himself as he is, and he is completely happy when he has done so.[78]

Froebel's child-centered educational theory and practice might well have been expected to provide a basis for infants' education in England's public elementary schools. But in England the first Kindergartens were private institutions; the first was opened in Bloomsbury in 1854 by a disciple of Froebel.[79] The Froebel Society was founded in 1874, and in the same year a Kindergarten was organised as an adjunct to one of the Girls' Public Day Schools. These were middle class institutions where fee-paying parents sent their children.[80]

As an adjunct to the curriculum, rather than as an underlying principle, Kindergarten as a distinct subject had already been employed in voluntary schools for the poor before 1870,[81] a subject taught once a week, which included building with wooden bricks, basket-making and clay modelling as in Huxley's curriculum. When Huxley presented the Board with his curriculum for infants' schools, he had also enumerated, beyond the three Rs, Morality and Religion, Singing, and Physical Exercise, the 'object lessons of a simple character, with some exercise of the hands as given in the "Kindergarten system"'.[82] Froebel's work – in its own way a deeply problematic image of child development – was acknowledged by the School Board for London, which appointed an Instructor in Kindergarten in 1873 to begin a series

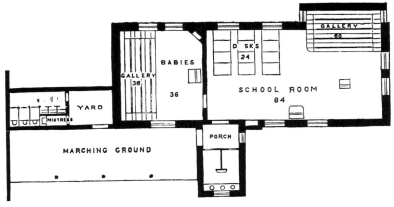

32] Suggested infants' school for 120, from E. R. Robson's *School Architecture*, 1874

of classes for Board teachers, but Froebel's 'paradise of childhood'[83] was never realised in the Board's infants' schools.

Robson gave passing mention to boxes of 'gifts',[84] but through the 1870s and 1880s Froebel's 'object lessons' remained merely one subject in the infants' school curriculum, and the accommodation provided owed more to the ideas of David Stow. Robson's *School Architecture*, for example, presented three plans for infants' schools, for 120, 170 and 300 children respectively [32–33]. Each plan provided for a large schoolroom with gallery space and adjacent accommodation for 'Babies', likewise equipped with a gallery [34]. The school for 300 included classrooms divided by a moveable partition. Education Department regulations permitted as many as eighty or ninety infants in a single gallery. Under Department regulations, accommodation for infants was calculated as only 8 sq. ft (0.74 sq. m) per infant and only 9 sq. ft (0.83 sq. m) for older children, though increased somewhat in

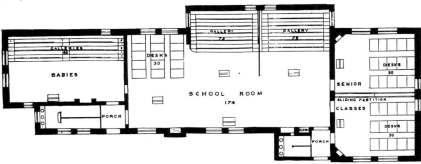

33] Suggested infants' school for 300, from E. R. Robson's *School Architecture*, 1874

1877 to 10 sq. ft (0.92 sq. m).[85] According to Robson, 'The greatest number of infants which can be managed with comfort by an average mistress appears to be 250, though some can control 300.'[86] Moreover, the gallery, according to Robson, was 'universally used in the Board Schools of London . . . [its] use depends on the mistress being able to see the expression of face of each child, and each child that of the mistress.'[87]

In 1882 a new Code was introduced which made specific reference to Kindergarten instruction as a means of judging excellence, conditional on excellence in instruction of the three Rs.[88] In 1888 the Board requested the Education Department to grant certificates to teachers who sat examinations in the principles of Kindergarten; even so, it would seem to have taken more than the removal of official hindrances to transform London's infants' schools. In 1891 an educator touring England stated that he 'did not find one true Kindergarten in connection with any English public elementary schools', and he went on to say that the interest that did exist in instilling preliminary skills – particularly eye and hand co-ordination – was in connection with manual work and preparation for industry, rather than to Froebel's concepts of developing the whole child.[89]

In 1893 the Board issued a circular to its Inspectors informing them that the Education Department was 'desirous of giving further encouragement to the employment of Kindergarten methods.' The circular made reference to 'two leading principles . . . the recognition of the child's spontaneous activity . . . and the harmonious and complete development of the whole of a child's faculties [as] a sound basis for the education of early childhood.'[90] But the testimony of teachers suggests that infants' school overcrowding lay in the way of any real transformation in the curriculum. In 1896 teachers gave evidence before the Board's School Management Committee concerning the difficulties of carrying out Froebel's ideas, even though it had been a requirement since 1877 that there be at least one teacher qualified to undertake Kindergarten work in every infants' school.[91] The Headmistress of Montem Street School in Islington testified that

> It really means drilling them – it is little different – for there is no spontaneous activity in these games. Games necessitating spontaneous activity cannot be allowed for lack of room. I should look upon it as impossible to conduct a game with eighty children if you want perfection . . . I think that the size of classes almost precludes the Kindergarten games. . . . As a rule an Inspector is very fond of perfection . . . I must say that I, myself, through lack of knowledge of child life, have erred very much in this direction, but of late years I have allowed the children much freedom.

34] Gallery lesson, London Board School

She added that if there were forty children in the classrooms that at present held eighty, real Kindergarten games would be possible. She also suggested moveable desks which might be set at the sides of the room.

A former headmistress of several London infants' schools, hired by the Leicester School Board as an Inspector, described, in contrast to London practice, how she was permitted to design classrooms to accommodate Froebel's ideas of freedom and experience:

> In one school at least there was a classroom so fitted that with very little change it could be turned into a sea beach for the children to play in the actual sand . . . parts of the floor are so arranged that portions of it can be readily removed; the under floor is made of glazed bricks, and upon this the sand is placed. The whole of this can be adjusted by the Caretaker. The children go to the room to play when the teacher thinks it necessary. This was an attempt to solve the problem of free play in a class of 60 to 70; but always more than 50.

At Leicester she had had the galleries removed and replaced with moveable seats set half way around the room; the desks were light enough to be moved out of the way to make room for play at any time. This experiment appears to have been unique.

Central to Froebel's message was an emphasis upon making children aware of nature. Since London children were at a particular disadvantage, divorced from the countryside, modest efforts were made to make plants available to infants' schools. One teacher testified that

> A very large proportion of Froebel's suggestions are based upon the assumption that the children of whom he writes are living in cottages or farms, and are in daily contact with open-air and nature. But in London it must often be assumed that few of the children have ever watched any domestic animal except a harnessed horse, or perhaps a cat, or any plant except within railings of an enclosed space.

The teacher suggested ways in which the urban school premises might be made suitable for

> informal observations of natural processes that the country child enjoys outside [such as] a few plants in pots or half-a-dozen creepers, however woe begone, trained against the wall of the Infants' playground

The efforts made by the Board, however, to provide a garden in any sense were extremely limited. In 1898, noting the efforts of some teachers to provide window-boxes in infants' schools and playgrounds, the Board gave head teachers of infants' schools a maximum of 10s to purchase seeds and flower pots, and £1 for the purchase of boxes for playgrounds. In the spring of that year, following the example of municipal schools in Berlin, where specimens were acquired for botany

35] Roof playground seen from street level, Nightingale Street School, architect E. R. Robson, from *The Builder*

lessons, the Board arranged with HM Office of Works to have flowers, leaves and cuttings sent fortnightly from Royal parks for use in Drawing and Botany classes and for Object lessons. A gardener was hired in 1899, and 220 departments were supplied with plants in an arrangement worked out with Kew Gardens, Chelsea Botanic Gardens and the Royal Horticultural Gardens, Chiswick.[92]

In the end, there was no architectural prototype or even modification based on Froebel's ideas of a children's world in miniature, no child's garden, but only restriction of movement imposed by the confining galleries and the sheer numbers of children.

As for the 'uncovered schoolroom', which Stow had proposed, the playground was a feature of all Board Schools. Where space for a playground was limited, an infants' school might share it with the girls' school. The boys had a separate play area. In the most crowded districts, where it proved difficult to secure land at a reasonable cost, the buildings were raised on arches to allow for a playground underneath, or a flat roof, covered with asphalt, was provided as a roof playground [35–36]. The playground, as in the case of all expenses, was a feature on which the Board was divided. For example, a site in St Giles, only one-eighth of an acre in size, was purchased in 1872 for a school to accommodate 750 children; a school of this size would ordinarily have been one half acre, but Board members argued that in

36] Roof playground, Myrdle Street School, Mile End

this overcrowded neighborhood further accommodation would prove too expensive.[93] The playground was placed under the ground floor, approximately 90 ft by 40 ft (27.43 m by 12.19 m), and the building raised on arches. After unsuccessfully pleading to the Works Committee for a further purchase of land to secure an outdoor playground, Benjamin Lucraft – the only working class member of the Board at that time – appealed to the Board as a whole. The Board was divided. Some agreed, in support of Lucraft, that it was imperative, particularly in an overcrowded neighborhood, to 'teach the children to love light and fresh air, and if a better playground was costly so much the worse for the Board, but it should be had at any cost.'[94] Others spoke on behalf of the ratepayers: 'The site was an exceptionally expensive one, and it was thought that with due regard to economy they could not go beyond a covered playground.'[95]

What emerges from an examination of infants' education and school accommodation is a sharp discrepancy between the avowed concern for the child and the absence of educational theory informed by any serious study of child behavior and development, whether it be Froebel's or any other. In fact, it was in the United States and in Germany that child development studies were pursued. Committees were set up by the British Medical Association to study the potential of children, investigations were made by the COS, and in 1896 the Childhood Society was founded, which concerned itself largely with statistical data, but the most significant and original work relating to the development of children did not take place in England.[96]

It was in terms of practical education for the older children in the boys' and girls' schools, however, that the elementary school was modified in its aims and its architecture, under a new and formidable pressure – the National Efficiency Movement.

Notes

1 J. M. Crook, *The Dilemma of Style: Architectural Ideas from the Picturesque to the Post-Modern* (Chicago: Chicago University Press, 1987), p. 179.

2 SBL 1033: Subcommittee on Building of Works and General Purposes Committee, signed minutes of 11 June 1877, p. 364.

3 SBL 929: Works and General Purposes Committee, signed minutes of 2 March 1874, pp. 11–14.

4 E. R. Robson, *School Architecture* (1874; rpt. Surrey: Leicester University Press, Victorian Library edn, 1972), p. 5.

5 E. R. Robson, 'Art as applied to town schools', *Art Journal* (1881), p. 171.

6 Robson, *School Architecture*, p. 159.

7 SBL 927C: Works and General Purposes Committee, 10 March 1873, p. 319.

8 Robson, *School Architecture*, p. 159.

9 *Ibid.*, p. 8.
10 M. Seaborne and R. Lowe, *The English School: Its Architecture and Organization 1870–1970*, 2 (London: Routledge and Kegan Paul, 1977); their account portrays Robson as a 'pioneer' (p. 9), a view which does not withstand an examination of Board School plans of the 1870s.
11 Robson, *School Architecture*, p. 160.
12 *Ibid.*
13 A tradition of young prefects or monitors existed in the grammar schools in the sixteenth and seventeenth centuries but should not be confused with the dependence upon monitors under the supervision of a single teacher as employed by Lancaster or Bell in schools for the poor.
14 As quoted by G. Bartley, *The Schools for the People: Containing the History, Development, and Present Working of Each Description of English School for the Industrial and Poorer Classes* (London: Bell and Daldy, 1871), p. 50.
15 A. Bell, *An Experiment, made at the Male Asylum at Madras. Suggesting a System by which a school or family may teach itself under the superintendence of the master or the parent* (London: Cadell and Davies, 1797).
16 Bartley, *Schools for the People*, pp. 59–60.
17 Bartley, *Schools for the People*, pp. 60–1. The First Report with minutes of evidence of the Scheme of Education Committee, 21 March 1871, includes the testimony of Mr Moses Angel, the Master of Jews School, Spitalfields. He described visiting a school of 2,600 children, mostly immigrants, 'an ordinary Lancasterian School, with stone floors, and groups of teachers and monitors – he never liked the Lancasterian'; he explained, 'it wa like most cheap things, not good', p. 15.
18 C. Birchenough, *History of Elementary Education in England and Wales from 1800 to the Present Day* (London: University Tutorial Press, 1914), pp. 216–17.
19 *Ibid.*, p. 216.
20 *Ibid.*, pp. 226–7.
21 From a Report on the Midlands District, Minutes of the Committee Council, 1, 1845, as quoted by Birchenough, *History of Elementary Education*, pp. 246–7.
22 Robson, *School Architecture*, p. 52.
23 D. Stow, *The Training System of Education, including Moral School Training for Large Towns and Normal Seminary, for Training Teachers to Conduct the System* (London: Longman, Green, Longman, and Roberts, 1859), p. 185.
24 *Ibid.*, p. 184.
25 *Ibid.*, p. 187.
26 *Ibid.*, p. 188. Stow's ideas were particularly influential upon the design of Wesleyan schools which were intended for day as well as Sunday School instruction.
27 Robson, *School Architecture*, pp. 12–15, 170.
28 Birchenough, *History of Elementary Education*, pp. 269–73.
29 As a consequence of the system, 'Discretionary' subjects which were included in Huxley's initial scheme of education – domestic economy, algebra and geometry – could not be afforded by teachers dependent upon the performance of pupils in the subjects which were examined.
30 B. Simon, *Education and the Labour Movement 1870–1920*, Studies in the History of Education (London: Lawrence and Wishart, 1965), p. 115.
31 G. Sutherland, *Policy-Making in Elementary Education 1870–1895* (London: Oxford University Press, 1973), p. 183.
32 M. Arnold, 'General Report for the year 1869', Sir Francis Stadford (ed.), *Reports on Elementary Schools 1852–1882*, London: Macmillan, 1889), p. 136.

33 Arnold, 'General Report for the year 1880', *Reports on Elementary Schools*, p. 234.

34 Sutherland, *Policy-Making*, p. 71.

35 *Ibid.*, p. 67.

36 As quoted by Sutherland from Mrs Burgwin, Headmistress of the renowned Orange Street School; and Sutherland describes her as 'not one to share the more paranoid feelings of her colleagues', yet she 'stated flatly that an Inspector could wreck a teacher's career' *Policy-Making*: p. 67.

37 C. Cooper, 'Reminiscence of school life in the latter part of the nineteenth century', in J. Burnett (ed.), *Destiny Obscure: Autobiographies of Childhood, Education and Family from the 1820s to the 1920s* (London: Allen Lane, 1982). Cooper's memoirs were written when he was ninety-two years old and were unpublished until their inclusion in Burnett's anthology.

38 From E. Holmes, *What Is and What Might Be* (1911) as quoted by Simon, *Education and the Labour Movement*, pp. 118–19.

39 As quoted by Simon, *Education and the Labour Movement*, pp. 118–19.

40 S. Webb, *London Education* (London: Longmans, Green and Co., 1904), p. 22.

41 Joseph Payne, *A Visit to German Schools: Notes on a Professional Tour to Inspect some of the Kindergartens, Primary Schools, Public Schools, Public Girls' Schools, and Schools of Technical Instruction, in Hamburg, Berlin, Dresden, Weimar Gortha, and Eisenbach, in the Autumn of 1874 with Critical Discussions of the General Principles and Practice of Kindergarten and Other Schemes of Elementary Education* (London: Henry S. King, 1876), pp. 127–8.

42 *Ibid.*, p. 128.

43 *Ibid.*, pp. 129–30.

44 T. A. Spalding and T. S. Canney, *The Work of the London School Board Presented at the Paris Exhibition, 1900* (London: P. S. King and Son, 1900), p. 63.

45 SBL 927A: Read to the Works and General Purposes Committee, 11 December 1871, p. 168.

46 According to *The Building News* (16 February 1872), p. 139, E. Barry, Saxon Snell, Roger Smith, A. and C. Harston, Jarvis and Son, and A. Newman were competitors

47 SBL 927B: Works and General Purposes Committee, p. 2. Smith describes his design in *The Builder* (24 May 1872), pp. 414–15.

48 Spalding and Canney, *The Work of the London School Board*, p. 63.

49 SBL 927A, p. 122.

50 Seaborne and Lowe, *The English School*, p. 25.

51 Robson, *School Architecture*, p. 104.

52 *Ibid.*, p. 103.

53 *Ibid.*, pp. 72–3.

54 *Ibid.*, p. 71.

55 *Ibid.*, p. 83.

56 The German *aula* is essentially used for special occasions and as an examination hall rather than assembly hall as in an English school.

57 Robson, *School Architecture*, p. 304.

58 See for example SBL 1033, 1875–77.

59 T. Roger Smith, 'School buildings and fittings', *The Builder* (5 December 1874), p. 1015.

60 SBL 1331: Annual Report of Chairman, 1898. In 1898 it was decided to add assembly halls to the schools which had been built without them.

61 Smith, 'School buildings and fittings', p. 1015.

62 S. A. Smith, 'Alfred Waterhouse', dissertation, University of London, Courtauld Institute of Art (1970), pp. 504–6.

63 SBL 1537: Miscellaneous reports on buildings and works, 4 August 1879, p. 3.

64 'The Blackheath High School for Girls', *The Builder* 3 April 1880), p. 414.

65 Felix Clay, *Modern School Buildings Elementary and Secondary: A Treatise on the Planning, Arrangement and Fitting of Day and Boarding Schools having special regard to School Discipline, Organisation, and Educational Requirements with special chapters on the Treatment of Class Rooms, Lighting, Warming, Ventilation and Sanitation* (London: B. T. Batsford, 1902), p. 309. Clay was architect to the Education Department.

66 E. R. Robson, 'The planning of schools', *The Builder* (11 February 1888), p. 106.

67 Robson, 'The planning of schools', p. 196.

68 Birchenough, *History of Elementary Education*, pp. 55, 233.

69 SBL 927B: Signed minutes, 10 June 1872, p. 61. The subcommittee appointed to consider the questions raised by the Education Department with reference to the 'Rules for Planning and Fitting up Schools' considered and agreed in regard to infants' schools that 'In every case there should be two Class-rooms, one for Babies, and another for the most advanced Infants.'

   SBL 1025: the minutes of the Subcommittee of the Works Committee on Sites and Plans make reference to Babies' rooms as late as 1904, p. 43. Although expenditure on Babies' rooms was not included in the provisions of the Education Act, and, therefore, was open to question, the accommodation was understood to be a necessity if the attendance of older children was to be ensured: an Education Department official is quoted as saying, 'I do not see why these Babies may not be regarded as cloaks or bonnets for which provision must be made.' In Davin, 'The Childhood of Working Class Girls', n. pag.

70 Robson, *School Architecture*, p. 180.

71 G. R. Sims, *How the Poor Live* (London: Chatto and Windus, 1883), p. 32.

72 C. Morley, *Studies in Board Schools* (London: Smith and Elder, 1897), p. 154.

73 Sims, *How the Poor Live*, p. 32.

74 SBL 1324: First Report with minutes of evidence of the scheme of Education Committee, 1871, pp. 3–4, Professor Huxley, Chairman.

75 I. M. Lilley (ed.), *Friedrich Froebel: A Selection from His Writings* (Cambridge: Cambridge University Press, 1967), p. 68.

76 (Mrs) Charles E. Green, 'Teaching of standard subjects facilitated by the Kindergarten system', *Journal of the Froebel Society*, 1: 7 (July 1883), p. 50.

77 Froebel, 'Pedagogics of Kindergarten: a New Year's meditation', in Lilley, *Friedrich Froebel*, pp. 92–3.

78 Froebel, 'Plan of an institution for the education of the poor in the Canton of Berne: To Herr Schneider, president of the Society for Christian Ecuation', in Lilley, *Friedrich Froebel*, p. 164.

79 P. Gordon and D. Lawton, *Curriculum Change in the Nineteenth and Twentieth Centuries* (London: Hodder & Stoughton, 1978), p. 66.

80 J. Kamm, *Hope Deferred: Girls' Education in English History* (London: Methuen, 1965), p. 246.

81 Bartley, *Schools for the People*, pp. 40, 113–14.

82 SBL 1324, pp. 3–4.

83 K. Froebel, *Explanation of the Kindergarten: For Those Who are not Satisfied with the Present Results of Education, and Search for Principles which Promise Social Improvement* (London: George Philip and Son, 1875), p. 1.

84 Robson, *School Architecture*, pp. 189, 400–1.

85 From 'Rules of the Education Department' in Robson, *School Architecture*, Appendix B, p. 422.

86 Robson, *School Architecture*, p. 183.

87 *Ibid.*, pp. 183–5.

88 *Final Report of the School Board for London 1870–1904* (London: P. S. King and Son, 1904), p. 92.

89 W. Catton Grasby, *Teaching in Three Continents* (London: Cassell, 1891), pp. 63–4.
In *Educating the Respectable: A Study of Fleet Road Board School Hampstead, 1879–1903* (London: Woburn Press, 1991), the author, W. E. Marsden, describes the work of the Infants' Department Headmistress, Louisa Walker, and her interpretation of Froebel's principles, pp. 132–59. As the title of the book suggests, the Fleet Road Board School – located as it was in Hampstead – was an exception in significant ways. The author notes that some parents even moved to the area in order for their children to receive the superior instruction offered in the Infants' Department, p. 159.

90 SBL 717: Circular included in the summary of achievements compiled by the Subcommittee of the School Management Committee on Method in Infant Schools, 16 July 1897.

91 The following evidence presented by infants' school teachers is included in SBL 717 which contains the Report of the Special Subcommittee on Method in Infant Schools, July 1897. In addition to the testimony of English teachers, the Committee heard from an American teacher from the Boston Normal School who criticised English infants' school methods as being too much like military drill.

92 *Final Report*, p. 121.

93 A report of the debate at the weekly meeting of the Board in *The School Board Chronicle*, 10 January 1874, pp. 27–9.

94 Mrs Herbert Cowell, School Board member, as quoted in *The School Board Chronicle*, p. 28.

95 Chatfield Clarke, School Board member, as quoted in *The School Board Chronicle*, p. 28.

96 R. J. W. Selleck, *The New Education: 1870–1914* (London: Sir Isaac Pitman and Sons, 1968), pp. 277–8.

CHAPTER FIVE

The Board School and the movement for National Efficiency: the 'regeneration' of the working classes

The last school designed by Robson, who stepped down from his position as the Board's Chief Architect in 1884, was in the Queen Anne style which had become the hallmark of the London Board School. In reviewing Robson's last school, Latchmere Road School in Lambeth [37], *The Builder* described it as 'looking like a school . . . the nature and intention of the building could hardly be mistaken.'[1,2] Schools designed by his successor and former assistant, T. J. Bailey, used essentially the same vocabulary [38], though Bailey's were often simpler and more symmetrical as the buildings were designed with plans for extension already drawn. By the time Bailey was designing schools the basic features were well known to the public and with the simplest reference to the style 'the nature and intention . . . could hardly be mistaken'. The meanings and associations that had deemed the architecture of the Queen Anne Revival an appropriate dressing for the London Board School now had become self-referential and remained in place.

In contrast, the internal organisation of the schools finally adopted the 'Prussian system' of separate classrooms and its assembly hall. The Latchmere Road School [28] suggests some of the features that were incorporated into Board School planning by the 1880s. While the façade of the elementary school retained its essential references to the Queen Anne Revival, the elementary school had become a more complicated institution designed to serve more efficiently

South Elevation

37] Elevation, Latchmere Road School, architect E. R. Robson, from *The Builder*, 20 April 1889

an ever-growing number of functions, as it became increasingly confident as a tool of social regeneration.

In December 1892 the School Board, in an effort to demonstrate its own progress, empowered the Works Committee to obtain plans in

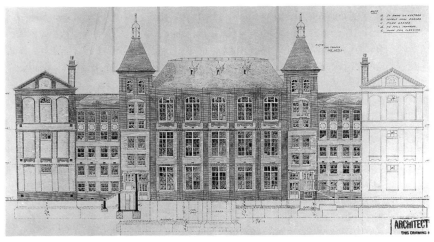

38] Elevation, Old Palace School, Tower Hamlets, 1894–6, architect T. J. Bailey

an open competition for an elementary school for 1,200 children. The President of the Royal Institute of British Architects was to be the assessor, and successful entries were to be awarded £150, £100, and £50.[3] The competition was advertised in daily newspapers and trade journals, and 112 architects applied for instructions; sixty-one sent in designs.[4]

The site selected was on open ground in Fulham. Although the Board awarded prizes, in the end it did not use any of the winning designs. Rather, the competition was interpreted by the Board as an affirmation of its own plans. The winning design was compared to 'some of the best board school plans', including Bailey's design for Lavender Hill School[5] [**39**]. A full report on the competition made by the Chairman of the Works Committee and the Chairman of the Subcommittee on Sites and Plans was submitted to the Board in April 1894; it concluded that the schools of the Board were being erected on what could be considered the most approved plans and at a cost that was modest in view of the estimates that had been submitted along with the competition entries.[6]

All the entries to the open competition were exhibited at the Hugh Myddleton Board School in Clerkenwell for public view.[7] The episode can certainly be interpreted on one level as an exercise by the Board to demonstrate to a public critical of Board expenditure that its achievement in school planning represented the best that the architectural profession could offer. In addition, however, this very public display of the Board's achievement – as the work of the Board was inevitably compared with the winning entries – suggests a considerable degree of assumed consensus and confidence regarding what was considered appropriate in the planning of a public elementary school by the 1890s.

By the 1890s, that is, there existed something of a recognised 'official model' for school planning. In fact, a writer in *The Building News* complained that those 'more or less trained in School Board traditions' possessed an unfair advantage in open competition. Acknowledging that there was a 'typical plan which has an official recognition', the writer compared the specialisation that was emerging in school architecture to that of 'well-known specialists in bath- and washhouses, polytechnics, town halls, and free libraries.' After his resignation Robson worked as a consultant to the Education Department and pursued a private practice. The career of T. J. Bailey, who succeeded Robson in 1885, was spent entirely in the service of the School Board for London and its successor, the London County Council; exempted from retirement in 1908 he worked for the LCC until early 1910, six months before he died.[8]

i   The decline of the nation

The hesitancy displayed in the aftermath of the Education Act to implement a national system of education comparable to that of the nation's competitors was transformed in the 1880s and 1890s by a new commitment to an expanded role of the state in education. Whereas Continental rivals had long understood the power of the state to direct cultural apparatus, it was only at the end of the century that a growing fear for the nation's future was translated into a national movement to direct the experience of the country's working class children far beyond the Liberal tradition.

The reasons for a redefinition of the role of the state were manifold. A series of events spurred the nation's leaders across the entire political spectrum, often making for strange bedfellows, to respond to what became increasingly seen in the 1890s and early years of the twentieth century as a crisis.

The so-called 'Great Depression' which lasted from 1873 until 1896 was accompanied by Britain's decline relative to her Continental and American rivals. Although fears for Britain's economic position had been voiced as early as 1870, her overseas trade at that time had still exceeded that of France, Germany and Italy combined. But by the end of the century, her position had deteriorated and she was but one industrial nation among many.[9] In the context of nineteenth century capitalism, Britain's unplanned and uncontrolled economy meant that the various economic sectors proceeded in terms of immediately perceived *self*-interest rather than long-term benefits which could not necessarily be proven to produce eventual profit.[10] Despite rhetoric asserting the need for technological advance, the situation was not in fact perceived as grave enough or desperate enough to effect real changes and investment in the industrial plant. In fact, there was an alternative which was quickly seized: British investors turned to the American West, Australia, and Argentina in the 1880s, South Africa in the 1890s and Canada, Argentina, and Brazil in the early twentieth century.[11] Annual investments abroad began to exceed Britain's net capital formation at home around 1870. Britain's 'parasitic' role, 'living off the remains of world monopoly, the underdeveloped world, the country's past accumulations of wealth and the advance of its rivals',[12] was noted by contemporaries. From 1885 onward the press discussed Britain's stagnating exportation, lost markets, and technological obsolescence, in contrast to Germany's growing industrial output, business methods, and salesmanship.[13]

Fears for Britain's place among industrial nations arose not only from the declining economic position but also from her military capability. Not only was her position of naval superiority threatened, but her dependence upon a small volunteer army, in contrast to the institution of conscription among other European states, was a growing cause for concern. In the rhetoric of the period the 'German threat', in the aftermath of Bismarck's unification of Germany, loomed the largest; the outcome of the Franco-Prussian War had only confirmed British fears. Similarly, the Northern victory in the American Civil War was evidence of the strength of yet another industrialising nation. And there were other threats as well to British superiority: with the British occupation of Egypt in 1882, for example, there came a rapprochement between France and Russia, uniting Britain's most formidable naval rivals.[14]

In London economic depression, the structural decline of some of the older industries, chronic shortage of working class housing, and an emerging socialism threatened to unite the working classes. Growing unemployment blurred the distinctions between the respectable working class and the 'residuum'. London's poor, it has been argued, were seen in the 1880s as potentially revolutionary;[15] the riots of 1886 were described by William Morris as 'the first skirmish of the Revolution'.[16] Whereas in the 1870s discussion of the condition of London's poorer population was confined to specialised journals, after 1883 the wider press was full of warnings that reform was urgently needed if revolution was to be averted.[17]

What was different in the 1880s was the re-emergence of Christian Socialism and the foundation of socialist organisations in London: the Democratic Federation, later to be called the Social Democratic Federation (SDF), founded by Hyndman in 1881; in 1884 Eleanor Marx and William Morris formed the breakaway organisation, the Socialist League; in 1886 the Metropolitan Radical Federation was founded, uniting a number of clubs and associations. The Fabian Society was founded in 1884. In contrast to the SDF and the Socialist League, the Fabians believed in the 'inevitability of gradualness', arguing that Britain was in a unique position to institute gradual, evolutionary, rather than revolutionary, change since it already possessed democratic institutions. The Independent Labour Party was founded in 1893, the Labour Representation Committee in 1900.

Documentation of poverty in the capital continued to bring home the extent of destitution to a middle class public.[18] Adding to the growing fears was the theory of Social Darwinists that the struggle for survival would leave the less fit nations of the world behind. Signs of a declining birthrate were seen as an alarming omen, as it was the nation's poorest, the least 'fit', who continued to increase their numbers while the middle and upper classes tended to limit their family size. Britain's population increased more slowly than that of almost any other European country in the decades between 1870 and the First World War.[19]

Herbert Spencer's theories of social evolution, first based upon the work of Lamarck and then upon Darwin, were summoned to explain and to justify Victorian *laissez faire* capitalism: supplementing the Malthusian argument, evolutionary theories substantiated the view that the individualistic, competitive society was ordained by nature and guaranteed progress.[20] Whereas Spencer had used Darwinian concepts to explain the role of individuals within society, there now emerged a different interpretation of Darwin's concepts to explain the relative progress of tribes, races and nations. This application of Darwin's theories to social progress gained currency in the last decade of the century; it was used in the defense of imperialism and had implications for the ways in which Britain perceived rival nations, her own colonies, and the physical and mental fitness of her own population. War, according to adherents of Social Darwinism, was a natural law of history. If, in fact, Britain was engaged in a dire struggle for survival, then there was little time to be wasted in fashioning a population that would be able to compete.

Related to Social Darwinism was the newly emergent 'science' of 'eugenics', the word coined by Sir Francis Galton, biologist and founder of the movement which dates from 1869 with his work, *Hereditary Genius*, and whose first full-scale study of the subject appeared in 1883, *Inquiries into Human Faculty and its Development*. The movement promoted the idea that it was scientifically possible to regulate and improve the racial stock of a nation. The eugenic solution was eventually supported by a wide range of political leaders, scientists and intellectuals in the late nineteenth and early twentieth centuries. If the nation was to retain her position of superiority, it was argued, attention must turn to the vast numbers of the working classes, the casual labor and the unemployed, who continued to reproduce more than the educated classes.[21]

The recruitment figures of the Boer War highlighted the problem of the physical debility of the British working classes, particularly in large cities: of 11,000 men offering themselves for service in Manchester in 1899, 8,000 were rejected as physically unfit.[22] In 1887 Lord Brabazon, a philanthropist and outspoken proponent of physical fitness programs for the working classes, quoted the Director-General of the Army Medical Department to substantiate his claim that the situation was an urgent one: the Director-General, he claimed, had 'adduced certain very pertinent facts concerning the question of race decay.' Drawing from recruitment statistics, he compared the numbers of able-bodied men examined over two decades. In the period from 1860 to 1864 inclusive, the number of rejections for medical reasons had been 371.67 per 1,000; by 1882 to 1886, however, the number had risen to 415.58 per 1,000. The statistics could be explained in 'one way only', according to the Director-General: the masses from which the army recruits were chiefly taken 'are of an inferior physique to what they were twenty-five years ago.' That, according to Lord Brabazon, was the 'plain unvarnished truth . . . by no means of a palatable kind to those who regard the national welfare as a thing to be conserved and prized.'[23] These and similar statistics were used in the debates concerning hereditary and environmental factors in saving the nation.

The fears expressed by Lord Brabazon and others in the 1880s appeared to be borne out by the long struggle of the Boer War, a war that by all calculations should have been won quickly and efficiently. The conflict cost approximately £200,000,000; nearly half a million British and Colonial soldiers were used against an army of scarcely one-fifth the size, including women and children and old men.[24] As the Boer War had virtually denuded the Empire's forces, it was considered by many nothing short of a miracle that Russia had not invaded India, that Britain's food supply had not been blockaded, and that there had been no invasion from the Continent.[25]

The Boer War focused the anxieties which had been growing for the nation's military future. As one writer in the *Nineteenth Century and After* phrased it,

> our failures have been even greater and more surprising than our successes . . . the contest has been one between a giant and a pygmy. And yet no life-and-death struggle against one of the first class Powers of Europe could have cost us more precious blood than that which has been shed in reducing a country of 300,000 inhabitants . . . our Empire has escaped destruction by a hair's breadth

And the author's attention soon focused upon Britain's greatest rival, Germany, noting the connection between military preparedness and universal elementary education:

> Continental militarism, whatever its evils, at least forms part of the national life and vigour. . . . Universal schooling on the one hand, and universal conscription on the other, are two pillars on which the most powerful state of Europe is raised.[26]

A movement for 'National Efficiency' united various factions that had been concerned with the apparent economic, military, and physical decline of the nation. National Efficiency as a rallying point involved a variety of interrelated commitments and allegiances. Emulating the Germans, and later the Japanese, the movement emphasised scientific and technological advancement and rationalisation of the nation's resources and skills in government and industry. It drew support from disparate quarters. The leaders were drawn from Liberal politicians like Lord Rosebery and R. B. Haldane, civil servants like Robert Morant, who had served in the Education Department, imperialists like Alfred Milner, who served in Egypt and then as High Commissioner for South Africa, the Fabians, most notably the Webbs, and independent journalists like Arnold White, author of the inflammatory *Efficiency and Empire*, a cry to the nation to act quickly in order to avert national suicide. Lords Rosebery and Haldane represented a movement within the Liberal ranks that sought to reconcile Liberal ambitions with a pro-imperialist stance. These sentiments were first espoused in the 1880s, but the Boer War forced the issue, dividing the anti-imperialist Radicals who opposed the war from those who supported the conflict. The issue was one that divided the Fabian Society as well, culminating in a debate in the autumn of 1899 and a vote on the issue in February of 1900, 250 votes in favor of a pro-imperialist position and 217 opposed.[27]

The ambitions and concerns of Liberal Imperialists and the 'National Efficiency' group merged: the desire for British supremacy at home and abroad was now articulated in terms of the need to develop a strong and efficient population. Sidney Webb wrote:

> What is the use of talking about Empire, if here, at its centre, there is always to be found a mass of people, stunted in education, a prey to intemperance and congested beyond the possibility of realising in any true sense either social or domestic life?[28]

The Efficiency movement, in its desire to make Britain competitive, partook of and grew out of the sense of crisis; its goals were expressed in terms of Social Darwinism, eugenics, and imperialism. Central to its vision was its new attitude toward state and local government, a commitment to the idea that it was not only within the power of the state to effect change, but was, in fact, its duty. Indeed, education was now redefined from the notion of individual redemption to a matter of national urgency. The interests of imperialists, their desire to produce an imperial race, merged therefore with the ambitions of social reformers who had concerned themselves with health conditions and social welfare in general.

In opposition to traditional Liberal fears of state intervention, the new coalition of social reformers and Liberal Imperialists saw the state in a new light. The defense of Empire abroad and the breeding of an imperial race at home *required* state intervention, particularly in the field of education. In a letter to *The Times*, Samuel Smith, MP, put forward the case:

> No country has ever suffered more from the abuse of the idea of individual liberty than England has done. Owing to this overstrained idea we did not get compulsory education until long after the advanced nations of the Continent, and still are far behind them in the care we take of our children. It is intolerable that the state of things should continue longer. Democratic government everywhere insists upon good education, and expects each citizen to fulfill its duties to the state.[29]

Education became one of the focal points of the Efficiency program. The goals stated were not new. The fear of foreign competition, both military and industrial, had been articulated during the debates surrounding the Education Act of 1870, but, under pressure of economic decline, greater dependency upon the Empire, a perceived military inferiority and social unrest at home, the commitment toward changing educational provision strengthened. Thomas Huxley exemplifies the nature of this heightened concern:

> in a densely populated manufacturing country, struggling for existence with competitors, every ignorant person tends to become a burden upon, and, so far, an infringer of the liberty of his fellows, and an obstacle to their success.
>
> Under such circumstances an education rate is, in fact, a war tax, levied for purposes of defence.[30]

ii   An explicitly gendered education

In contrast to an apparent lack of will to create an infants' school modeled on the lines of the most current theories of childhood development, the education of older boys and girls was provided with purpose-built accommodation in response to the concerns voiced by the Efficiency movement.

Whereas the 1870s saw the building of Board Schools based upon planning techniques that recommended themselves primarily for reasons of their economy and their conception of mass education for the working class, the 1880s and 1890s witnessed a far greater concern with bringing English schools in line with those of Continental rivals. Working class boys and girls were to be not only 'rescued' but trained for their future roles in an increasingly competitive world. The relative complacency with which Continental and American prototypes in school planning were dismissed in the 1870s could no longer be indulged in if this was a contest of nations. The demand for 'childhood' was now followed by an emerging concept of 'youth' by the end of the century, also a separate and defined stage in human development, with its own needs and requirements, likewise to be accompanied by protective legislation and educational measures.[31]

The school of the 1890s was still designed with the essentials of the 'LSB style', yet, as noted, built into the design was the expectation of expansion [39]. Designed on the separate-classroom system, each classroom was now intended for fewer children, approximately sixty, a figure which had become the recommended standard in 1889, with reduction to fifty and even forty in some cases.[32] Whereas schools in the 1870s were designed to provide 9 sq. ft (0.83 sq. m) per child in boys' and girls' schools and 8 sq. ft (0.74 sq. m) for infants, by the 1880s the space was reckoned at 10 sq. ft (0.92 sq. m) per child. Both the boys' and girls' schools had assembly halls.[33] The increased number of classrooms and the inclusion of corridors in order to eliminate the need to pass through and thereby interrupt lessons, as well as the reduction in class size, were only a few of the ways in which the schools were made more efficient. The school of the 1890s was better lit, with greater attention paid to the placement of windows, and was better ventilated and warmer than the Board School of the 1870s, though the Board was still involved in experiments to secure warmer and purer air.[34]

More importantly, as a socialising agency, as a substitute for the atmosphere of home and street, the elementary school became increasingly defined not only as an agent of social regeneration, but also the place in which cleanliness, physical fitness and gender roles were explicitly taught.

Encouraging a fitter population, preparing children to assume the roles that would devolve upon them in later life, meant the initiation of a curriculum designed in accordance with roles defined by gender. As Lord Brabazon stated in a letter to *The Times*, 'it is imperative that our boys should be taught to labour, and our girls to become good housewives.'[35] That a working class education should include training in practical skills as well as a foundation in the three Rs was not a new idea, although it assumed a significant role only in the 1880s.

Criticism of the Board's initial curriculum, which had lacked practical training, had been voiced as early as the 1870s. The education of girls had been often discussed in terms of training appropriate for later life, either as wife and mother or as domestic servant. Running for the first School Board for London in 1870, Mrs. Grey had addressed a meeting in Chelsea on the eve of the School Board election:

> I do not know how far it may be possible to give technical education to boys in addition to the ordinary instructions. It would involve a very large expense for workshops and masters in the many different trades to be taught; but I am quite sure that girls ought to receive what I call their technical education, which is the same for all, because all must be trained in the habits which make home healthy and happy. . . . They should learn in short, as their proper business, all the arts by which the wife and home can compete with the public-house, and the mother be enabled to send her children to school prepared to get the most from it.[36]

There were warnings that a training in the three Rs was insufficient preparation for wifely duties and motherhood:

> 'Strange, indeed!' her teachers would say, 'she was a good grammarian, and could repeat long pieces of poetry, and could scramble very fairly through the needle work that had been cut out for her; . . . and she

39] Elevation, Lavender Hill School, architect T. J. Bailey, from *The Building News*, 8 April 1892

> was in Fractions in her sums.' And she was for a short – all too short – a time in service, and then she was married; and then very soon she was called upon to become purveyor and cook and laundress and dressmaker and needlewoman and nurse and family doctor in one; and she had not the smallest training in any one of these important offices! Then she failed in health for want of ordinary knowledge of the rules of hygiene; and then her looks went, and her temper suffered, and love flew out of a very dirty window[37]

As Mrs Grey put it, 'truly it was a wise man who said he would begin the training of the child "twenty-five years before he was born" – that is, he would begin with the mother and teach her to train the child.'[38]

Whereas both boys and girls in the 1870s had received the same instruction in the three Rs, with the exception that girls took needlework as a compulsory subject, by the 1890s the sexual division of labor which existed in the middle class model of home life was replicated on the schoolgrounds. Girls learned domestic skills in purpose-built model homes resembling artisans' dwellings, and boys acquired manual training in centers modeled on the workshop: a division of labor and hence, a division of knowledge, based on a middle class concept of family.

The historian Anna Davin has argued that the reasons usually put forward to explain the passage of the Education Act of 1870 fall short of explaining why girls were included in the measure at all. In political terms, the newly enfranchised electorate did not include women, and in economic terms, the desire to make Britain's work-force more skilled and competitive likewise had little to do with women who were, by and large, excluded from skilled and technical employment. Rather, the framers of the Act had in mind from the start the provision of an alternative to the working class home, a place in which the bourgeois model with its division of labor – breadwinner father and domestic, homebound, dependent mother – could be taught.[39]

The middle class family model carried a potent image of the family as central to harmony and civilisation; fears of social disharmony then could be located in the 'failure' of the working class family, and the palliative would be the reintroduction of 'morality through family life. . . . Education was to form a generation of parents . . . to establish (or as they believed to re-establish) the family as the stabilising force.'[40] Davin's examination of textbooks used in the Board Schools from the 1870s onward demonstrates how a gendered image of the middle class family was conveyed to children: the families as presented in children's literature, even in the animal world, consistently have breadwinning fathers and housekeeping mothers.[41] Now school architecture suggested in its very imagery and its divisions, the middle class conception of the appropriate division of labor between boys and girls.

In the 1880s and 1890s the school became the place in which home life was concretised in the design of the school, and in a sense enacted, as girls learned domestic skills in centers designed for instruction in cookery, laundry, and housewifery and boys were instructed in woodworking and metalcraft in manual training centers. Manual Training Centres were built within the boys' school playground, approximately 60 ft by 20 ft (18.28 m by 6.09 m), raised on arches, essentially workshops fitted with benches [40–41]. Within the girls' and infants' school playground there were built two-storey cottages,

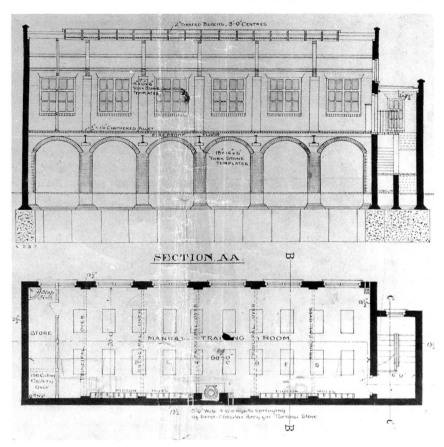

SECTION AA.

MANUAL TRAINING ROOM

40] Manual Training Centre, Old Palace School, drawing, 1892

from the outside resembling the schoolkeeper's house, which was also on the premises. The girls' brick detached 'house', with slate roof and white sash windows, provided accommodation for cookery lessons on the ground floor and a laundry on the second. Though rejected, there were even suggestions that girls be trained in domestic skills in real middle class homes.[42]

That a particular concept of home life was being taught is evident from Charles Morley's contemporary description of a visit to a Housewifery Centre at an East End Board School:

> Down in that gray wilderness of bricks and mortar we call Bethnal Green . . . is a certain four-roomed house, in which the girls of the quarter are daily instructed in the mysteries of housekeeping. It is a most delightful establishment, I do assure you – a truly model dwelling.

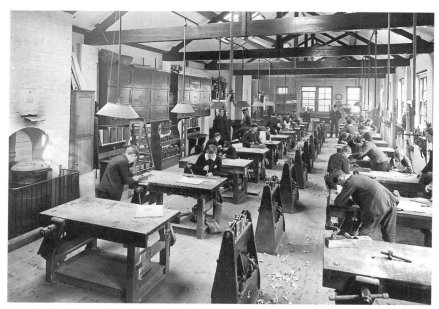

41] Woodworking
Centre, Bellenden Road
School, Camberwell

42] Domestic Economy
Centre, Surrey Lane
School, West Lambeth

43] Housewifery Centre,
Mordern Terrace
School, Greenwich

44] Housewifery Centre,
Denmark Hill School,
Camberwell

There is a cosy parlour, nicely furnished, which is swept and dusted twice daily for five days a week. . . . There are bedrooms in which the beds are made with equal frequency. There is the kitchen (with the usual appurtenances) which is also faithfully dealt with by numerous zealous little women.[43]

Asked how she will divide up her week's work, one girl explained to Morley that she would set herself a schedule of chores day by day,

'And on Saturday I should clean up the passage, and polish up the front door . . . and do my best to get finished before . . . *he* come home'[44]

The training of working class girls in domestic skills took place within a building designed and furnished to resemble the middle class notion of working class home life, or rather, working class home life as the middle class thought it ought to be.[45] Purpose-built houses or neighboring houses acquired by the Board,[46] fitted up as Housewifery Centres by the female members[47] of the Board, became part of the school in the 1890s, one center sometimes serving a number of neighboring Board Schools. In its most elaborated form the Domestic Economy school, as it was called, combined Cookery, Laundry and Housewifery in a single center [42]. The Housewifery Centre generally included a lecture room, a bedroom, sitting room and kitchen and

45] Cookery Centre, Kilburn Lane School, Paddington

scullery [**43–44**]. The rooms, according to the Superintendent of Domestic Economy for the London School Board,

> are furnished and fitted as a model working-man's house, . . . By careful arrangement of colours the children are taught that usefulness and art may be combined, and comfortable substitutes for cheap stuffed furniture are placed before the children's eyes. All the utensils provided in these centres are those used by the artisan class. A cottage stove is fixed in the kitchen, and the children cook daily the dinners for themselves and the teacher[48]

Cookery lessons would have taken place in a kitchen presumably 'fitted up with such appliances as are suitable for an ordinary artisan's home, with the addition of a gas stove'[49] [**45**].

In spite of assertions that 'the work is done under the ordinary conditions of the working-man's home',[50] the facilities provided and the instruction given in Cookery, Laundry and Housewifery Centres were a far cry from what most Board School girls would have known as home life: the majority of Board School girls in the late 1880s, probably 60 per cent according to Charles Booth's survey of poverty in London, came from homes in which the family struggled to survive in overcrowded conditions on £1 a week or less.[51] The Board School recipes, however, included rabbit, beef, meat pies with veal stuffing,

46] Laundry Centre, Beaufort House School, Camberwell

and sultana puddings.[52] The laying of a proper table with cloth, cruet, saltcellar, dessert spoon and forks, knives and carving knife, or the cleaning of marble or sweeping of carpeted floors[53] had little bearing upon home life for most girls. Ostensibly the girls were taught the 'general routine of a day's work in the house of a working-man'.[54] That girls were now being trained for domestic service was an issue raised by Samuel Smith, MP, among others, who urged a 'system for transforming the slatternly girl of the slums into the neat and tidy domestic servant.'[55] The Education Department, however, never acknowledged this as a goal; the Education Department Code of 1897 described instruction in Housewifery:

> It is not intended that this teaching should resolve itself into a class for training children for domestic service, but it is intended to be a course for the various household duties which devolve more or less upon all women.[56]

The contrast between the realities of home life and the model offered by the Board School did not go unnoticed by contemporaries. One journalistic account described a visit to a Housewifery Centre: 'On the door of one structure, an ordinary small London House, is the mysterious word "Housewifery". An ordinary house, "but how extraordinarily clean", your first remark is'.[57] Morley visited a Cookery Centre where he noted 'the pale and hungry faces of many of the little cooks', and added wryly, 'However, it is notorious that cooks are not great eaters'.[58] 'Alas! like those ravens who mourn and even brought food to Elijah, they were, *"Though ravenous, taught to abstain from what they brought"'.*[59]

The Laundry Centre, equipped with 'ironing tables, ironing-stove, sand box, sinks, gas copper, and open fire-range, with hood over latter appliances to carry off steam',[60] was also described by the Board as a facility 'fitted up with such appliances as are suitable for an ordinary artisan's home'[61] **[46]**. The garments listed for laundry instruction in the syllabus, however, included print collars, cuffs, handkerchiefs, serviettes, table damask, pillow slips, chemises, and sheets, as well as lace.[62] Washing materials included soap, starch, blue, soda, borax, turpentine, sanitas, salt of lemon, white wax, and bath brick. A family living on £1 a week might spend at best 4d. on soap and soda per week.[63]

In the 1880s and 1890s the contrast between school and home was again made visible and tangible, the model home juxtaposed with the reality of life in the London slum. Accompanying the campaign to provide domestic economy lessons in schools was a critique of home life, again in the language of child rescue. 'Our girls,' wrote Miss Headdon on the Council of the National Association for the Promotion of Housewifery, an association which campaigned for the inclusion of domestic economy in the Board School curriculum, 'are reared in untidy, ill-managed homes by shifty housekeepers.' And she summed up the problem as she saw it: 'What hope,' she asked, 'can there be for a nation when there is thriftless ignorance on the part of the mothers and thorough inefficiency on the greater number of domestic servants . . .?'.[64] The elementary school was now more than ever the alternative to the home. The rescue mission was realised in architectural terms as girls from the slums were taught household chores within a model working class home.

While Board School girls were instructed in 'their natural duty of turning a mere house into a healthy home',[65] boys were taught the skills and discipline of the workshop. The provision of manual training centers for boys was also argued for in terms of national survival in an increasingly competitive world:

> At present our industrial classes were like badly drilled soldiers fighting a battle with antiquated weapons – it was like sending our soldiers into the field, armed with Brown Bess, to meet the best armed soldiers of Europe.[66]

Acknowledging a debt to Huxley, the Marquis of Hartington, presiding at the distribution of prizes in the fields of science, art and commercial classes at the London Polytechnic in that same year (1887), warned his audience that defeat in industrial competition would mean

> instead of being what we are now, we should be hewers of wood and drawers of water, the slaves and the servants of the rest of the world, instead of being the leaders and masters of the world. . . . Just as we could not in preparations for actual warfare afford to disregard the teachings and experience of the rest of the world, and allow ourselves to be behindhand in the possession of the necessary scientific knowledge and appliances which modern warfare required, still less could we afford to be behindhand in the preparations for the industrial warfare[67]

Both speakers asserted that German workers were better prepared for industrial competition than their English counterparts. Other anxious commentators pointed to accomplishments in the United States, France, Belgium, Austria, Holland, and Sweden.[68]

The education of boys in industrial skills, like the education of girls in domestic skills, was promoted as a means of averting class tensions and ensuring social harmony. Lord Brabazon warned that

In our very laudable desire to obtain for the nation a high standard of general culture and in omitting to teach them the use of the tools by which the mass of them will hereafter have to earn their living, we are unintentionally leading them to believe that the bread which has been gained by the sweat of the brow is less honourably earned than that which is the result of mechanical quill-driving.

Such misguided boys would be 'useless at home, useless as emigrants, and, with bitterness and despair in their hearts', who in their desperation

are ready to blame everyone – Providence, society, capitalists – for the miserable condition of their existence, the real culprit all the time being, in my opinion, in a great measure the national system of education.[69]

Those who feared that Board School education had become overly literary and out of touch with the needs of society were assured that the vast majority of children would 'remain at the bench, the anvil, the loom, the engine, the plough . . .' so therefore, 'after the child has learnt to read, write and cypher well, he should at once be inducted into at least the rudiments of some branch of technical industry.'[70] Manual training would 'remove the unfortunate notion that education leads to clerkship and gentility.'[71] By practical experience 'the nobility of labour' could be taught.[72]

In 1883 Professor Gladstone, Chairman of the Board's Sub-committee on Technical Education, moved that arrangements be made for instruction in the use of woodworking and iron for 'Boys Schools situated in manufacturing neighbourhoods' and urged the Education Department to provide a grant 'similar to that allowed for the practical teaching of Cookery to girls.'[73] His proposal was met by the combined resistance of the School Board for London, the City and Guilds of London Institute, and the Drapers' Company in 1886,[74] as the legal power of the Board to provide practical training remained in doubt.[75] Efforts went ahead on a limited basis when the Board provided for teaching both boys and girls practical skills, while the Institute and the Drapers' Company provided the necessary funding. By 1890 woodworking was included in the Code of the Education Department as part of the grant-earning syllabus; by 1904 there were 188 centres for instruction in woodworking in London with 188 instructors and 114 assistant instructors. In addition, there were seven centres that taught metalwork[76] [47]. Typically, Manual Training Centres were built on the boys' playground, the centers resembling workshops: long, narrow rooms fitted with carpenters' benches at right angles to the row of windows. Tool racks stood by each bench either on the wall or in the center of the room.[77]

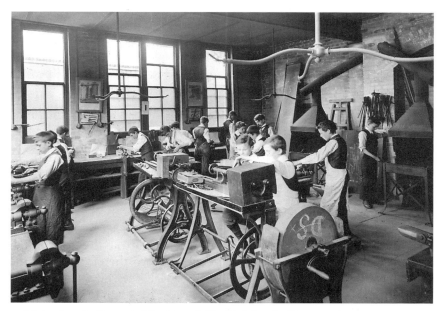

47] Metalwork Centre, Blackheath Road School, Greenwich

Expressing themselves in Social Darwinian terms of survival, fired by the cries of eugenicists and the distressing recruitment figures of the Boer War, proponents of physical training promoted their own agenda. Concern for the physical well-being of the nation merged with patriotic fervor and defense of empire.[78] It was not simply 'superior generalship' which had been found wanting but rather 'the material of which the Prussian army was then composed', as English recruits were 'wanting in hardihood, in physical strength, and in love of country'.[79] A sense of 'disaster averted' lay behind the interest in the military in Edwardian Britain, seeking 'Both within government, and at a popular level, a search commenced for a military panacea to arrest and reverse the evident process of national decline.'[80]

In elementary schools this was realised in public displays of drill and physical exercise performed by Board School children at the Royal Albert Hall and attended by Field Marshal Rt Hon. Lord Roberts. There was also the foundation of the Lads' Drill Association to promote the formation of cadet corps in elementary schools (later subsumed under the National Service League), the initiation of Empire Commemoration Day, and the flying of the Union Jack over Board Schools. Whereas the military spirit attached to these activities, particularly to the teaching of military drill, had its critics on the Board, there was a firm consensus in favor of physical training among Board members[81] [48].

Although the Huxley curriculum of 1871 had proposed 'Drill' as an essential subject, and an instructor had been appointed to train all male teachers, followed by training for female teachers in 1876, it was not until 1897 that allocation of a specific time for combined drill and physical exercise was made compulsory. In 1900 it was required that instruction in drill and physical exercise be given three days a week in twenty-minute lessons for boys and girls and fifteen for infants.[82] Gymnastic equipment was introduced into London Board Schools by a donation from Lord Brabazon.[83] By the turn of the century a limited number of gymnasia were being built by the School Board. Instruction in swimming was authorised by the Education Department, primarily dependent, however, on swimming baths built by London boroughs.[84]

In addition to playgrounds for drill and physical exercise, schools of the 1890s often had a room set aside within the main school building for medical inspection. The first Board Medical Inspector was appointed in 1891, although systematic inspection of the hygienic conditions of elementary schools, eyesight testing, weighing of children and the certification of teachers in Hygiene were instituted only after the turn of the century.[85] Blind and deaf children received instruction from 1872 onward; but it was in the 1890s that the Board became concerned with the education of children with other disabilities as well.

Growing interest in the health of the nation's children 'whose energy is the chief of the national assets', as a memorandum from the Board's Medical Officer reminded Board members,[86] led to a proposal for a survey of the physical condition of Board School children 'to show the relations between (a) The educational status (b) The physical condition and (c) The social position' of the pupils. Measurements of height, weight, cleanliness, and condition of clothing were to be gathered and School Attendance Visitors were to supply information regarding the particular family circumstances.[87] The passage of the Education Act of 1906 permitted schools, at last, to offer some free meals, and it introduced 'Care Committees' to see that recommendations of medical officers were followed and that selected children were fed.

The persistent rhetoric that children needed protection from parents is evident in the discussion of health: for example, with respect to scalp diseases, the Medical Officer noted that, 'There is serious danger that the parents may find out, and apparently already found out, that a dirty head is a safeguard against compulsory school attendance', as children with lice were forbidden in school. Medical inspection

48] Boys at drill, Upper Hornsey Road School, Islington, 1906

carried with it recommendations of prosecution of parents who did not comply.[88] Municipal authorities under the Cleansing of Persons Act of 1887 had the power to disinfect homes. 'As a uniform practice does not prevail over London as regards the putting in force of this Act,' a system of warning notices separating out the 'worst offenders' was used. It was suggested that 'each child so separated should have some distinguishing mark, for instance a white diamond-shaped label, fixed on the front of her desk.'[89]

In general, schools were seen as

> exercising guardianship over every child, protecting him when necessary from neglectful, cruel or ignorant parents, from the manifold evil effects of poverty and vicious unhealthy surroundings and lastly, of getting the child as good a start as is practicable, when he is finally released from the control of the Educational Authority and compulsory attendance.[90]

iii   The end of the Board School era

In 1903 the School Board for London was subsumed under the rationalised educational authority of the London County Council (LCC), and empowered to provide both secondary and technical education, going far beyond the powers that had been granted to the School Boards by the Education Act of 1870. The Education Acts of 1902 and 1903 instructed the London County Council to 'provide anything and everything that it deemed necessary in the way of education – physical, mental, moral, elementary, secondary, university, manual, literary, artistic, scientific, commercial, technological, or professional.'[91]

That year Sidney Webb, a fervent supporter of National Efficiency, looked back over the life of the Board and recalled its 'arrest of a nation's suicide'.[92] '[T]he present working class population of London – taken, as a whole, perhaps the least turbulent, the least criminal, and the most assiduous in its industry of any of the world's great capitals – has been fashioned.'[93] Reaffirming the accomplishments of the School Board for London as a 'systematic attempt to rescue the whole of the children of London',[94] Webb lauded the vast building program and its achievements:

> These five hundred new public buildings, occupying 600 acres of valuable land, existing now in every one of London's fifty-eight electoral divisions, four to the square mile of the whole of London's surface, erected at a cost of fourteen millions sterling, constitute by far the greatest of our municipal assets . . .
>
> Imperceptively public opinion gained a new point of view. The leaders of all the political parties unconsciously absorbed the idea that national efficiency depended on our making the most of the capacities of the whole population, which form, after all, as truly part of the national resources as our iron and coal. . . . Public education has, therefore, insensibly come to be regarded, not as a matter of philanthropy undertaken for the sake of the individual children benefited, but as a matter of national concern undertaken in the interest of the community as a whole.[95]

Though, as an established building type, the Queen Anne 'homes of education' continued to display the architectural vocabulary of child rescue, the ambitions of the School Board focused on physical fitness and industrial and domestic training, as well as the three Rs, to transform the working class child still further, to make him or her fit for England's struggle. The work of reformers and political leaders had secured education for all children. The nature and assumptions defining that education would continue to be debated, but the presence of nearly five hundred Queen Anne 'homes of education' – in the language of child rescue – spoke eloquently of their intended mission in every corner of the abyss.

Notes

1 'A London Board School: Latchmere Road', *The Builder*, (20 April 1889), p. 298.

2 The elementary school was not only reassessed in terms of its internal organisation, but the Board saw fit to put its own house in order in the 1880s with an investigation into the 'whole of the existing arrangements relating to the work of the Works Department.' The investigation and report are contained in SBL 1133: Special Committee on the Work of the Works Department. The Committee, including an outside architect and quantity surveyor, concerned itself with cases referred to it by the Board or by the Works Committee that involved allegations regarding inferior materials or work executed under contracts with the Board. Complaints included claims that the Board had paid for depths of foundations that had not been carried out to specification, for inferior material under tarpaving of playgrounds, or none at all, or that in the case of bricks and mortar, woodwork, and lead, requirements had not been followed and that procedures regarding payment – specifically a requirement to withhold 20 per cent of a builder's fee for six months after completion of a school – had not been followed. It had come to the Board's attention that an inordinate amount of money had been spent on repair work of relatively new buildings.

   Although the Board had passed rules in 1879 regarding methods of inspection for schools upon completion, the investigation found that they had not been followed. The procedures regarding repair work were even more lax. The investigation uncovered the fact that although the Board had experimented with obtaining tenders from both a limited list of builders as well as in open competition, 'advantage has been taken . . . by a class of Builders deficient alike in experience of sound work, in the requisite capital, and in legitimate habits of business.'

   The investigation revealed that Robson as Chief Architect had failed to follow rules that required him to personally inspect 'when foundations were dug to see all "bottoms"'. Although the investigation led to accusations of negligence on the part of Robson – the Board even suggested that he personally provide compensation – the Report of the Committee concluded in the end that it was impossible to apportion blame because of the amount of work that had been carried out with insufficient staff. The Committee pointed to improvements made in the Architect's Department, including more careful supervision of requisitions, reports submitted by the Clerks of Works weekly, more Clerks of Works employed and less work entrusted to each, payments made only upon completion of work and no portion of the retention fund paid prior to the expiration date of the terms of the contract, with a formal certificate of completion to be forwarded from the Architect to the Finance Department. Although never formally found guilty, Robson was again accused of negligence in a case in which the School Board sued a builder, The School Board for London v. Wall Brothers. For questioning of Robson see SBL 1535, pp. 38–9, 1891.

3 SBL 1533: Works Committee Annual Reports (1890/1–1902/3), Third Annual Report, pp. 8–9. The competition was announced at the meeting of the School Board, 15 December 1892.

4 *Final Report of the School Board for London 1870–1904* (London: P. S. King and Son, 1904), p. 40.

5 'School planning and design', *The Building News* (29 December 1893), p. 848.

6 *Final Report*, p. 40.

7 'School Planning and Design', *The Building News* (29 December 1893), pp. 848–9. Unfortunately none of the competition entries survive although a description of the winning plan is given in this account.

8 The issues raised by Bailey's career in terms of the development of the architectural profession, both the work as an employee of a public authority and the specialisation in a single building type, have received little attention from architectural historians to date. Whereas Robson received a salary of £1,000 with permission to maintain an outside practice, Bailey was contracted for £600 per annum to increase by £100 per annum to a maximum of £900. His contract stipulated that he could take no outside work. SBL 944: Works Committee Minutes, 12 January 1885, p. 14.

9 G. R. Searle, *The Quest for National Efficiency: A Study in British Politics and Political Thought, 1899–1914* (Oxford: Basil Blackwell, 1971), p. 12. For an examination of Britain's industrial decline see D. H. Aldcroft and H. W. Richardson, *The British Economy 1870–1939* (London: Macmillan, 1969), pp. 101–25.

10 E. J. Hobsbawm, *Industry and Empire: An Economic History of Britain since 1750* (London: Weidenfeld and Nicolson, 1968), pp. 157–8.

11 W. Ashworth, *An Economic History of England, 1870–1939* (London: Methuen, 1960), pp. 157–60.

12 Hobsbawn, *Industry and Empire*, p. 161.

13 Searle, *The Quest for National Efficiency*, p. 20.

14 *Ibid.*, p. 8.

15 G. Stedman Jones, *Outcast London: A Study in the Relationship between Classes in Victorian Society* (Oxford: Oxford University Press, 1971), pp. 290–6.

16 As quoted by Stedman Jones, *Outcast London*, p. 194. For a description of the riots of 1886 see D. Rubinstein, 'The Sack of the West End', D. Rubinstein (ed.), *People for People: Radical Ideas and Personalities in British History* (London: Ithaca Press, 1973), pp. 139–44.

17 Stedman Jones, *Outcast London*, p. 290.

18 The 1880s saw a series of exposés, referred to earlier in the context of child rescue, including A. Mearns's *The Bitter Cry of Outcast London: An Inquiry into the Condition of the Abject Poor* (1883; rpt. Leicester: Leicester University Press, 1970), George Sims's articles in *Pictorial World* (1883), later republished as *How the Poor Live and Horrible London* (1889), W. T. Stead's articles on housing reform in his *Pall Mall Gazette*, and William Booth's *In Darkest England and the Way Out* (1890). These sensational exposés were followed by the lengthy studies of poverty produced by Charles Booth between 1889 and 1907, followed by Seebohm Rowntree's study of York, *Poverty: A Study of Town Life* (1901).

19 Searle, *The Quest for National Efficiency*, p. 9. According to Searle, at the time of German unification the population was forty million, that is, about ten million more than that of the United Kingdom; by 1914, the gap had doubled. America was in even more striking contrast to the UK, with a population of nearly one hundred million by 1914: 'The success with which the northern states had preserved the American Union and the absorption of the various German states into a Federal Empire,' wrote Searle, 'seemed to show that the future lay with large units of power, capable of mobilising correspondingly large manpower resources', p. 9.

20 B. Semmel, *Imperialism and Social Reform: English Social-Imperial Thought 1895–1914* (London: George Allen and Unwin, 1960), p. 29.

21 J. Gillis, *Youth and History: Tradition and Change in European Age Relation 1770–Present* (New York: Academic Press, Studies in Social Discontinuity, 1974). Gillis estimates that between 1890 and 1899 the English professional middle class family averaged 2.80 persons, which was about half the size of the family of manual laborers which were still pre-industrial in size, averaging 5.11 members, pp. 40–1.

    For an examination of the impact of eugenics upon education in Britain see R. A. Lowe, 'Eugenicists, Doctors and the Quest for National Efficiency, An Educational Crusade, 1900–1939', *History of Education*, 8:4 (1979), pp. 293–306.

22 A. Summers, 'The Nation in Arms: militarism in Britain before the Great War', *History Workshop: A Journal of Socialist Historians*, 2 (1976), p. 111.

23 Lord Reginald Brabazon (Earl of Meath) (ed.), 'Are we Decaying?', rpt. from the *Scotsman* (1886) in *Prosperity or Pauperism? Physical, Industrial and Technical Training* (London: Longmans, Green and Co., 1888). This volume is a valuable collection of essays dealing with the physical and technical training of working class children. Also dealing with the same theme are two other volumes edited by Lord Brabazon: *Some National and Board School Reforms* (London: Longmans, Green and Co., 1887) and *Social Arrows* (London: Longmans, Green and Co., 1886).

24 Searle, *The Quest for National Efficiency*, p. 38, or see R. Shannon, *The Crisis of Imperialism, 1856–1915* (1974; rpt. London: Paladin Grafton Books, 1986).

25 Summers, 'The Nation in Arms', p. 111.

26 C. C. Perry, 'Our undisciplined brains – the war test', *Nineteenth Century and After* (December 1901), pp. 894–904.

27 Semmel, *Imperialism and Social Reform*, p. 68.

28 As quoted by A. Davin, 'Imperialism and motherhood', *History Workshop Journal*, No. 5 (spring 1978), p. 18.

29 Samuel Smith, MP, in a letter to *The Times* during a visit to Berlin, rpt. in *Prosperity or Pauperism?*

30 T. H. Huxley, 'The struggle for existence: A programme', *Nineteenth Century*, (February 1888), p. 177.

31 J. Gillis, 'Youth in History: Progress and Prospects', *Journal of Social History*, 7:2 (winter, 1974), pp. 200–7. In the context of examining recent work on juvenile delinquency, Gillis traces the emergence of the concept of 'youth' and deviations from an accepted norm, 'juvenile delinquency'. In so doing, he points to the failure of a number of historians to recognise the ways in which such concepts as 'youth', 'adolescence', and 'juvenile delinquency' are historically determined.

    See also J. Gillis, 'The evolution of juvenile delinquency in England 1890–1914', *Past and Present*, No. 67 (1975), pp. 96–126.

32 SBL 793: Signed minutes of the special Subcommittee of the School Management Committee, V, p. 331. According to SBL 717, in 1897 the average class size was 53.71 for boys, 55.33 for girls and 54.21 for mixed departments – of which there were a limited number – and 60.59 for infants. According to SBL 1533, in 1899 the Board resolved that standards VI and above should not exceed forty pupils, in standards IV and V, fifty, and in standards I, II and III, sixty.

    The seventh standard was added gradually as the number of children remaining at school increased. In the first instance, however, there were few children who remained at school for standard VII so that it was not uncommon to find standards V, VI, and VII taught together under one teacher. For the development of the 'Higher Grade School' see F. G. London in T. A. Spalding and T. S. Canney, *The Work of the London School Board Presented at the Paris Exhibition, 1900* (London: P. S. King and Son, 1900), pp. 193–9, and postscript pp. 268–9.

33 *Final Report*, p. 36. It was not until 1891 that the Education Department agreed to calculate the amount lent for building a school so as to grant a special loan for an assembly hall. Before that date the assembly hall was calculated within the loan limit; the hall would then have been either extremely small or would have been used for regular classes as well as assemblies, pp. 37–8.

34 Although experiments in heating apparatus began even in the 1870s, early schools were all equipped as well with open fires; 'On town and country schools', *The Builder*, 30 May 1874, p. 458, describes two London schools in which a system of hot water pressure was used to warm the schools. In SBL 1000: Works and General Purposes Committee, 28 March 1898, p. 209, the Architect reported that open fires were being provided in some new schools; in the same year it was decided that the appropriate means of warming would be determined for each new school or enlargement.

   Although Board Schools were usually lit by a three-light pendant hung in a row over the center of the rooms, fitted with flat-flame gas burners, in the last schools built under the supervision of the Board, as well as in some enlargements, incandescent gas lighting was used. Eighteen Board Schools in the early twentieth century were equipped with electric lighting, but this was considered an expensive alternative to gas. *Final Report*, pp. 56–7.

35 Lord Brabazon, 'Industrial training in elementary schools', letter to *The Times*, rpt. in *Prosperity or Pauperism?*, p. 143.

   For an account of education available for working class girls before 1870 see J. Purvis, 'Schooling and working-class girls', in *Hard Lesson: The Lives and Education of Working-class Women in Nineteenth-century England* (Minneapolis: University of Minnesota Press, 1989), pp. 71–94.

36 M. G. Grey, 'Meeting of working men and women at the Cadogan Rooms, address delivered 28 November 1870', *The School Board for London: Three Addresses of Mrs William Grey in the Borough of Chelsea with a Speech by William Groves, Esq., QC, FRC* (London: W. Ridgeway, 1871), p. 20. Narrowly defeated in her campaign for the School Board, Maria Grey and her sister, Emily Shirreff, founded the National Union for the Education of Girls of All Classes above the Elementary, in 1871, later known as the Women's Education Union.

37 C. A. Leigh, 'For lack of knowledge', letter to the Editor, *The Daily News*, rpt. in *Prosperity or Pauperism?* p. 148.

38 Grey, 'Public Meeting at the Chelsea Vestry Hall in support of Mrs William Grey's Candidature', from an address delivered 14 November 1870, in *Three Addresses*, p. 11.

   For an examination of the relationship of Social Darwinism and imperialism to the education of girls in late nineteenth century England see C. Dyhouse, 'Social Darwinistic ideas and the development of women's education in England, 1880–1920', and *History of Education*, 5:1 (1976), pp. 41–58, and by the same author, 'Working-class mothers and infant mortality in England, 1885–1914', *Journal of Social History*, 12 (1979), pp. 252–67, and 'Good wives and little mothers: social anxieties in the schoolgirl's curriculum, 1890–1920', *Oxford Review of Education*, 3:1 (1977), pp. 21–35. The subject is also examined in C. Dyhouse, *Girls Growing Up in Late Victorian and Edwardian England* (London: Routledge and Kegan Paul, 1981). Also see Davin's 'Imperialism and motherhood'.

39 A. Davin, '"Mind that you do as you are told": reading books for Board School girls, 1870–1902', *Feminist Review*, 3 (1979), pp. 88–98.

40 *Ibid.*, p. 89.

41 Analysing textbooks used in girls' departments, David concludes that the message presented to Board School girls was that their 'ultimate aspiration' ought to be 'either a good place, and the trust and respect of their mistress, or a good husband, who equally would value their thrift and industry . . . few of the stories are about school situations: home and family loom much larger', pp. 94–6.

42 M. Headdon, 'Industrial training for girls', in *Some National and Board School Reforms*, p. 133.

43 C. Morley, *Studies in Board Schools*, (London: Smith and Elder, 1897), p. 135.

44 *Ibid.*, p. 137.

45 With the Education Code of 1878, Domestic Economy became a recognised subject for girls, followed by grants for Cookery in 1882 and Laundry in 1890. Between 1897 and 1903 Cookery, Laundry and Housewifery were united in a general scheme of Domestic Economy. *Final Report*, pp. 122–6.

46 See for example SBL 703: Signed minutes of Subcommittee on Domestic Economy of the School Management Committee for a discussion of acquiring such houses for use.

47 SBL 703, p. 69. The Subcommittee was composed of 'Lady Members of the Board' who selected the furnishings.

48 SBL 1423: Curricula and Methods of Teaching, Manual Training, Miscellaneous Papers which include a Memorandum for the Press at the Distribution of Prizes, February 1893.

49 Public Record Office (PRO): ED 14–37, 1883.

50 Emily Briggs (Superintendent of Cookery), 'Cookery', in Spalding and Canney, *The Work of the London School Board*, p. 228.

51 Davin, "Mind that you do as you are told", p. 89.
   The classic study of the daily expenditures of working class mothers in London was conducted between 1909 and 1913 in the district of Lambeth. Compiled by Maud Pember Reeves, *Round About A Pound A Week* (1913; rpt. London: Virago Press, 1979), and a committee of the Fabian Women's Group, the investigation shed light on the conditions that most Board School girls were to experience. Even at this later date, the study was conducted in order to demonstrate that it was neither ignorance nor degeneracy but lack of sufficient income which made the struggle for survival desperate for the majority of the population. The study was made of respectable working class families earning from 18s to 30s a week: 'respectable men in full work, at a more or less top wage, young, with families still increasing, and they will be lucky if they are never worse off than they now are. Their wives are quiet, decent, "keep-themselves-to-themselves" kind of women, and the children are the most punctual and regular scholars, the most clean-headed children of the poorer schools of Lambeth', pp. 2–3.
   Albeit a number of years earlier, the Housewifery examination of 1893 dealt with the preparation of a budget for a family on 30s a week. The reality of conditions encountered by the Fabian women was a far cry from the lessons on ventilation, carpet-sweeping, airing linen, and decorating a house included as subjects for examination, SBL 1423: Manual Training, Theoretical Examination. According to the Fabian study, a family with three or more children would spend between 7s and 8s a week on rent: 'The kind of dwelling to be

had for 7s or 8s a week varies in several ways. If it be light, dry, and free from bugs, if it be central in position, and if it contain three rooms, it will be eagerly sought for and hard to find' (p. 29). And the writer went on to describe the alternatives, often cramped quarters, often damp, with vermin a constant problem. The study provides an in-depth examination of how families earning approximately £1 a week struggled to survive.

52 SBL 692: School Management Committee, signed minutes of the Subcommittee on Cookery, 1884, p. 38.

53 Charles Morley described the laying of a table: *Studies in Board Schools*, pp. 141–2. Further descriptions of the syllabus can be found in SBL 405: Report of the Joint Committee on Manual Training, First Report, December 1893, p. 33.

54 SBL 405: Report of Joint Committee on Manual Training, p. 32.

55 Smith, 'The industrial training of destitute children', *Prosperity or Pauperism?*, p. 77.

56 SBL 706: School Management Committee, Subcommittee on Domestic Subjects, 5 March 1897, p. 255.

57 H. A. Kennedy, 'Board School London' in *Living London*, 1, p. 93.

58 Morley, *Studies in Board Schools*, p. 124.

59 *Ibid.*, p. 127.

60 SBL 1423: from a brochure entitled, 'Instruction in Laundry Work', 25 March 1892.

61 SBL 1423, from scheme and syllabus, n. pag.

62 *Ibid.*

63 Reeves, *Round About a Pound A Week*, pp. 75–93.

64 Headdon, 'Industrial training for girls', p. 130.

65 SBL 794: School Management Committee Special Subcommittee on House-wifery, Mrs Homan, Chair, 27 June 1895, p. 110.

66 A. J. Mundella, MP and President of the Board of Trade in 1886, presenting a deputation to the government in 1887 urging that School Boards and local authorities be empowered to establish and assist in the promotion of technical and commercial education, drew from a letter written by Huxley to *The Times*, as quoted in 'Technical and Commercial Education', in *The Times* (22 March 1887), rpt. *Prosperity or Pauperism?*, p. 129.

67 Marquis of Hartington, 'Speech on Technical and Trade Instruction', *Standard* (16 March 1887), rpt. *Prosperity or Pauperism?*

68 Sir Philip Magnus, 'Manual training in school education', *Prosperity or Pauperism?*, pp. 92–104.

69 Lord Brabazon, 'Industrial training in elementary schools', *Prosperity or Pauperism?*, pp. 144–5.

70 E. J. Watherston, 'Technical Education in Elementary Schools: The Form It Should Take', *Prosperity or Pauperism?*, p. 200.

71 SBL 405: Report of Joint Committee on Manual Training: Mr Wade, Headmaster at Halford-road, Fulham, Board School in memorandum summarising his experiences to the Committee.

72 SBL 1331: Annual Address 1887, Revd Diggle, p. 6.

73 SBL 790: Signed minutes of the Special Subcommittee of the School Management Committee on Technical Education, 12 November 1883, p. 185.

74 SBL 405: Report of Joint Committee, 1887.

75 At the time the Government Code had no provision for Manual Instruction, which meant in practical terms that there could be no financial assistance for such training. After an unsuccessful appeal, the School Board turned to the

City Guilds for voluntary contributions. In 1889 the Technical Instruction Act was passed by Parliament, which contained a clause forbidding government assistance to elementary schools for such training. In the same year, however, the Liverpool School Board received legal advice that they could in fact offer Manual Training and defray the cost from the school fund. The London School Board followed suit. The following year Manual Training was recognised by the Education Department. *Final Report*, pp. 112–13.

76 *Final Report*, p. 333.

77 F. Clay, *Modern School Buildings*, 2nd edn (London: B. T. Batsford, 1906), pp. 419–22.

78 Lord Brabazon (Earl of Meath) in his own activities exemplifies something of this attitude. As has been noted, he was deeply involved in promoting industrial and technical training in elementary schools – and his wife, Mary, Lady Brabazon, was an enthusiastic proponent of domestic training for girls – but he was, above all, associated with the movement to ensure a healthier population. As Chairman of the Metropolitan Public Gardens Association from its foundation in 1882 until his death in 1929, he was an advocate of increasing the open spaces available for physical exercise and recreation in urban areas, and he served as the first Chairman of the Parks Committee of the London County Council. He was likewise active in pressing Parliament to require physical exercise as a compulsory subject in Board Schools. He was also associated with the establishment of Empire Commemoration Day in elementary schools and the champion of the custom of flying the Union Jack, in his words the 'emblem of our imperial heritage', over Board Schools. In addition he was the founder and first president of the Lads' Drill Association and Chief Commissioner of the Boy Scouts in Ireland. Reginald, 12th Earl of Meath, MP, *Memories of the Nineteenth Century* (London: John Murray, 1923).

79 Lord Brabazon, 'Physical Training', an address given by the Earl of Meath at the Liverpool Gymnasium, 12 October 1887, rpt. *Prosperity or Pauperism?*, p. 55.

80 Summers, 'The Nation in Arms', p. 111. 'In the 19th century,' Summers writes, 'sympathetic concern for the individual soldier and the impulse to reform the army as a whole were always expressions of a desire to bring military standards into line with those in civil life. In the Edwardian period, it was civil society which required regeneration, and it was through, and indeed for the army that the process of renewal was to take place. Before, the army had been domesticated; now, society was to be militarised', p. 112.

81 Lord Brabazon described the conflict that his proposal for flag flying engendered among School Board members, resulting in 'a compromise between my proposals and the violent opposition of the advanced Radicals, some of whom described the proposal . . . as "a ritual in keeping with that semi-barbaric worship of national fetishes known as 'Jingoism'"', *Memories*, p. 332. The nature of drill as a subject was a matter for debate. As physical exercise it was acceptable to the Progressives on the Board, as 'military' drill and marching it was not.

82 *Final Report*, p. 115.

83 SBL 790: Special Subcommittee of the School Management Committee, vol. 2, 2 August 1883, p. 242. The Board resolved 'That a "Physical Education Committee" be formed which shall take the management and control of Physical Education generally including gymnastics, drill, Swedish exercises, the use of playgrounds, and the furnishing and management of the gymnasiums about to be erected through Lord Brabazon's generosity.'

84 *Final Report*, p. 114

85 SBL 287: General Purposes Committee, signed minutes of the Subcommittee, the Medical Officer's Department, 11 December 1899 – 28 April 1904. The first meeting of the Committee took place 14 February 1900. In 1901 the Committee issued special guidance to teachers; in 1902 eight oculists were appointed; the weighing of students began in 1903.

86 SBL 1462: Memorandum by the Chairman of the School Management Committee on the medical inspection of schoolchildren, 26 June 1900.

87 SBL 287: 14 October 1903, p. 170.

88 SBL 287: 19 November 1903, pp. 178–9.

89 SBL 288: 25 February 1904, pp. 12–13.

90 M. F. Davies, 'School Care Committees', *School Hygiene*, 2 (1 February 1910), p. 93.

91 S. Webb, *London Education* (London: Longmans, Green and Co., 1904), p. 3.

92 *Ibid.*, p. 4.

93 *Ibid.*, p. 3

94 *Ibid.*, p. 5.

95 *Ibid.*, p. 9.

CHAPTER SIX

'The best for the lowest': the Settlement movement

Kindly and enthusiastic millionaires build for us art galleries, collec-
tions of paintings and statuary, museums filled with stuffed beasts and
the products of foreign lands. We gaze on their imposing facades as we
hurry to work in the morning, or hurry at evening to rest. Amiable
young men elevate us by frequent lectures on the ethics of Dante, the
poetry of the Renaissance, and similar pleasing topics. [1]

Whereas the Board School provided striking visual evidence in every
poor neighborhood that children were being rescued and transformed
within Queen Anne 'homes of education' provided by the State
through the rates, private philanthropy, for its part, built a variety of
institutions designed to bring culture to the East End and other poor
neighborhoods of late nineteenth century London. Such contact, it was
hoped, would engender warmer feelings between classes. It was argued
that the plight of the poor stemmed not only from the want of the basic
necessities of life but from the 'absence of anything more civilising than
a grinding organ to raise the ideas beyond the daily bread and beer.'[2]
The city's poorest neighborhoods were 'deadly dull, jerry-built, God-
forsaken-looking stacks of brick and mortar'[3] and the inhabitants 'have
no resources in themselves'.[4]

> narrow ill-lighted, ill-kept, ill-policed streets, are the drawing room of
> the people. . . . Their entertainment is at best a cheap cinema, at
> worst a street fight; a young man's hospitality is given in a Public House
> or a Coffee Stall, to a girl whose literature is the divorce news in the
> Sunday press; their art is the posters of bottled beer. For their
> architecture and their music, they have strings of houses or returning
> drunks[5]

Philanthropists increasingly pointed to the cultural deprivation the poorest districts as a source of serious division in the capital: as ne writer in south London phrased it, 'There is more lost to dwellers in South London than good wages, free education, or any measures of heroic legislation can restore. Religion, light, refinement, were never considered when South London grew.'[6] The solution was seen as necessarily coming from outside. 'What is needed to-day,' were 'men of purpose who will become repairers of the breach and bridge-builders, messengers who will bring brightness into dark places and the gospel of the fulness of life and joy.'[7]

It was in the task of bringing 'light and refinement' to the poor that university students followed in the steps of Arnold Toynbee, many coming to live and work amidst the poor. A variety of private and Church-sponsored institutions shared the ambition of bringing middle class culture and refinements to the city's poor. These efforts represented piecemeal attempts to deal with the social problem, in contrast to the large scale centralised organisation on behalf of the child population. The architectural expression of these institutions spoke again of origins and ambitions. Utilising popular myths about the past – rich and poor joined together in rituals of hospitality – they contrasted, like the Board Schools, with the homes of the poor. Lacking the obvious economic utility of the Board Schools, they offered more scope for perpetuating a fantasy symbolism in their architecture.

The institution that *epitomised* the middle class cause of bringing culture to the poor was the Settlement House. In a structured way university students and graduates were brought into daily contact with the poor, living in the city's poorest communities in Settlement Houses and participating in community activities, providing the 'leavening influence of residents with minds more richly endowed', 'the best for the lowest'.[8] The Settlement was distinct from missions, as their prime concern was not proselytising but rather providing 'contact with higher and fuller lives than their own',[9] for only 'by close contact with the slowly-acquired Best possessed by the race can a human being gain the high intellectual or moral level from which his own power can have a chance of adding to the moral or intellectual wealth of the world.'[10]

Activities at a Settlement House were wide-ranging, emphasising cultural and intellectual pursuits as well as practical advice for visitors of all ages. This included at various Settlements such disparate functions as evening courses, lectures, picture exhibitions, theatre clubs, music societies, chess clubs, legal advice, travellers clubs, evenings for children, mothers' meetings, clubs for young adults, and use of a library. Lectures might be given on subjects ranging from

women's suffrage and current parliamentary debate
music and Spanish antiquities. Speakers were drawn
Liberals and other cultural lights of the day, from
Watts, for example, to H. H. Asquith, MP, or Per

That the Settlement was contrived, an 'art
best, designed to compensate for some of the grea
Victorian city, was freely admitted even by its adhere
as the warden of one Settlement said, 'a Settlemen
artificial expedient, and can only faintly set forth the g
come if men of different ranks and interests lived tog
intercourse and cooperation.'[11] Settlements, as anothe
tained, were 'artificial, not growing up naturally as in a r
planted as a protest against the disastrous cleavage betw
West'.[12] And yet, that a 'solution', however artificial, was
firmly held by the wardens who organised and ran the Settle
by the many residents who came to live and work in them fo
months or years. By the First World War there were twent
residential Settlements in London, thirty-nine throughout the co
Settlements were founded by Oxford and Cambridge colleges,
Cheltenham Ladies College, and by persons of various religiou
political persuasions. There were also Settlements that were
denominational or non-religious in orientation. All, however,
assumptions about the relationship of Settlement residents to the
populace.

The concept of a Settlement was first proposed by Canon San
Barnett in a lecture which he delivered to an enthusiastic audience
St John's College, Oxford, in 1883, the same which had inspired
Toynbee.[14] Critical of the role of the Church in dealing with the
growing gulf between rich and poor in the metropolis, he proposed
individual service among the poor: 'The grand idea which moved the
College, the idea which, like a new creative spirit, is brooding over the
face of society, . . . making men conscious of their brotherhood finds
no adequate expression in the district church machinery with which,
in East London, I am familiar.' Describing Church government as
'unreformed' in 'an age of reform', he proposed the foundation of a new
institution which could channel the ambitions of sympathetic men who
would 'under a wiser Church government' have found their outlet
through service as clergymen.[15]

Canon H. Scott Holland later recalled how

> Barnett came down and preached in our College Halls, and the whole
> University laid hold of his idea and understood. He came as a prophet
> just when it was wanted, and men saw in his Settlement proposal

opportunity which their gathering interest in the problems
emanded for its exercise and fulfillment. [16]

isioned an institution that would provide a place for
etween classes, a means of mitigating class suspicion
knowledge and experience of each other. 'Poverty,
Sin threaten the city. Free Trade, the Suffrage, the
 have been tried, and the doom still impends. What is
ed Barnett. Central to the Settlement movement was
o *individual* service. Barnett believed that

ns are good, just in so far as they are vivified by personal
aws are good as they allow for the free play of person on person
s persons who save; and if today fifty – a company – of righteous
ould be found in London, the city might be spared and saved. [17]

e model for the Settlement worker came from the example of
rd graduates in the 1860s, J. R. Green, a clergyman who had
ced his orders after working in the East End, and Edward
n, son of the Bishop of Salisbury. As early as 1867 Ruskin had
ith Denison, J. R. Green, Revd Brooke Lambert, the Vicar of St
s, Whitechapel, and possibly Revd H. Scott Holland to discuss
could be done for the poor. Both Denison and Green had
mended that university men live among the poor as Denison was
, but the matter was not pursued. [18] But at Oxford in 1883
ett's plea for such a movement found resonance in an atmosphere
which such ardent supporters of personal service as the Master of
lliol, Benjamin Jowett, the late T. H. Green and Arnold Toynbee
had already entreated students to seek fulfillment in duty to the
community. It was at the Settlement House that the philanthropy and
service stressed by T. H. Green in his lectures at Oxford found their
clearest expression.

In 1884 Henrietta and Samuel Barnett opened the first Settlement
House, Toynbee Hall, named after Arnold Toynbee, who had died the
previous year at the age of thirty-one. Toynbee Hall, located in
Whitechapel, was designed by the architect Elijah Hoole. Although
little is known about Elijah Hoole, the son of a missionary to Madras,
it is known that he designed working class housing for Octavia Hill,
including the Red Cross Cottages and Hall, not far from the Bermondsey
Settlement. [19] According to family memory, his work for Octavia Hill
began in 1870 at the urging of his wife. [20] At the age of forty,
disappointed with Wesleyan Methodism, he converted to the Anglican
Church. [21] Barnett described Hoole's building in a letter to his brother
as a 'manorial residence in Whitechapel' [22] [**49–50**].

The design, as executed, was of a manor house of red brick with stone dressing in the Elizabethan manner, replete with dog-tooth patterns and mullions. The major components of the building – the warden's residence, the library, classrooms, conversation room, drawing room and accommodation for sixteen residents – surrounded a courtyard which set the building back from the hubbub of the street.

The interior provided the comforts of a West End parlour for Settlement activities [51]. In describing the interior decoration, Henrietta Barnett explained that 'we finally decided to make it exactly like a West-End drawing room, erring, if at all on the side of gorgeousness.'[23] The *Cambridge Review* likened the decor to that of a 'comfortable country house'.[24] The interior was decorated along the fashionable lines of the day: the walls were painted a sallow green and hung with Japanese prints; the lattice-paned windows were draped with heavy, warm-colored curtains, fitted with cushioned seats below. In one corner of the drawing room stood a grand piano, in another was a fireplace with glazed Gothic revival tiles; a huge gilded screen stood before a comfortable nook, and Oriental rugs were strewn over the floor. As one observer noted, 'the picture is completed by the china cabinets and the tables heaped with albums.'[25]

In what ways did the architecture of this new institution express the ambitions of its founder? What would explain the place and function of a 'manorial residence in Whitechapel' in the 1880s? In order to answer these questions it is critical to understand the mission of the Settlement movement.

Fundamental to Barnett's vision of a harmonious, cohesive society was the belief in a social hierarchy:

> Classes must exist. A body in which every member is a hand could do no work, and a city of one class would have no life. The classes in our great cities are many, but the terms 'rich' and 'poor', if not exact definitions, represent the two great classes of society. Their unity means strength, their division means ruin.[26]

But, as noted by many who lamented the loss of the traditional role of charity in the nineteenth century, the once close relationship was 'broken up', sending the rich and poor 'to live apart and think apart'.[27] As in the development of the Board School, the awareness of the transformed nature of charity played a vital role. The Settlement movement was a self-conscious attempt to reconstruct a more 'natural', organic relationship between classes. It cast a look backward to a period before the industrial revolution which was imagined to have been more peaceful and caring. Liberal ideology glanced back longingly:

TOYNBEE·HALL·Commercial·Street·Whitechapel·London·E·   M.ʳ E.Hoole ғʀıʙᴀ·ᴀʀᴄʜıᴛᴇᴄᴛ·

49] Toynbee Hall, architect Elijah Hoole, from *The Builder*, 14 February 1885

> A few generations ago . . . England was the population of the English
> countryside: the 'rich man in his castle', 'the poor man at his gate'; the
> feudal society of country house, country village, and little country
> town, in a land whose immense wealth still slept undisturbed. . . . The
> little red-roofed towns and hamlets, the labourer in the fields at
> noontide or evening, the old English service in the old English village
> church, now stand but as the historical survival of a once great and
> splendid past . . . the one single system of a traditional hierarchy has
> fissured into a thousand diversified channels, with eddies and break-
> waters, whirlpools and sullen marshes, and every variety of vigour,
> somnolence, and decay.[28]

A central feature of this 'great splendid past' was its 'traditional
hierarchy'. In London in the eighteenth century the poor lived adjacent
to their more affluent neighbors, inhabiting the alley-ways behind
fashionable squares. In the countryside the gentry and the peasant, it
was asserted, had had mutual responsibilities.[29] Whereas in provincial
towns 'wealth and poverty' were still 'neighbours',[30] in the contemporary
city distance had transformed the relationship between classes.

Active in East End charity, the Barnetts were keenly aware of
the debates on the role that charity played in defining the relationship
between classes: whereas charity administered by the wealthy had been
a central feature of the old order, the geographical gulf that now
separated rich and poor had rendered giving an anonymous act. Barnett

50] Toynbee Hall, from Henrietta Barnett's *Canon Barnett*

contended that 'The resentment common among the poor who receive help is largely caused by gifts which are given without the giver.'[31] But further, it has been argued, distance now meant that giving no longer

51] Toynbee Hall, drawing room, from Henrietta Barnett's *Canon Barnett*

entailed being repaid with obligations, with deference and respect, with 'cheerfulness, submission and gratitude'.[32]

In urging university men to come to East London, Barnett inquired whether there was not a general awareness 'that all our social system is arranged on the tacit assumption that there is a leisured class in every locality who will see that the laws are carried out and generally keep the social life going?' And he continued, 'Do you realise that there is no such class in East London, where it is most wanted?' The Settlement movement drew its inspiration from an image of the past which it sought to recreate in poor neighborhoods. The Settlement worker with a superior education was to become an active leader within the working class community, joining working-men's clubs, giving lectures, and standing in local elections. As one church leader said, the Settlement worker would 'by some *je ne sais quoi* in himself . . . preserve their freely accorded social homage.'[33] He urged university men to 'Come and be that class, not in a patronising spirit but in a spirit of neighbourliness.'[34] Barnett warned of the dangers of a Settlement with fewer than twelve members, as residents in small groups might find it more difficult to remain aloof, risking the potential of being overwhelmed by the influences of the local neighborhood, by the 'slovenliness and cheapness and want of manners which often distinguishes industrial neighbourhoods.'[35] A worker at Oxford House, a Settlement in Bethnal Green founded by the Keble College Anglicans as a distinctly religious institution, in contrast to Toynbee Hall's non-denominational outlook, described the Settlement worker's role in the Working Men's Club at the Settlement as 'the *Kyning* of the new feudalism which is springing up in this present time, raised on the shields of his kin, for that in their hearts and consciences they acknowledge his superiority.'[36]

Revd H. Scott Holland described the aims of the movement as

> simply the restoration of the natural conditions which our whole public life assumes. It gives back the very people who alone can functionalise on behalf of the body. It restores the right relation of people to one another. It re-establishes a graded variation of conditions which will allow for the interchange of services.[37]

And the feudal language became explicit when he implored university men to 'Come and be the squires of East London'.[38]

The notion of a feudal hierarchy in Barnett's conception of the Settlement was subsequently borrowed by other Settlements designed on the Toynbee Hall model. For example, Barnett conceived of the Settlement House as the seat of hospitality in the neighborhood. In 1895 Barnett described the essence of the Settlement:

> Hospitality was, in old days, if not the secret, then to a large extent, the source of the power of the chief. The feudal lord entertained his followers and welcomed strangers. The master was the host of his apprentices, and national events were marked by feasts in which all shared. They thus met, as it were, off their guard. They learnt to know one another's thoughts and manners, they discovered points of likeness, and came into quiet possession of a common inheritance.[39]

The 'chief', 'the master', or 'feudal lord' 'welcomed strangers' who found their 'common inheritance' by participating in the Settlement movement. Barnett saw other efforts at entertainment provided for the working class as falling short of that function, mere gifts that

> do not rise to the level of sharing; they do not make at one giver and receiver; they do not reveal the thoughts and manners of his home; they do not provoke a sense of common possessions by interest in one another's possessions: they do little, therefore, to increase peace and good will between the nation of the poor and the nation of the rich.[40]

In contrast, 'University Settlements claim to show a way of entertainment which is more nearly hospitality . . . It is perhaps the one large house of the neighbourhood – the one house in which it is possible to enjoy social life.'[41] The residents of a Settlement 'are able to use their powers of hospitality to bind their friends together.'[42]

The movement was backward looking and its nostalgia for a lost feudal world as conjured up by the imagery of a 'manorial residence in Whitechapel' recalls, as noted, E. P. Thompson's observations on the rituals of paternalism and deference which characterised eighteenth century culture:

> The great gentry . . . met the lower sort of people on their own terms . . . just as their formidable mansions imposed their presence, apart from, but guarding over, the village or town. Their appearance has much the same studied self-conciousness of public theatre. . . .
> We have studied an elaborate hegemonic style, a theatrical role in which the great were schooled in infancy and which they maintained until death. And if we speak of theatre it is not to diminish its importance . . . what matters is a continuing theatrical style. What one remarks of the eighteenth century is elaboration of this style and the self-conciousness with which it was deployed.[43]

The Settlement House was the 'theatre' for an on-going drama which constantly reaffirmed the mutual roles of the participants. That some residents felt awkward and uneasy is not surprising[44] in a deeply self-conscious movement which tried to recreate a feudal world in the urban slum. Contemporary criticism could, in fact, be quite caustic. An article in the *Spectator* in 1885 characterised the Settlement movement as possessing 'an artlessness . . . which savoured a little of the academic prig . . . inhabitants of East London . . . were to be regenerated by the efforts of undergraduates and the sight of aesthetic furniture and Japanese fans'.[45] Alas, most local visitors left no memoirs of these events. The theatre, however, was one which was enacted and re-enacted in the Settlement movement for years to come.

The appearance and placement of the Settlement House were critical in setting the terms of the rituals to be enacted. Whether purpose-built or an existing accommodation taken over and made into a Settlement, the site was separate and distinct from the rest of the community, affording the local poor visitor to the Settlement a 'glimpse of a new, fresh, and pleasant way of looking at the world.'[46] Barnett was clear about the potential of culture to raise men and women, akin to a spiritual transformation:

> It seems a hard thing, but I believe that it is on the line of truth, to say that the dock labourer cannot live the life of Christ; he may be loving and trusting, live a higher life than that lived by many rich men, but he cannot live the highest life possible to men of his time. To live the life of Christ is to make manifest the truth and to enjoy the beauty of God. The labourer who knows nothing . . . which, by admiration, can lift him out of himself, cannot live the highest life of his day, as Christ lived the highest life of His day.[47]

The Barnetts saw the design itself of the Settlement House as one part of their larger cultural program for East London, of bringing 'the best to the lowest'. In decorating St Jude's, for example, they had employed William Morris and had taken great satisfaction in the decoration of the church. Barnett described how he had viewed the attention paid to the decor:

> The great want of this East End of London is beauty; the streets are ugly, and few signs of taste are anywhere apparent; it is therefore well that it should be possible for both inhabitants and passers-by to enter a building which by its grace and beauty, should remind them of a world made beautiful by God's Hand.[48]

In answering criticism that perhaps Settlements should be more modest in appearance – decorated without carpets, pianos and pictures – Barnett asserted that it was 'in part by contact with these despised luxuries that unity will be reached . . . in a very true sense it is only familiarity with good furniture and fine clothes which will breed contempt of them as barriers against fellowship.'[49] Like the residents themselves, fine things would have an influence on those who came into contact with them:

The resident in a settlement, who has made his room his home, furnished it with his favourite books and pictures, marked it by his daily habits, is able to entertain his friends with a power impossible in strange quarters, or amid the artificial creations of asceticism. It is sufficient to say that the power is used – the result must be imagined.[50]

The idea of providing a glimpse of a finer home life was an important feature of Henrietta Barnett's work with local women even before the founding of Toynbee Hall. She arranged that well-to-do women with houses and gardens in other localities invite women from Whitechapel for annual teas.

Very pregnant of influence are these introductions to a house scrupulously clean and tastily furnished – a house kept as the dwelling of every human should be kept. Do we not know ourselves, if we go to visit a friend with a higher standard of art, morals, or culture, how subtle is the influence; how from such visits (albeit unconsciously, or at least hardly with deliberate resolve) is dated the turning toward the new light, the intention to be more perfect?[51]

In writing of his 'Ideal city' Barnett similarly noted the importance of providing beautiful buildings, even for humble building types:

Halls, galleries, libraries, baths, hospitals, colleges, asylums, prisons (many of them brilliant with mosaic) will catch and raise the thoughts of men, as in old days the thoughts of their citizens were caught by the public buildings of Florence or Venice.
  A visitor to the IDEAL CITY would be charmed by its first aspect: its variety of architecture, its beauty of colour, its freshness and purity[52]

Barnett understood as well the symbolic function that the Settlement building had, as it

touches at many points the life of the industrial centre in which it is established. Its associations tend to be more important than its achievements: it stands for more than can appear in visible results; its moral significance in the eyes of a wider public becomes perhaps its most distinguishing characteristic.[53]

The architecture and decor of the institutions, which so clearly represented the culture and refinements of another class, had a didactic function: 'Settlements will best do their work,' wrote Barnett, 'when by what they are as well as by what their residents do, the people of East London understand how the rest of London lives.'[54]

  The tone that runs through the movement would seem to verify E. P. Thompson's observations on the nature of paternalism:

> paternalism as myth or ideology is nearly always backward looking. It
> offers itself in English history less as actuality than as a model of an
> antique, recently passed, golden age from which present manners are
> a degeneration. . . . Paternalism . . . tends to offer a model of the
> social order as it is seen from above; it has implications of warmth and
> face-to-face relations which imply notions of value; it confuses the
> actual and the ideal.[55]

The Settlement movement developed a self-consciously paternalistic
architecture which tallied with the movement's nostalgic view of
history. Toynbee Hall drew its architectural vocabulary from the 'Old
English' style popularised by the architects George Devey, William
Eden Nesfield and Norman Shaw in their manor house designs of the
1860s onward, a style that evoked nostalgia for the picturesque
vernacular architecture they had sketched in the countryside of Kent
and Sussex.[56] The 'Old English' style drew loosely on Tudor-Gothic
and Elizabethan models. Here, now, in the middle of East London,
Elijah Hoole designed Toynbee Hall along the lines of an English
manor house, with heavy chimney stacks, stone dressing and brick, a
material widely available since the fifteenth century.[57]

A paucity of documentation makes the plan of the Settlement
difficult to analyse in terms of a country-house model,[58] but it is clear
that the requirements of an institution designed for twenty residents,
as well as the provision of accommodation for lectures, presented
planning problems different from those of a country house. However,
it does appear that Hoole followed at least some of the planning ideas
available to the country-house architect, ideas which found expression,
for example, in Robert Kerr's *The Gentleman's House* of 1864 and J. J.
Stevenson's *House Architecture* of 1880. These writers urged a pleasant,
sunny aspect, preferably south-east, for the drawing room, with a view
of the garden or landscape.[59] The country-house architect was
instructed to assure sufficient wall space for furniture and decorations
such as curiosity cabinets, piano, and sofas. However, the architectural
handbooks distinguished between the decor deemed appropriate for the
drawing room and the dining room: whereas the '*character* to be aimed
at in the Drawing-room is especial cheerfulness, refinement of elegance,
and what is called lightness as opposed to massiveness . . . entirely *lady-
like*', the 'dining-room . . . is in almost every way one of contrast.'[60]
An echo of these instructions appears at Toynbee Hall. In contrast to
the drawing room, the dining room partook of the Medieval Revival,
an exercise in decoration supervised by the designer and architect
C. R. Ashbee after he had given a series of lectures on Ruskin and
labor at Toynbee Hall in 1887. The room was decorated with a free-
hand design on the walls, punctuated by modeled bosses or medallions,

the coats of arms of Oxford and Cambridge colleges in clay, cast in plaster and painted and gilded. In each medallion was a stylised tree, the 'T' of Toynbee Hall putting forth leaves and branches, the whole incorporated into a frieze along the top of the wall.[61]

Although Barnett likened Toynbee Hall to a manor house, the architecture of the Settlement has also been compared to that of the Oxford and Cambridge colleges from which the residents came. According to one contemporary account, on arrival 'You pass through a narrow passage beneath an archway; you find yourself before a fine range of buildings comprising three sides of a quadrangle. You might think yourself in an Oxford collegiate edifice'.[62] According to an American visitor,

> Toynbee Hall is essentially a transplant of university life in Whitechapel. The quadrangle, the gables, the diamond-paned windows, the large general rooms, especially the dining room with its brilliant frieze of college shields, all make the place seem not so distant from the dreamy walks by the Isis or the Cam.[63]

The suites of the residents, a sitting room and bedroom or bedsitter, differed, according to the *Cambridge Review*, 'in no essential aspect from an ordinary college room' except for the bright colors which Henrietta Barnett preferred to institutional ones.[64] That Barnett imagined that one day Toynbee Hall might develop into a university for East London is widely acknowledged. As early as 1882 he had written that 'the scheme by which a kind of East London college may be established is already fully shaped in my mind.'[65] In the late 1880s two residential units were added to Toynbee Hall, Balliol House and Wadham House, for which Oxford and Cambridge were the models.[66] In the Seventh Annual Report of Toynbee Hall, in reference to the addition of Balliol House in 1890–91, mention was made that 'what may grow in time to be part of an East London residential university is full of anxious promise.'[67]

The language of paternalism which ran through the Settlement movement and which found visual form at Toynbee Hall was realised as well at Oxford House in Bethnal Green which, though also founded in 1884, did not have its own purpose-built building until 1892, designed by Arthur Blomfield [52]. Again the design was an English manor house of red brick with stone dressings. Its most elaborate addition to the Toynbee Hall model was a chapel.

It was at the Bermondsey Settlement in south London, however, founded by the Methodist Conference in 1891 and opened in 1892, that the imagery of a pre-industrial England found its fullest expression [53]. The task of Settlement workers in Bermondsey was seen in much the same way as Barnett had conceived the role of workers in Whitechapel. In fact, the founder and warden of the Settlement freely acknowledged that the model for this Settlement was Toynbee Hall and that it was to the Barnetts that he turned for advice.

The contrast between Victorian Bermondsey and Bermondsey of an earlier period ran through the literature of the Settlement: contemporary Bermondsey was 'almost submerged in dullness . . . a district without cabs and without bookseller's shops'.[68] The district offered 'nothing . . . betwixt heaven and hell – betwixt the mission room and the tap-room.'[69] But this state of things had not always been the case. According to the organisers of Settlement activities, Bermondsey had once been a center of 'chivalry and romance, of learning and sanctity'.[70] Bermondsey's importance had come from the fact of its being a Royal Manor, an occasional residence of the sovereigns, and the site of the great Abbey of St Saviour.[71] In the Middle Ages royal processions and knights and barons had passed through. Crusaders were seen on their way to the Abbey. It was down Bermondsey streets that, in the beginning of the reign of Queen Mary, Sir Thomas Wyatt had led his insurrectionary forces. There had been 'the stately monastery, with the good cheer in its refectory, and High Mass in its Chapel'.[72] Great

52] Oxford House, drawing, from Henry Walker's *East London Sketches of Christian Work*, 1896

53] Bermondsey Settlement, 1892, architect Elijah Hoole

events had transpired in Bermondsey: 'Parliaments have been held in the Abbey, Councils deliberated on great affairs of State, Judges held their courts within its precincts, Princes of the blood and Princes of the Church have lodged in the monastery'.[73] That rich, but to the poor, unknown, local history was self-consciously used in the Settlement's mission to revitalise and enrich Bermondsey.

The warden, John Scott Lidgett, again employed the architect Elijah Hoole, whose family was active in Methodist affairs and who was married to one of Lidgett's aunts. Although Lidgett lamented that Hoole's design had to be modified due to cost, the building was, in fact, even more imposing than Toynbee Hall. Like the latter, it was built of red brick and decorated with stone dressing, but it had a massive tower and oriel window over the entrance and high-pitched roof and dormer window. The *Methodist Recorder* described how the building appeared in relation to its surroundings:

> Here in the middle of a paved space, rose up a high, red building with a very wide frontage, solid, aggressive, reassuring, confronting cowering lines of curtainless, hopeless dirty dwellings[74]

The striking contrast of this building amidst the 'curtainless, hopeless dirty dwellings' suggests again how the authority of a new institution was conveyed by its sheer scale as well as style.

The imagery of 'Old England' was found not only in the grand castle that towered over the neighborhood, but was extended to the smallest details of the Settlement. It was within this medieval world that social relationships would be recast. At Bermondsey the language of an explicitly pre-industrial world informed all activities: a 'Guild of Play' was established for the children, a 'Guild of the Poor Brave Things' for the disabled of all ages in the community, 'St Olave's Guild' for young servant girls of the district, and a 'Mothers' Guild'. Girls sang 'Old English and Scotch Ballads'.[75] The children of this south London slum sang 'Round and Round the Village',[76] and throughout the neighborhood 'pretty old English games are sung by ragged little barefooted maidens in many a Bermondsey court and street'.[77]

The nostalgic element which found expression in the revival of old English traditions was epitomised by the programs of the Guild of Play, an organisation which was founded at Bermondsey and which was replicated at other London Settlements. Focusing attention on the children of the district, the Guild of Play was committed to reviving the historical associations of the district, conjuring up an image of a Bermondsey with ties to its glorious past through the revival of 'old English singing games, country dances, customs, etc, for which the Bermondsey of the Middle Ages was famed far and wide, and which festivals Royalty singled out to visit.'[78] It was asserted, in a variant of the language of child rescue, that

> In the spacious days of Elizabeth, England played more than to-day, and everyone was expected to dance, and found no favour at Court if heavy upon their feet. In the medieval times in Bermondsey, colour and pageantry ran riot on this very spot, where long grey streets cover the once green fields and orchard ways.[79]

The Guild organised play in which the central theme was the 'revival of all that is national and traditional . . . for there is but little doubt that the historical method is the right one.' The aims of the Guild of Play were tied to the larger ethos of the Settlement movement. The Guild was committed to 'the cultivation of politeness and courtesy . . . the amenities of polite society'.[80]

May Day was celebrated with the traditional crowning of the May Queen and the plaiting of the maypole by children dressed in old English costumes [54]:

> There was first the crowning of the May Queen. . . . So little Harriet . . . was arrayed in spotless white and garlanded with daisies, and walked past the Lord Mayoress, Adeline Duchess of Bedford, and the Countess Somers. And all of them kissed her, the Countess presenting her with a purse. . . . Village youths and maidens, shepherdesses and

54] Guild of Play, maypole drill

milkmaids, Robin Hood and his inseparables, Friar Tuck, Little John, and Maid Marian, sweeps and Morris dancers, Jack-in-the-Green and hobby horse, and everybody else whom tradition has connected with May Day did their part remarkably well.[81]

A program of events reminded the participants that

In Bermondsey of the Middle Ages, which was the time of Bermondsey's glory, May Day was a great festival. Bluff King Hal rode a-maying from Greenwich to Shooter's Hill with Queen Katherine and a retinue of lords and ladies.

And an old English proverb was quoted: 'When Maye-Daye cometh, with blythe jolite, Haste ye good friend to merrie Bermondsey.'[82]

Exposure to traditional song and dance had, however, a further aim:

The great message of the national dance is undoubtedly the preparation for future citizenship . . . it is never difficult to rouse the enthusiasm of children, and anything connected with the British flag will always strike a good, imperial, and patriotic note[83]

That the songs and games had a didactic function was spelled out by the organisers:

True play is the carrier of social traditions, not only those traditions which carry the form of play, dances, ceremony, and games, but even more than this, those traditions which prevent the strong from trampling the weak, that give to each equal opportunity. This scheme

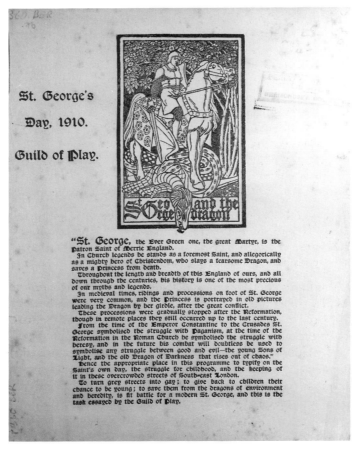

St. George's
Day, 1910.
Guild of Play.

"St. George, the Ever Green one, the great Martyr, is the Patron Saint of Merrie England.

In Church legends he stands as a foremost Saint, and allegorically as a mighty hero of Christendom, who slays a fearsome Dragon, and saves a Princess from death.

Throughout the length and breadth of this England of ours, and all down through the centuries, his history is one of the most precious of our myths and legends.

In medieval times, ridings and processions on foot of St. George were very common, and the Princess is portrayed in old pictures leading the Dragon by her girdle, after the great conflict.

These processions were gradually stopped after the Reformation, though in remote places they still occurred up to the last century.

From the time of the Emperor Constantine to the Crusades St. George symbolised the struggle with Paganism, at the time of the Reformation in the Roman Church be symbolised the struggle with heresy, and in the future his combat will doubtless be used to symbolise any struggle between good and evil—the young Sons of Light, and the old Dragon of Darkness that rises out of chaos."

Hence the appropriate place in this programme to typify on the Saint's own day, the struggle for childhood, and the keeping of it in these overcrowded streets of South-east London.

To turn grey streets into gay; to give back to children their chance to be young; to save them from the dragons of environment and heredity, is fit battle for a modern St. George, and this is the task essayed by the Guild of Play.

55] Guild of Play program, 1910

of play is not for the well-behaved, clean, beribboned and pinafored children alone, for whom it is always an easy thing to work, but for the crude and uncouth, the noisy, impudent little street Arabs who have had false starts in life, with everything against them.

The writer went on to explain the 'value of traditional songs, dances and games'. In the Guild of Play 'stress is laid on all imitative play calling for gesture and impersonation of either period, or racial feeling and for social order, and the best good of all.'[84]

That contemporary Bermondsey was no longer the Bermondsey described in the novels of Sir Walter Scott was duly noted in the Settlement programs, which were printed in old English script [55]: 'There is something pathetic,' it was noted in the program to one festival, 'in the Bermondsey of to-day, where the children hold their

May-Day revels'.[85] And yet the festivals 'link our lives indissolubly with the generations who have preceded us.'[86]

The revival of Gothic and Elizabethan imagery with its potent and evocative contrast between the reality of the nineteenth century slum and the vision of a more harmonious and pleasing world, was central to the Settlement movement. The grace and loveliness of civilisation and culture were bestowed upon the poorest neighborhoods of the city and offered to the children, the future generation of working class citizens. Providing the local population with a feeling for tradition was understood as one means of reclaiming the lost populace, offering a sense of heritage and duty. The warden of one Settlement outlined the ambitions of the movement:

> the problem is, how to make the masses realise their spiritual and social solidarity with the rest of the capital and the kingdom: how to revive their sense of citizenship, with its privileges which they have lost, and its responsibilities which they have forgotten.[87]

It was for the Settlement as a 'theatre' for enacting a restored sense of community through revived tradition, and for providing 'hospitality', as Barnett phrased it, with the mutual roles that that notion entailed, that the architecture was designed. Style created an image of largesse made visible, the relationship of giver to recipient, as the feudal manors towered over the two-up, two-down workers' cottages of London's working class neighborhoods, concretising the values of a charity which, as before, required in return subservience, subordination, and respect.

Notes

1 C. F. G. Masterman, *From the Abyss: of Its Inhabitants by One of Them*, (London: R. Brimley Johnson, 1902), p. 22
   An earlier verson of this discussion of Settlement arctitecture appeared as 'The architecture of Victorian pilanthropy: the Settlement House as manorial residence', in *Art History* (June 1990), pp. 213–27.
2 Edward Denison as quoted by G. Stedman Jones, *Outcast London: A Study in the Relationship between Classes in Victorian Society* (Oxford: Oxford University Press, 1971), p. 258.
3 *A Week at Mansfield House* (Canning Town: Mansfield House, 1893), p. 11.
4 P. Parker, 'A day in Canning Town', *The Temple Magazine*, 1:1 (1896–97), p. 278.
5 Mansfield House Settlement, 1932.
6 'The Outlook', *Cambridge House Magazine*, 56 (December 1901), p. 35.
7 *Ibid.*
8 C. E. Grant, *From 'Me' to 'We' (Forty Years on Bow Common)* (London: Fern Street Settlement, 1940), p. vii.
   Henrietta Barnett described the phrase 'the best for the lowest' as a 'guiding principle . . . often quoted to each other'. H. Barnett, *Canon Barnett*, 1, p. 300.

9 J. Scott Lidgett, Warden, as quoted by Mary Simmons, *Report of the Bermondsey Settlement, Some Account of Women's Work*, 1897, p. 6.

10 *The Toynbee Journal and Student's Union Chronicle*, 1 April 1886.

11 T. C. Collings, 'The London Settlements', *Leisure Hour* (1893?), pp. 739–44.

12 Grant, *From 'Me' to 'We'*, p. 35.

13 W. Picht, *Toynbee Hall: The English Settlement Movement*, trans. Lilian A. Cowell (London, 1914). In W. Bliss (ed.), *The Encyclopedia of Social Reform* (New York and London, 1909), p. 1109, there is an even longer list of Settlements, many of which were probably small or whose definition may overlap with that of a mission or hostel.

14 S. Barnett, 'University Settlements', rpt. *Practicable Socialism: Essays on Social Reform*, ed. S. and H. Barnett (London: Longmans, Green and Co., 1888; rpt. New York: Books for Libraries Press, 1972), pp. 96–108. The lecture was given in November 1883, and the text appeared in *Nineteenth Century* the following February.

15 S. Barnett, 'University Settlements', *Practicable Socialism*, p. 168.

16 Canon H. Scott Holland quoted in H. Barnett, *Canon Barnett. His Life, Work and Friends* (London: John Murray, 1918), 1, p. 309; originally printed in *The Commonwealth* (July 1913).

17 S. Barnett, 'The work of righteousness', *Practicable Socialism*, pp. 253–4. This sermon was originally preached at St Jude's, Whitechapel, in the same year.

18 G. Kitson Clark, *Churchmen and the Condition of England 1832–1885: A Study in the Development of Social Ideas and Practice from the Old Regime to the Modern State* (London: Methuen, 1973), pp. 280–2.

19 The RIBA members' index lists a variety of work done for the Wesleyan community, both chapels and schools, as well as industrial dwellings in the 1870s and 1880s.

20 I am grateful to Irene Brewer and Richard Green, who generously shared the Hoole family tree and memorabilia. Hoole's decision to work for Octavia Hill is recorded in a personal memoir written for the family by Irene Brewer's grandmother, daughter of Elijah Hoole (1837–1912) and Judith Lidgett (1845–1932).

21 According to a letter written to Irene Brewer from Elizabeth Hoole Brewer. For information concerning the cottages in Southwark see 'Cottage homes for artisans', in *London* (9 May 1895), pp. 336–7, and 'Southwark cottages', in *The Lady* (29 January 1976), pp. 177, 194. For an illustration of the Red Cross Hall, wall panels by Walter Crane, see *The Builder* (9 November 1889), p. 1360.

22 As quoted from a letter to his brother in H. Barnett, *Canon Barnett*, 1, p. 314.

23 *Ibid.*, 2, p. 42.

24 H. F. Wilson, 'Toynbee Hall', *Cambridge Review* (18 February 1885), p. 214.

25 J. A. R. Pimlott, *Toynbee Hall: Fifty Years of Social Progress 1884–1934* (London: J. M. Dent and Sons, 1935), pp. 74–5. Pimlott's account includes a description of the drawing room. In a caustically satirical account of the tea parties given by the Barnetts at Toynbee Hall, the Arts and Crafts designer and architect C. R. Ashbee, who had worked with the Barnetts at Toynbee Hall, recalled the furnishings of the drawing room in *The Building of Thelema* (London: J. M. Dent, 1910), pp. 170–1.

26 S. Barnett, *Towards Social Reform* (London: T. Fisher Unwin, 1909), p. 26.

27 *Ibid.*, p. 27.

28 C. F. G. Masterman, *The Condition of England* (1909; rpt. London: Methuen, 1960), pp. 11–12.

29 E. P. Thompson, 'Patrician society, plebian culture', *Journal of Social History* (1974) pp. 382–90.

30 Collings, 'The London Settlements', p. 739.

31 S. Barnett in 'Philanthropists and the poor', *The Service of God* (London: Longmans, Green and Co., 1897), p. 56.

32 J. Barrell, *The Dark Side of the Landscape: The Rural Poor in English Painting, 1730–1840* (Cambridge: Cambridge University Press, 1980), in describing the relationship between classes in the eighteenth century, p. 3. The importance of the gift relationship is described in depth by G. Stedman Jones in 'The deformation of the gift', *Outcast London*, pp. 240–61.

33 Revd J. (James) Adderley as quoted in B. Simon, *Education and the Labour Movement 1870–1920* (London: Lawrence and Wishart, 1965), p. 83. When Adderley published his own book he used the name 'James Adderley'.

34 Samuel Barnett as quoted by James Adderley, *In Slums and Society: Reminiscences of Old Friends* (London: T. Fisher Unwin, 1916), p. 48.

35 Samuel Barnett in the Introduction to the Sixth Annual Report of Toynbee Hall, p. 8.

36 Gerard Fiennes of Oxford House, 'The Federation of Working Men's Social Clubs: What It Is, and What It May Be', J. M. Knapp (ed.), *University and the Social Problem* (London: Rivington, Percival, and Co., 1895), p. 218.

37 H. Scott Holland, *A Bundle of Memories* (London; Wells Gardner, Darton Co., 1915), p. 91.

38 Canon H. Scott Holland as quoted by Adderley, *In Slums and Society*, p. 48.

39 S. Barnett, 'Hospitalities', in *The University and the Social Problem*, ed. J. Knapp (London, 1895), p. 53.

40 *Ibid.*, p. 59.

41 *Ibid.*, p. 60.

42 *Ibid.*, p. 61.

43 Thompson, 'Patrician society, plebian culture', p. 389.

44 Standish Meacham, *Toynbee Hall and Social Reform, 1880–1914* (New Haven and London: Yale University Press, 1987), p. 49.

45 Pimlott, *Toynbee Hall*, p. 41.

46 *Cambridge House Magazine*, 9 (January 1898), p. 3.

47 S. Barnett in Revd V. A. Boyle (ed.), *Perils of Wealth and Poverty* (London: George Allen and Unwin, 1920), p. 20.

48 Barnett as quoted from 1875 in H. Barnett, *Canon Barnett*, 1, pp. 219–20.

49 S. Barnett in introduction to the Seventh Annual Report of Toynbee Hall, p. 10.

50 S. Barnett, 'Hospitalities', p. 62.

51 H. Barnett, 'At home' to the poor', *Practicable Socialism*, p. 159. This article first appeared in *Cornhill* in May 1881.

52 S. Barnett, *The Ideal City* (Bristol: Arrowsmith, 1895), p. 10.

53 S. Barnett, Twelfth Annual Report of Toynbee Hall, p. 15.

54 S. Barnett in introduction to the Seventh Annual Report of Toynbee Hall, p. 10.

55 E. P. Thompson, 'Eighteenth-century English society: class struggle without class?', *Journal of Social History*, 3:2 (1978), pp. 135–6.

56 For a discussion of 'Old English' see A. Saint, *Richard Norman Shaw* (New Haven and London: Yale University Press, 1976), pp. 24–44, and M. Girouard, *The Victorian Country House* (New Haven and London: Yale University Press, 1979), pp. 71–3.

57 Saint, *Richard Norman Shaw*, p. 76.

58 No plans of Toynbee Hall have survived – only the ground plan from *The Builder* of 14 February 1885. The building received major damage during the Second World War. However photographs and drawings do exist as well as written descriptions. Unfortunately no plans or photographs of Bermondsey Settlement survive and the building has been demolished. Oxford House still stands, altered considerably except for the chapel; no plans have been located.

59 See for example R. Kerr, *The Gentleman's House or How to Plan English Residences* (London: John Murray, 1864), p. 109.

60 *Ibid.*, p. 107.

61 A. Crawford, *C. R. Ashbee: Architect, Designer and Romantic Socialist* (New Haven and London: Yale University Press, 1986), p. 27. Today little of the design survives.
   Contemporary literature on the English manor house describes the 'impressive' passage from the drawing room to the dining room. See H. Muthesius, *The English House* (Berlin, 1904, rpt. London: Granada Publishing, 1979), p. 83. At Toynbee Hall, however, only a corridor which passed the Lecture Hall connected the drawing room to the dining area.

62 According to 'The Oxford House and Toynbee Hall', in *The Leisure Hour* (1888), as quoted by Seth D. Koven, 'Culture and poverty: the London Settlement House movement 1870 to 1914', Dissertation, Harvard 1987, pp. 114–15.

63 R. A. Woods, 'The social awakening in London', in *The Poor in Great Cities* (New York: Charles Scribner's Sons, 1895), p. 19.

64 Meacham, *Toynbee Hall*, p. 46.

65 Pimlott, *Toynbee Hall*, p. 57.

66 Meacham, *Toynbee Hall*, p. 47.

67 Seventh Annual Report, p. 25.

68 Report of the Settlement, 1897.

69 J. Cowan, 'A social solution: some phases of work in the Bermondsey Settlement', *The Methodist Recorder* (12 September 1901).

70 'Programme of the May-Day Festival: The Guild of the Poor Brave Things and the Guild of Play', 3 May 1902.

71 'Programme of the Yule-Tide Festival and Carolling at the Town Hall', Spa, Bermondsey, Guild of the Poor Brave Things and The Guild of Play, 1902?

72 May Day Programme, 3 May 1902.

73 'Programme of the Yule-Tide Festival', 1902.

74 Cowan, 'A social solution'.

75 Report of the Bermondsey Settlement: Some Account of the Women's Work, 1897, p. 15. Reports of the Bermondsey Settlement are held by the Southwark Local Studies Library.

76 *Ibid.*, p. 20.

77 *Ibid.*, p. 18.

78 'Programme of the Yule-Tide Festival', 1902.

79 'A Plea for a Children's Settlement in Bermondsey', from the *Programme of Masque of the Children of the Empire*, Guild of Play, 1911.

80 G. T. Kimmins, *Guild of Play Book*, introduction (London: J. Curwen and Sons), p. ix.

81 'Lady Mayoress in Bermondsey: "Poor Brave Things" Fete-Day: Duchess and Countesses as Spectators', *London Gazette*, 15 May 1901.

82 'A Bermondsey Revival: Interesting May Day Festival', *Daily Graphic*, 5 May 1901.

83 *Guild of Play Book of National Dances*, p. 6.

84 'The Child of Play', p. 2, a fund-raising brochure, Southwark Local Studies Library.

85 'Programme of the May-Day Festival', 3 May 1902, p. 3.

86 'Programme of the Yule-Tide Festival', 1902.

87 Revd J. (James) Adderley as quoted in Simon, *Education and The Labour Movement* p. 82.

CHAPTER SEVEN

The People's Palace: Walter Besant and the slum pastoral

Of all novels with a purpose, 'All Sorts and Conditions of Men', has been the most immediately and the strikingly successful. It was in the pages of that book that the People's Palace was built, and committees, subscribers, and architects have merely been translating it into a different material. [1]

Government blue books documented the social problems of the metropolis, but political leadership failed to provide viable solutions. How to cope with the social ills of late Victorian London, how to devise settings in which the poor might learn middle class values, was not only a subject debated among journalists, politicians, churchmen, philan-thropists, and School Board members. Writing to a middle class public keenly aware of social problems, a few novelists responded with imaginary, if not fantastic, solutions to the city's problems. Their extraordinary and unprecedented popular success attests to the serious-ness of the tensions that these fantasies addressed.

In the context of growing frustration, fear and bewilderment in the 1880s, one finds social experiments inspired by images drawn from contemporary fiction: Mrs Humphry Ward's bestselling novel, for example, *Robert Elsmere*, which served as the model for a Settlement House, and Julia Ewing's *The Story of a Short Life*, [2] a popular children's story of a disabled child coping with hardship, which inspired the founding of the Guild of the Poor Brave Things at the Bermondsey Settlement and a children's hospital in Sussex. In many cases, those involved in creating these philanthropic institutions were also involved in shaping the Board Schools.

The realisation of these fictive solutions speaks of the concern

56] People's Palace, cover design for a fund-raising brochure, E. R. Robson, 1886?

57] People's Palace, Queen's Hall, architect E. R. Robson

and desperation with which a solution was sought for the contemporary crisis – short, that is, of government intervention.

The *Pall Mall Gazette*, quoted above, was reporting the opening of the People's Palace by Queen Victoria, the first official gesture of her Jubilee Year. The 'palace' was built on Mile End Road in the very heart of the East End. According to its early fund-raising campaign it was to accommodate a variety of activities for the benefit of the working population of the district. It was to include an assembly hall, class-rooms, a conversation room, a library and reading-room, workshops, warm and cold swimming baths, a gymnasium modeled on the German *Turnhalle*, an outdoor garden with fountains and botanical specimens, and a winter garden with tropical shrubs[3] [56]. Queen Victoria opened the first portion of the scheme, the Queen's Hall, the largest assembly room in East London, in 1887 [57].

As the *Pall Mall Gazette* noted, 'what makes the People's Palace unique is that it is built upon a book.'[4] In 1882 Walter Besant had published his novel, *All Sorts and Conditions of Men: An Impossible Story*, which became a bestseller [58]. The *Saturday Review* credited the novel with having 'probably done more than any other to familiarise the general public with the true character of that dark continent called the East End.'[5] Another critic asserted that the book had 'shocked and aroused the conscience of all England.'[6]

In the novel, a young heiress, a recent graduate of Newnham College, Cambridge, disguised as a simple seamstress, goes to live and work in the East End, the source of her personal fortune, to see for herself the condition of the poor. Her perception of the East End, not dissimilar from the Barnetts' – as she is guided by a well-educated young man whose circumstances have left him to work and live in Stepney – was that of endless tedium and the sheer monotony of existence among local residents, a flat quality pervading the lives of those who lacked the leisure and culture known to the West End:

> It is the joylessness of the life . . . the ignorant, contented joylessness, which weighs upon one. And there is so much of it. Surely there is no other city in the world which is so utterly without joy as this East London.[7]

Besant told his readers that the district was utterly devoid of 'gardens, avenues, theatres, art galleries, libraries, or any kind of amusement whatever.'[8] The young hero of the novel declares:

> What we want here . . . is a little more of the pleasures and graces of life. To begin with, we are not poor and in misery, but for the most

part fairly well off. . . . When all our works are in full blast, we make quantities of money. See us on Sundays, we are not a bad-looking lot; healthy, well-dressed, and tolerably rosy. But we have no pleasures.[9]

The heroine of the novel sets out to provide enjoyment in the district with the endowment of a 'Palace of Delight':

58] *The Period*, cover, 29 June 1886

> Life is full, crammed full, overflowing with all kinds of delights. It is
> a mistake to suppose that only rich people can enjoy these things. . . .
> You shall learn music, and forthwith all the world will be transformed
> for you; you shall learn to paint, to carve, to model, to design, and
> the day shall be too short to contain the happiness you will get out of
> it. You shall learn to dance, and know the rapture of the waltz. You
> shall learn the great art of acting, and give each other the pleasure
> which rich men buy. You shall even learn the great art of writing, and
> learn the magic of a charmed phrase. All these things which make the
> life of rich people happy shall be yours; and *they shall cost you nothing.*
> I will give you a house to shelter you and rooms in which to play. You
> have only to find the rest. Enter in, my friends; forget the squalid past;
> here are great halls and lovely corridors – they are yours. Fill them with
> sweet echoes of dropping music; let the walls be covered with your
> works of art; let the girls laugh and the boys be happy within these
> walls. I give you the shell, the empty carcase; fill it with the Spirit of
> Content and Happiness.[10]

It was the fantasy of a simple and safe palliative under the guidance of
the middle class which must have appeared so seductive to Besant's
readers and to the supporters of the building scheme that followed. It
may also have appealed to the readers' 'consciousness of sin'.

The ambition of bringing the cultural advantages of the West
End to the East End was not unique, of course, to Besant, but it was
Besant who first envisioned realising this ambition – and with it solving
the ills of the East End – in a single, monumental institution. Indeed,
it was only a year after the publication of Besant's novel that Samuel
Barnett first proposed the Settlement idea to an enthusiastic Oxford
audience as a means of bringing 'the best to the lowest'. Whereas
Barnett's solution grew out of his years of work in Whitechapel, and
out of an intellectual tradition that dated back to the efforts of
reformers like Denison working among the poor in the 1860s, Besant's
grew out of the imagination of a novelist who had researched the East
End but had never lived there.

The initial building program for a People's Palace would seem
to have taken as its starting point the needs as recounted in the novel,
the provision, that is, of the 'pleasures and grace of life'. The first
portion of the program completed included the Queen's Hall, which
was described in the fund-raising literature as a 'drawing-room for those
to whom high rents forbid the luxury of a drawing-room'. Ladies' 'social
rooms' were to enable 'any lady member to hold weekly receptions of
her friends in the Palace. A spacious apartment, being handsomely
furnished . . . replete with every modern convenience'.[11] The Ladies'
'social room' corresponded, in fact, to the drawing room provided for

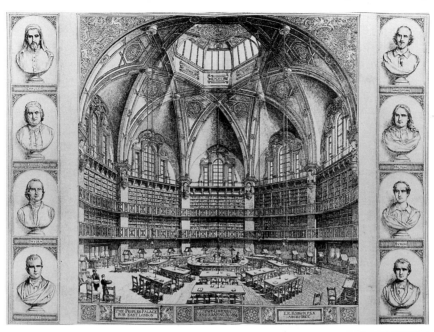

59] People's Palace, library and reading room, drawing, from *The Builder*, 7 September 1889

60] People's Palace, reading room as built

the working girls of Stepney by Besant's heroine; it was there that they had tea before playing lawn tennis, of which the reader is told they 'are as fond of . . . as [are] the students of Newnham'.[12] Their evenings were passed in music and dance, the provision of such a place of refinement lifting the girls 'above their neighbours'.[13] The gift of West End culture offered to the East End was most strikingly realised in built form by the construction of a reading room, self-consciously modeled, albeit on a smaller scale, on that of the British Museum [59–60].

Besant's portrait of the district is not that of the 'abyss', of 'outcast London', so often heard in the period. Rather, the novel presents an alternative problem to its readers, one which could be managed, to which a solution was easily at hand. The novel concludes:

> The Palace of Delight is in working order now, and Stepney is already transformed. A new period began on the opening night for all who were present. For the first time they understood that life may be happy: for the first time they resolved that they would find out for themselves the secret of happiness.[14]

This image of the East End, as compared with the journalistic exposés of the period, the experience of School Board Visitors or governmental reports, was surely a reassuring one. The reader is presented with a remedy that requires no fundamental changes in the social system.

The publication of the novel coincided with the availability of funds from a private trust which had as its object the provision of 'Intellectual Improvement and Rational Recreation and Amusement for the people living in the East End of London',[15] and which was at that time searching for an appropriate scheme. The private trust was the bequest of John Barber Beaumont, a Unitarian philanthropist, who had endowed the Beaumont Philosophical Institution in Beaumont Square, Mile End, Stepney, before his death in 1841. He stipulated that the money should be spent 'for the mental and moral improvement of the inhabitants of the said Square, and the surrounding neighbourhood', leaving £300 a year and a trust of £13,000.[16] Without proper leadership and such inadequate funding the Beaumont Institution closed its doors in 1879. In 1882, however, a new scheme for the Beaumont Trust was drawn up by the Charity Commissioners, and Sir Edmund Currie, a lifelong member of the Institution, heir to a distillery fortune in the East End and an active figure in East End politics, including service on the School Board for London, was appointed Chairman of the Beaumont Trustees.

The initial plans proposed by the Beaumont Trust and launched by Thomas Huxley to an enthusiastic gathering at Mansion House in

1884 were ambitious. The 'Palace' was to encompass both recreation and education. As one fund-raising pamphlet described it,

> Members may play or work, as they choose. Whether they resort thither for mental improvement or simply recreation each will be free to take his own path, though the number be twenty thousand. It is to be a vast club; it is to be a many-sided university; it is to be a playground and college.[17]

Supporters of the scheme described it as establishing in 'Darkest England . . . the seed of higher civilisation for the neglected courts and alleys.'[18] The scheme would 'stir certain civilising instincts, which may be trusted to work out the gradual redemption of the many lives which now seem drunk in low habits or crushed by the weight of sordid cares.'[19] The Palace was 'a scheme of broad philanthropy',[20] 'a truly philanthropic undertaking'.[21] 'Wealthy citizens of the Empire ought to vie with one another for the privilege of contributing to such an object.'[22] The founding of the Palace was understood as a testament to the fact that 'between the poorest and the wealthiest districts of London a real sympathy exists.'[23] It was even suggested that funds for missionary work abroad should be redirected to support the Palace.[24] The Prince of Wales donated £200, as did Queen Victoria, after the assurance that activities at the Palace would be conducted with propriety.[25]

E. R. Robson was entrusted with the design of the Palace. He had the task of 'translating' the 'Palace of Delight' in Besant's novel into architecture. Again Robson would have the job of finding an appropriate architectural expression for an utterly new institution, this time one that existed in the pages of a novel. What would a People's Palace look like? How would it relate to its surroundings? What message was to be conveyed and to whom on Mile End Road? How would the building accommodate the disparate functions that would take place under one roof?

The novel describes the many activities of the Palace but offers little in terms of a physical description of the building. Indeed, even the novel's illustrator did not venture to render it. The reader is told that it is 'not a beautiful building', that it is 'solid, big, well-proportioned, and constructed of real red brick',[26] and that to the uninitiated the nature of the building would be difficult to determine from the façade. It is noted that the building is 'without the "Queen Anne" conceits which mostly go with that material',[27] the only reference that Besant makes to style. In the novel the patron, interviewing architects for the job, seeks a practical plan without 'lordly staircases . . . nor

61] People's Palace, earliest design, for a fund-raising brochure

great ante-rooms, nor handsome lobbies.' But the reader is told that the heroine 'did not explain to her architect how she proposed to use this magnificent place of entertainment.'[28] As an institution existing solely in the pages of fiction such a description was obviously inadequate for Robson. The novel concentrated instead on the diverse activities that took place within: dancing rooms, a children's playroom, exhibition space, a theatre, a library, a reading room, a music room, billiard rooms, a tennis court, a raquet court, a card room, and classroom.

Robson was in the position of having to lure potential donors by a compelling design, a problem not encountered by the novel's heroine, described as the richest woman in England. The first design which Robson drew for purposes of fund-raising was reminiscent of the Crystal Palace [61]. In fact, the comparison was made in the novel. When the palace is first proposed it is described as something like the Crystal Palace 'with modifications'.[29] The design that Robson later exhibited at the Royal Academy in 1886, a version of which appeared in *The Builder*, departed from the Crystal Palace model. It was described as having an 'Oriental character, though the details are Renaissance in feeling'[30] [62]. The design was an elaborately decorated domed building surrounded by a long ground-storey arcade. Replete with minarets

62] People's Palace, 1886 version, from *The Graphic*, 26 June 1886

capped with gilded cupolas, the building was to have had Portland stone columns, arches and pediments set off against polychrome brick. The building was strikingly similar to Gabriel Davioud's Trocadero

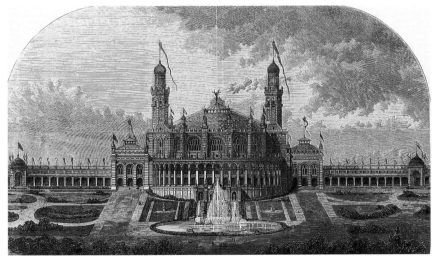

63] Trocadero, intended for the international exhibition, Paris 1878, architect Gabriel Davioud, from *The Builder*, 11 November 1877

Palace in Paris of 1878,[31] which opened, like the Crystal Palace, for a World Exhibition, but was a far cry from anything else on Mile End Road or, indeed, anything in England. Robson may well have seen the Trocadero illustrated in *The Builder*[32] in 1878, described as 'essentially the Palace of the People'[33] [63].

Robson's exotic neo-Byzantine design was described in a handbook about the scheme:

> The appearance of this building facing, as it does, on the great highway of half a million of people, will proclaim in the most lasting and effective way the aims and hopes of its founders.
> It is, therefore, planned to be large and rotund, with welcoming doors inviting 'all sorts and conditions of men' to enter and assemble themselves together. It is further made to tower above the low heights of the neighbouring buildings with minarets springing from its midsts, reaching upward to invite men to learn and to rise; and it is made to stand in the midst of gardens, where music and fountains make brightness, and where all can enjoy the recreation which is both pleasure and rest.
> By its very appearance the building will suggest Association and strength born of common life and common interests; Aspiration without which common life must lose half its value, and that restful Pleasure which has to be added to the lives of workers, to make either association or aspiration possible.[34]

The only description in the novel of interior space is the Great Hall, and Robson was a faithful translator. In the novel the East End friends of the heroine gather at the site:

> They found themselves in a lofty and very spacious hall. At the end was a kind of throne. . . . Statues stood on either side: behind them was a great organ: upon the walls were pictures. Above the pictures were trophies in arms, tapestry carpets, all kinds of beautiful things. Above the entrance was a gallery for musicians[35]

And they were told

> This Hall is your great Reception Room. You will use it for the ball nights, when you give your great dances: a thousand couples may dance here without crowding. On wet days it is to be the playground of the children.[36]

When on 14 May 1887 Queen Victoria opened the Queen's Hall and laid the foundation stone for the Technical School which was to be part of the scheme [64], the Queen's Hall stood as an isolated building, decorated for the occasion with colorful bunting to cover up the bare stock brick which awaited a palatial façade. But the interior of the hall,

130 ft by 75 ft (39.62 m by 22.86 m) and 60 ft (18.28m) high, had been completed with a sumptuous decor befitting the fictional description: the hall had a stained-glass roof, supported by buff-and-gold Corinthian columns, and a gallery supported by Greek caryatids,

THE ROYAL PROCESSION PASSING THE MANSION HOUSE ON THE WAY TO THE PEOPLE'S PALACE

THE ROYAL PROCESSION IN CHEAPSIDE

THE QUEEN AT THE CITY BOUNDARY—THE CIVIC CEREMONY AT HOLBORN BARS

64] The Queen's visit to the East End, from *The Graphic*, May 1887

designed to seat 240 people [57]. The central oval panels of the elaborate ceiling were decorated with the Prince of Wales' feathers, royal arms, royal monograms, and the arms of England, Australia, Canada, India, Wales, and Scotland.[37] Statues of twenty-three queens from history, culminating with a statue of Queen Victoria, lined the walls. The splendor of the hall was noted by the contemporary press. *The Illustrated London News* remarked that

> Not the Egyptian Hall, not the House of Lords, not even Henry VII's Chapel at Westminster, is nobler in design, or more graceful in detail, than the Queen's Hall of the People's Palace.[38]

According to *The Times*:

> Its marble statues, painted glass, and gilded balconies give an air of splendour and magnificence which is all the more striking for being met with in so unlovely a neighbourhood as that of the East-end of London.[39]

It would seem, however, that the fanfare that accompanied the Queen's highly publicised 'descent into Purgatorio'[40] did not represent a united vision of what the new institution should be. The building program moved forward in a piecemeal fashion, plagued by a lack of funds. No comments seem to survive from East Enders, who must have watched the building take form. Unlike the novel in which the narrative carried the reader to the speedy completion of the building, Currie's annual report of 1888 lamented that

> the difficulty has been the want of full accommodation. The Refreshment Rooms, the Gymnasium, and the Exhibition buildings have been . . . merely temporary iron buildings, standing only on sufferance of the authorities, and liable at any time to condemnation, while the Winter garden, the permanent Social Rooms, the rooms for the use of Benefit Societies, etc . . . of the original plan, are not in existence.[41]

Whereas in the novel the heroine finances the great experiment, in reality it was necessary to plead with potential subscribers. Even three years after the opening, the Queen's Hall faced Mile End Road bare; the bombastic design of 1886 had not been built. The exposed stock brick had acquired a 'sooty tinge', the building looking as 'dreary and depressing and unattractive as any plot of building land very well could look'.[42] *The Graphic* in a cautious understatement, described it as 'not picturesque'.[43]

While Besant's 'solution' to the social question was naïve and ill-defined, the success of his novel and the ensuing campaign to build the dream of the Palace – the fund-raising campaign reaching its peak during the crisis winter of 1886 – came from a sense of alarm and a need to find a solution, however implausible. The fantasy of a 'great building' which was 'destined to change the character of the Gloomy City into a City of Sunshine',[44] presented greater problems 'in translation' when the crisis atmosphere was gone. The inability to find an appropriate face for the People's Palace was aggravated by waning support for the scheme when the panic subsided after 1886. However, an examination of the history of the 'palace' suggests that more than financial considerations account for the delay in its completion. The difficulty in completing the scheme, particularly its main façade along Mile End Road, indicated an inability to define the nature of a People's Palace, its purpose, its direction, its role in the community.

Besant's vision of the East End, which he elaborated in *All Sorts and Conditions of Men* – a city whose inhabitants suffered above all from cultural deprivation – had first found expression in a novel which he serialised in 1879 with his then partner James Rice: 'No country town is so dull, none so devoid of society, distraction, and amusement as the East End of London.' It was a place 'destitute of the means of artistic grace', and they suggested to their readers,

> There ought to be a prefect of the East End: he should be one of the royal princes: he should build a palace among the people: there should be regiments of soldiers, theatres, picture-galleries, and schools, to wake them up and make them dismally discontented about their mean surroundings.[45]

Although Besant's scheme for a 'palace' was not elaborated until *All Sorts and Conditions of Men* in 1882, or taken on board seriously by public subscription until the social unrest of 1886, it was rooted in that pre-crisis period, when a vision of cultural transformation as an easy palliative to the social question might seriously be offered. Though exciting the imagination of its readers in the alarmist mood of the mid-1880s, it now competed with other proposals to solve the question of real distress in East London.

Further difficulties in the realisation of the scheme would seem to have stemed from assumptions and contradictions inherent in Besant's novel. Central to the definition and administration of the scheme were the questions of who was to be in charge of the Palace and for whom its activities were intended. In the pages of Besant's novel, the heiress bestows the Palace as a gift to the local populace, 'to be governed by them alone, in trust for each other'.

> Now it is yours, with all it contains. I pray God that it may be used worthily, and for the joy and happiness of all. I declare this Palace of

> Delight open, the property of the people, to be administered and
> governed by them and them alone, in trust for each other.[46]

And, writing in the *Contemporary Review* in 1887, Besant reiterated
that the Palace was 'to be governed by the people for themselves'.[47] In
reality, however, Currie and Besant, rather than the local residents,
were the overseers. As to the participants, Besant described those
whom he hoped would enjoy the activities of the Palace (from donkey
shows to flower shows, dances, art exhibitions, to debates): 'As a rule,
only the very poorest; and on this I lay the greatest stress. . . . We
want those who are too poor to go elsewhere.'[48] Currie admitted,
however, that he had felt the need to institute regulations, as well as
increased fees, in order to exclude undesirable elements.[49]

Recalling his employment with the Beaumont Trustees, the
novelist Arthur Morrison satirised the Palace in his novel, *The Child
of the Jago*:

> The triumphs of the East End Elevation Mission and Pansophical
> Institute were known and appreciated far from East London, by people
> who knew less of that part than of Asia Minor. Indeed, they were
> chiefly appreciated by these. There were kept, perpetually on tap for
> the aspiring East Ender, the Higher Life, the Greater Thought, and
> the Wider Humanity . . . specifics all for the manufacture of the
> Superior Person. There were many Lectures given on still more
> subjects. Pictures were borrowed and shown, with revelations to the
> Uninformed of the morals ingeniously concealed by the painters. . . .
> And there were classes, and clubs, and newspapers, and games of
> draughts, and musical evenings, and a brass band, whereby the life of
> the Hopeless Poor might be coloured, and the Misery of the Submerged
> alleviated.

Morrison described the class of people who actually partook of these
activities: 'The wretches who crowded to these benefits were trades-
men's sons, small shopkeepers and their families, and neat clerks, with
here and there a smart young artisan of one of the especially respectable
trades.'[50] In his autobiography Besant conceded that those with whom
he worked on the *Palace Journal* were 'young clerks chiefly'.[51]

Besant's literary output suggests inconsistencies implicit in his
notions of social reform which necessarily came to the fore in determining the administration of a scheme that he had both imagined and
in which he actively participated. Although Besant continually asserted
that it was social and economic disadvantage that divided men and
women, rather than inherent qualities of birth, his stories repeatedly
showed the upper class – even when disguised as members of the

working class – guiding the poor. This is central to the depiction of his heroine and hero in *All Sorts and Conditions of Men*. Besant's second novel dealing with the East End, *Children of Gibeon* of 1885, likewise a great success, has among its central characters two young women raised as sisters since birth, one the daughter of a poor washerwoman, the other of noble birth. Not even the women themselves know which is of humble and which is of noble origin. Their appearance is virtually identical, and it is only a birthmark that eventually betrays the secret. Yet here, even in a story which is constructed to illustrate the equality of all, stressing the importance of nurture over nature, it is the woman of noble birth who – like the heroine of *All Sorts and Conditions of Men* – descends to the East End, equipped with her superior wisdom to instruct the poor.

The novel has been aptly called a 'slum pastoral' by the literary historian P. J. Keating. Borrowing a definition of 'pastoral', he exposes the framework of Besant's novel:

> The essential trick of the old pastoral, which was felt to imply a beautiful relationship between rich and poor, was to make simple people express strong feelings (felt as the most universal subject, some-thing fundamentally true about everybody) in learned and fashionable language (so that you wrote about the best subject in the best way). From seeing the two sorts of people combined like this you thought better of both; the best parts of both were used. The effect was in some degree to combine in the reader or author the merits of the two sorts; he was made to mirror in himself more completely the effective elements of the society he lived in.[52]

But the commitment to an inevitable leadership of the middle and upper classes, necessarily emerged when the fantasy of the novel of the 'slum pastoral' was realised in the heart of London's East End.

Criticism of the scheme came from a variety of quarters. Whereas the Working Men's Club at Oxford House in Bethnal Green raised £17 for the scheme and the Borough of Hackney Working Men's Club voted £3 and invited Currie to their meetings to promote the project,[53] the critique from the Left was cynical. The journal of the Socialist League referred to the enterprise as 'the-bone-to-the-dog business'. and warned the 'proletarian' not to mistake 'the bone for the meat'; the stone-laying ceremony with the Prince of Wales in attendance was described as 'consisting of all classes of society, of high degree and no degree, fleeced and fleecer.'[54] A writer in *Justice* described the scheme as 'social chloroform'.[55] William Morris, writing in *Commonweal* in 1886, described the scheme as providing 'a place where [the working classes] can play at being comfortable so long as they behave like good children, between the spells of their stupid weary work and their miserable and hideous "homes".'[56] The lion's share of the donations, it was noted by George Bernard Shaw, was received in the aftermath of the riots of 1886 which had so frightened middle class London; as calm returned, the donations dwindled.[57]

From those who declined to contribute there were other accusations.[58] As one letter to the fund-raisers stated, 'Friends, your scheme is too pompous and ambitious'; another complained that too much was already being done for the working classes, that soon 'they will have *Castles* too'. Others scoffed that the distress of the workers was due to their improvident ways: 'I am persuaded,' wrote one angry gentleman refusing to contribute, 'that those that *won't* work "neither shall they eat" – nor have Palaces to lounge in'. That Edmund Currie's personal fortune came from a distillery was noted with anger by those who attributed the social problem to drink. One writer noted that if 'Beer and Gin Palaces' were closed there would be no need for such a scheme. Others associated Currie with extravagance because he had been a Progressive on the School Board for London. Responding to the appeal for funds, many pointed to the elaborate Palace illustrated on the fund-raising brochure: 'too much ornament in design and too much finery in decoration' was scrawled across the picture of the Palace returned to the fund-raisers. Another letter urged that money not be wasted on 'a palace in the most squalid part of London, for the use of the very poorest of her people' and pointed to the 'splendid' workhouses built for them.

The purpose of the institution, which in the novel was that of generally raising the tenor of the neighborhood by the introduction of culture and taste from the West End, required a clearer definition when translated into reality. Competing interests sought to define the role of the institution. Though it was often stated that the Palace was to 'prove the sympathy of the West-end for the East-end',[59] that it was to be a place where 'sympathies are extended', there was a widespread concern with what had become known as the 'Leisure Problem', as the length of the working day was shortened and workers worked only half a day on Saturday.[60] How could a concerned middle class hope to compete with traditional working class entertainments and still provide activities that would develop qualities of thrift, sobriety, and orderliness? Ultimately the answer would be in the program and rhetoric of the movement for 'Rational Recreation'.[61]

Besant had seen the Palace as a place for recreation alongside education, but the scheme attracted the attention of supporters with a more utilitarian viewpoint. In the initial plan the dual functions of the

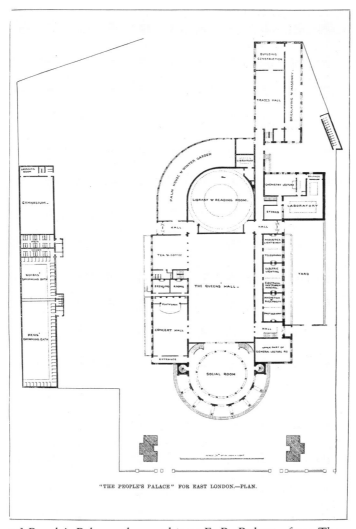

"THE PEOPLE'S PALACE" FOR EAST LONDON.—PLAN.

65] People's Palace, plan, architect E. R. Robson, from *The Builder*, 26 June 1886

Palace, leisure and education, were placed on either side of the Queen's Hall, both wrapped in a garb associated with leisure [**65**]. Arguments were soon made, however, in language that anticipated the Efficiency movement, for the need to focus on the education of the working classes, to provide practical vocational skills rather than amusement. Drawing on a recent speech by Huxley, Lord Hartington was quoted in the fund-raising pamphlets for the Palace on the need for scientific education:

66] Sidney Webb's ladder from board school to university

It is impossible in actual hostilities to extemporise effective armaments; 'the possession of scientific knowledge and perfect appliances' is essential in warfare, and the same holds good for industry. In both the prize goes to those who are best prepared to run the race. The comparison is impressive; the consequences are far-reaching.

67] People's Palace, drawing, architect E. R. Robson, from *The Illustrated London News*, 8 June 1891

68] People's Palace, 1895, from Mile End Road

The advice given was to spend generously in order to protect the nation's industrial prowess:

> to be not niggardly in providing industrial education and diffusing scientific knowledge . . . [the] drawing, mechanics, mathematics, chemistry, and other sciences or arts which aid the artisan in his daily work may be imparted, and on the spread of such knowledge may depend the continuance of industrial supremacy.[62]

And 'rich men, of whom in spite of trade depression, there are still many, with noble balances at their banker', were told of this particularly 'Advantageous investment . . . of most extraordinary and securely profitable description.'[63]

Fund-raising literature was addressed to the 'Merchants of London',[64] with fear of foreign competition used as the inducement to business men to make their contributions. Reference was made to the large number of boys coming from Board Schools in need of further technical training:

> To our regret we see our shops filled with foreign manufacturers . . . and we are told that our artisans are not sufficiently trained to use the complicated tools necessary to produce these articles. We turn to America, to Germany, and to France, and we find them well provided with excellent technical schools; whereas London is almost destitute of them. Is this state of things to continue?[65]

Another issue that featured in the development of the Palace, as it did in the Board Schools, was the physical fitness of British youth, an issue high on the agenda of the National Efficiency movement. Lord Rosebery, a figure prominent in the movement, contributed £2,500 toward the building of swimming-baths at the Palace.

Running through all the arguments on behalf of the scheme was the ubiquitous fear that the geographical gulf between rich and poor would lead to social unrest. The Palace, Lord Rosebery alleged, was one means of bringing classes together:

> We are inside what is called the police radius of London. We have inside that radius two or three populations which would be counted as nations on the Continent of Europe, and the danger is that they should become nations as distinct as any that there are on the Continent of Europe. I hold that it is a great and sacred responsibility, not merely for our statesmen . . . but for all our leading citizens, in whatever capacity it may be given to them to lead, to endeavour to prevent the formation of those distinct nations within our metropolis . . . I believe this People's Palace may do much, not merely to raise the population of

the East-end of London, but also to prove the sympathy of the West-end for the East-end.[66]

With the growing strength of the movement for National Efficiency, Besant's dream and Robson's neo-Byzantine fantasy were replaced by a more austere vision. The Drapers, the City Company which also contributed to the provision of manual training in Board Schools, financed the completion of the façade in 1890, allowing a generous £15,000; the clock-tower was added three years later. From the outset the Drapers had been supportive of the educational program of the Palace and now they rescued the fledgling institution but insisted on a redefinition of its goals: the People's Palace was to become a technical education school for the working classes. Out of the Drapers' scheme the East London Technical College developed, becoming part of London University in 1907. Today it is Queen Mary College, University of London. In the Palace's transformation to a school of higher learning one could see, however, in some sense, the realisation of Sidney Webb's ambition to develop an educational 'ladder' from the Board School to the university in a rationalised educational system [66].

Robson's third design, a neo-Classical façade, had associations very different from his bombastic design of 1886 for a pleasure palace [62]. The austere design finally projected on to Mile End Road was in keeping with the sober image of an educational institution [67, 68].

Notes

1 'The Hero of the Hour', *Pall Mall Gazette* (14 May 1887), p. 8.
   An earlier version of my research into the People's Palace appeared as 'The People's Palace: an image for East London in the 1880s', in D. Feldman and G. Stedman Jones (eds), *Metropolis London: Histories and Representations Since 1900* (London: Routledge, 1989), pp. 40–56.

2 *The Story of a Short Life* first appeared in *Aunt Judy's Magazine* in July 1882 as 'Laetus Sorte Mea'. The Heritage Craft Schools and Hospital at Chailey were founded in 1903.

3 As described in a publication of the Beaumont Trust, 6 November 1882, in the Greater London Record Office (GLRO).
   Records of the Beaumont Institute and People's Palace are located at the Greater London Record Office; see A/BPP/1/1–4 for reports, letters, accounts, and programs, etc., relating to the Beaumont Institute and J. T. Barber Beaumont, 1842–73. For documents relating to the Beaumont Trust and People's Palace, see A/BPP/2/1–3, 1881–91. Additional material, including correspondence between the Beaumont Trust and E. R. Robson, is preserved in the archives of the library of Queen Mary College, University of London, which occupies the site of the People's Palace.

4 *Pall Mall Gazette*, 14 May 1887, p. 1.

5 As quoted by Fred W. Boege, 'Walter Besant: Novelist, part 1', *Nineteenth Century Fiction*, March 1956, from *Saturday Review*, 27 November 1886, p. 70.

6 As quoted by Fred W. Boege, *Cosmopolitan*, 1891, p. 257.

7 W. Besant, *All Sorts and Conditions of Men* (London: Chatto and Windus, 1882; 1883 2nd edn), p. 101.

8 *Ibid.*, p. 132.

9 *Ibid.*, p. 50.

10 *Ibid.*, p. 138.

11 Announcement of 'Ladies' Social', *The Palace Journal*, 1:1 (16 November 1887), p. 6.

12 Besant, *All Sorts and Conditions of Men*, p. 104.

13 *Ibid.*, p. 105.

14 *Ibid.*, p. 331.

15 Bequest of John Barber Beaumont.

16 GLRO, A/BPP/1–4.

17 Fund-raising brochure reprinting an article from *The Times*, 15 January 1886.

18 As quoted by A. Chapman from the *Western Mercury News*, 25 June 1886, 'The People's Palace for East End: a study in Victorian philanthropy', MPhil, Hull, 1978, p. 73.

19 As quoted by Chapman from the *Sussex Daily News*, 27 May 1885.

20 As quoted by Chapman from the *The Times*, 12 June 1886, p. 73.

21 As quoted by Chapman from the *Saturday Review*, p. 70.

22 As quoted by Chapman from the *The Lambeth Post*, 30 January 1886, p. 70.

23 'A Real Jubilee Offering', 23 April 1887, *Saturday Review*, p. 574.

24 As quoted by Chapman, 'Charity at home and abroad', *Saturday Review*, 14 October 1885.

25 Chapman, 'The People's Palace for East End', p. 129.

26 Besant, *All Sorts and Conditions of Men*, p. 255.

27 *Ibid.*

28 *Ibid.*, p. 135.

29 *Ibid.*, p. 51.

30 'The People's Palace for East London', *The Builder* (26 June 1886), p. 914.

31 I wish to gratefully acknowledge Emily Davies for this observation. Surprisingly, the contemporary architectural press did not make the observation.

32 *The Builder* (11 November 1876), p. 1097.

33 'In Paris this week', *The Builder* (17 November 1876), p. 1142.

34 *Handbook and Guide to the People's Palace*, n.d. (1886–87?), Queen Mary College, PP Bundle 3, p. 3.

35 Besant, *All Sorts and Conditions of Men*, p. 310.

36 *Ibid.*, p. 311.

37 *Handbook and Guide*, p. 11.

38 'The Queen's Visit to East London', *The Illustrated London News*, 21 May 1887, p. 4.

39 'The People's Palace', *The Times*, 14 May 1887, p. 17.

40 'The Hero of the Hour', *Pall Mall Gazette*, 14 May 1887, p. 8.

41 Report of E. H. Currie, 1 October 1888, p. 8. GLRO, A/BPP/2.

42 'Additions to the People's Palace', *Daily News*, 14 January 1890, p. 8.

43 *The Graphic*, 21 May 1887, p. 538.

44 Besant, *All Sorts and Conditions of Men*, p. 135.

45 W. Besant and J. Rice, 'The Seamy Side; a New Novel by the Authors of *Ready-Money, Mortiboy*, etc.', *Time*, 2, October 1879, p. 87.

46 Besant, *All Sorts and Conditions of Men*, p. 327.

47 W. Besant, 'People's Palace', *Contemporary Review*, February 1887, p. 233.

48 'Echo Portrait Gallery', *Echo*, 14 May 1890.

49 Sir Edmund Currie, 'The working of "The People's Palace"', *The Nineteenth Century* (February 1890), pp. 346–7.

50 A. Morrison, *The Child of the Jago*, pp. 18–19.

51 See also W. Besant, *Autobiography of Sir Walter Besant* (London: Hutchinson, 1902), p. 245.

52 From William Empson's *Some Versions of the Pastoral* as quoted by P. J. Keating in *The Working Classes in Victorian Fiction* (New York: Barnes and Noble, 1971), p. 102.

53 Chapman, 'The People's Palace for East End', p. 127.

54 H. A. Baker, 'A People's Palace', *Commonweal: The Official Journal of the Socialist League* (1886).

55 As quoted by Chris Waters, 'Socialism and the Politics of Popular Culture in Britain, 1884–1914', unpublished dissertation, Harvard University, 1985, pp. 228–9.

56 As quoted by C. Waters, *British Socialists and the Politics of Popular Culture 1884–1914* (Manchester: Manchester University Press, 1990), p. 82.

57 G. Bernard Shaw, 'Blood money to Whitechapel', to the editor of *The Star*, 24 September 1888.

58 The files of Queen Mary College include the subscribers to the scheme as well as letters from those who responded but refused to donate. The following quotations are from letters in these files.

59 Lord Rosebery, quoted at a meeting at the Drapers' Hall convened by the Beaumont Trustees, 19 April 1887.

60 Waters, *British Socialists*, pp. 25–7.

61 *Ibid.*, pp. 79–81.

62 Lord Hartington, quoted in fund-raising pamphlet, 'Scheme of Training Workshops for Teaching Handicrafts', including an article from *The Times*, 17 March 1887, on the 'Importance of scientific training for artisans', GLRO, A/BPP/2.

63 Pamphlet reprinting article form *The Times*, 15 January 1886, GLRO, A/BPP/2.

64 Fund-raising appeal dated 27 October 1886, signed by E. H. Currie.

65 Pamphlet, 'East London Technical and Science Schools, Mile End', announcement of opening 12 September 1887.

66 Lord Rosebery, quoted at a meeting at the Drapers' Hall convened by the Beaumont Trustees, 19 April 1887.

CHAPTER EIGHT

Robert Elsmere: Mrs Ward and the New Theology

Mrs Humphry Ward's *Robert Elsmere* of 1888, which described the foundation of a Christian brotherhood as a means of reaching London's working population, was *the* most successful novel of the period, engendering at last an International Copyright Bill,[1] and even a review by William Gladstone.[2] Walter Besant wrote of the great popularity of Mrs Ward's novel:

> The success of that book, apart from its very great literary merits, was undoubtedly due to the fact that it appealed to the thoughts of thousands who were ready for broader views of humanity and religion, for proclaiming things which they themselves felt but wanted the power to clothe with words.[3]

Like Besant's book, *All Sorts and Conditions of Men*, Mrs Ward's novel was the inspiration for an institution which opened the doors to its own new building in 1897, the Passmore Edwards Settlement at Tavistock Place in Bloomsbury. Like Walter Besant, Mrs Humphry Ward wrote of the efforts of well-meaning individuals devoted to social service. The hero of Mrs Ward's novel, *Robert Elsmere*, founds the Elgood Street Brotherhood in the East End of London. Unlike the People's Palace it is an avowedly Christian experiment, but it shares many of the ambitions of both the Settlement movement and the People's Palace: James Knowles, editor of *The Nineteenth Century*, writing to Gladstone, noted the similarity:

> I cannot say whether or not 'Elgood Street' represents her practical convictions and desires – but I incline to think so. To what extent in that respect she is following Besant's successful enterprise in 'all sorts and conditions of men' I wonder.

And he concluded that the solution proposed in the novel – the Brotherhood – was 'a new confirmation of the way in which the "enthusiasm of humanity" has got hold of our Century.'[4]

Mrs Ward was uniquely placed to give voice to the religious debates, the growing commitment to individual public service and the impulse to disseminate culture from the 'best to the lowest'. Born Mary Arnold, she was the granddaughter of Dr Thomas Arnold of Rugby – clergyman and headmaster – and the niece of Matthew Arnold. Her father, Thomas Arnold, an Oxford graduate, suffered grave religious crises, converting to Catholicism and back again and then returning to Catholicism, teaching history at Oxford and at Dublin University for Newman. The Arnold family was committed to public service and education. They married within a circle that shared their convictions: Jane Arnold, Mrs Ward's father's eldest sister, married W. E. Forster; Mrs Ward's younger sister married Leonard Huxley, son of Thomas Huxley; Mrs Ward married Thomas Humphry Ward, Oxford tutor, editor and art critic; and their daughter Janet married the Oxford historian, G. M. Trevelyan.

In its focus and vantage point, *Robert Elsmere* is closely allied to that intellectual tradition, so crucial to Liberal notions of popular education and the Settlement movement. Its concern with a contemporary Christianity, demythologised and realised through social service, has been likened to the writings of Matthew Arnold, who, though gravely dissatisfied with Christianity, refused to live without it[5] and desired 'to preserve faith through the demolition of dogma, to the end that ethics might emerge and fraternity prevail.'[6] In a letter referring to his forthcoming review of the novel, Gladstone described Mrs Ward as 'a fruit, I think, of what must be called Arnoldism'.[7]

The novel drew also upon Mrs. Ward's experiences at Oxford in the 1860s and 1870s. As a woman, Mrs Ward was unable to receive a formal education. (In later years she worked for the foundation of a woman's college at Oxford.) Instead, she studied independently in the Bodleian Library, following readings suggested by a network of supportive scholars, and she ultimately became an authority on medieval Spanish literature. Among those who took an interest in her scholarship during her Oxford days was Mark Pattison, a formidable scholar and Rector of Lincoln College, Benjamin Jowett, and T. H. Green.

The teachings of T. H. Green and Benjamin Jowett, who urged, it will be recalled, a New Theology, entreated students to fulfil their Christian duty through public service. The New Theology argued for a Christianity that could be embraced by intellectuals. Mary Ward recalled the turbulent times in *A Writer's Recollections*:

beating round us all the time were the spiritual winds of an agitated day. The Oxford of thought was not quiet; it was divided . . . by sharper antagonisms and deeper feuds than exist to-day. Darwinism was penetrating everywhere; Pusey was preaching against its effects on belief; Balliol stood for an unfettered history and criticism, Christ Church for authority and creeds; Renan's *Origines* were still coming out, Strauss's last book also; my uncle was publishing *God and the Bible* in succession to *Literature and Dogma*; and *Supernatural Religion* was making no small stir. And meanwhile what began to interest and absorb me were *sources – testimony*. To what – to whom – did it all go back – this great story of early civilization, early religion, which modern men could write and interpret so differently?[8]

It was this search for a New Theology that Mrs Ward's novel explored in *Robert Elsmere*.

The story revolves around a young clergyman, a recent Oxford graduate, who marries a deeply religious Evangelical woman. Together they commit their lives to social service. Mrs Ward's hero – like many of her contemporaries – deeply questions his faith in the light of the scientific and historical movements of the century, examining the historical record and calling into question the miracles of Christ. Robert Elsmere, with great pain to his wife and after much personal anguish, denounces his orders and leaves the Church. There follows Elsmere's search for a form of social service to which to devote himself. He begins by moving to London where he works with a Broad Churchman vicar. Elsmere offers evening classes and undertakes rent-collecting, which he finds unsatisfactory, as the vicar believes in working within the Church Reform movement. Elsmere feels instead that in working with the Church there is a 'perpetual divorce between thought and action'.[9] Elsmere then works closely with a Unitarian minister who establishes a successful mission in London's East End and who argues that there are 'changes creeping over the modern Unitarian body', which in the past had little appeal to the poor. In the end, however, Elsmere sets out on his own and founds the Elgood Street Brotherhood of Christ among the working men of the East End, 'what is practically a settlement among you', as he describes the venture.[10]

Mrs Ward's novel was peopled with characters borrowed from the Oxford she had known. Robert Elsmere's Oxford tutor, Professor Grey, was a thinly disguised T. H. Green, to whom she dedicated the book;[11] Mrs Ward had described Green as representative of the 'spiritual and liberating forces' at Oxford and as a 'great thinker and teacher, who was also one of the simplest, sincerest and most practical of men – which Oxford will never forget, so long as high culture and noble character are dear to her.'[12] The importance of this teacher to the development of the central character is made abundantly clear in the novel:

> [Professor Grey's] mere life, that he was there, on English soil, within a measurable distance, had been to Elsmere in his darkest moments one of his thoughts and refuge. At a time when religion which can no longer be believed clashes with a scepticism full of danger to conduct, every such witness as Grey to power of a new and coming truth holds a special place in the hearts of men who can neither accept fairy tales, nor reconcile themselves to a world without faith. The saintly life grows to be a beacon, a witness[13]

Other characters have been identified, although Mrs Ward denied that they were based on specific individuals. Rather, what is important is that they so closely followed the lives of so many of her contemporaries. Robert Elsmere was likened to the historian, her friend J. R. Green, who had been a curate for two years to her father-in-law, Revd Henry Ward, and who had befriended all his children,[14] and who, like the hero of the novel, had renounced his orders. Comparisons were made as well between Elsmere and A. H. D. Acland, in the circle around Green, who had a deeply religious wife and who, too, broke with the Church.[15] While denying these connections, Mrs Ward did admit to inspiration from the life of Charles Kingsley.[16] The Squire who leads Elsmere through his library of German philosophers has been likened to Mark Pattison, former follower of Newman and a sceptic who fought to make university appointments dependent upon scholarship rather than religious beliefs;[17] the character of Langham has been likened to Amiel, whose *Journal* Mrs Ward had translated. Newman appears as 'Newcome', a Ritualist Anglican priest.[18] In preparing the lectures which Elsmere would give to the 'Brotherhood' she drew on T. H. Huxley's lay sermons as well as on Edward Denison's letters and books about the East End. The death of J. R. Green, who had labored among the poor and died of tuberculosis, provided Elsmere's death from the same ailment.[19] But as Jowett commented, the success of the book is 'really due to what everybody else is thinking'.[20]

The book appeared on 24 February 1888, and was an overwhelming success, into its third edition in April.[21] In May the review by Gladstone appeared, defending the Church of England against the novel, a rare distraction from the statesman's obsession with Ireland and Home Rule. The urgency of the review speaks of the way in which the novel touched some of the deepest anxieties of the day. Sales continued to soar.[22]

Following publication of the book, Mrs Ward visited Toynbee Hall, an experience which moved her, and in the library she found a well-worn volume of *Robert Elsmere*. At the Settlement she encountered a newly formed working men's club which had borrowed ideas from the 'New Brotherhood' of the novel.[23] Although the description of Elsmere's social work is limited in the novel – Elsmere gives a series of story-telling evenings and founds a 'Scientific Sunday School' – the under-lying concept that modern Christianity must deal with the social question was one for which Mrs Ward sought to find 'expression in some living form', as her daughter phrased it.[24] And, indeed, 'the New Brotherhood of *Robert Elsmere* . . . [became] some sort [of] a realised dream.'[25]

Mrs Ward sought to found an institution, modeled on the Settlement idea, which would have its foundation and its emphasis in Modernism, that is, in the New Theology, what has been called a 'Toynbee Hall of Liberal Theology'.[26] In the year following the publication of *Robert Elsmere* her idea for such an institution found support among Unitarians and Liberal churchmen, including such eminent men as the Unitarian leader Dr James Martineau, the Irish radical Revd Stopford A. Brooke, who had defected from the Church of England in 1880, the Earl of Carlisle, and Dr James Drummond of Manchester College, Oxford. Although it was feared that the selection of a Unitarian warden would cause the experiment to be perceived as propagating a particular faith, after much searching – and with the assistance of Canon Barnett[27] – Philip Henry Wicksteed, economist, Dante scholar, the foremost English disciple of the Modernists of Holland and the Unitarian minister of Little Portland Street, was persuaded to accept the position.[28]

Mrs Ward envisioned an institution which would emphasise Liberal Christianity through its dual functions as center of religious study and social work. Mrs Ward had hoped that Biblical criticism would be high on the agenda of the new institution. According to the memoirs of the first warden

> it is certainly true that she hoped to shape the Settlement into something far more like a direct manifestation of the ideals of Robert Elsmere than turned out possible.

And he described in detail her initial ambitions:

> to found a kind of school of free Biblical and ecclesiastical study, to be conducted with a wide philosophical, literary and historical outlook, and always to be associated with the direct consideration of social movements and problems. Such a school was to be no seminary, but

it was to be the educational side and the specific characteristic of a 'Settlement', as the term is usually understood, and was to form a basis and a support for all the practical and popularising work of such as found in its animating idea the source of their own inspiration. Naturally a body of Residents closely interested in the School, and themselves devoting their leisure to the practical side of the work, was not only an essential feature of the scheme but was to be its central organ. [29]

The Settlement was founded in an existing residence hall, University Hall, Gordon Square, in Bloomsbury in 1890, and it also used a 'little dingy hall in Marchmont Street, where the residents of the Hall started clubs and classes'. [30] The institution was located in a fashionable part of London, as it was in the pockets of poverty amidst plenty that the Settlement sought to offer its help. According to house-to-house surveys conducted by the *Pall Mall Gazette* in East London and in South and West London 'the conditions of life are not better in the proximity of the Squares than in the heart of the slums. Everywhere if you choose to see it there is the same poverty to be seen'. [31] The 'astonishing experiment,' as Mrs Ward described it, [32] was still, however, very much 'attached . . . to a growing movement', [33] part of the 'spirit of fraternisation . . . in the air' allied to 'an ardent wish to break down the local and geographical barriers that separated rich and poor, East End and West End.' [34]

A circular announcing the foundation of University Hall stated that

> It is intended that the Hall shall do its utmost to secure for its residents opportunities for religious and social work, and for the study of social problems, such as are possessed by the residents of Toynbee Hall or those at Oxford House. There will be a certain number of rooms in the Hall which can be used for social purposes, for lectures, for recreative and continuation classes and so on. [35]

And potential applicants were assured that public transportation was such that

> it would be comparatively easy for the residents to take part in any of the organisations already existing in the East or South of London, for the help of the poor and the study of social problems.

But that aspect of the theological debates, social service, which the novel had explored, was not sufficiently addressed in the minds of many of the residents. They turned to the social work at nearby Marchmont Hall, where they reduced the sense of hierarchy, establishing a system whereby local residents, both men and women, became 'associates' of the Hall.[36] Involving the local working population, eliminating the religious element entirely, and functioning without a warden in authority, this off-shoot experiment functioned in stark contrast to Mrs Ward's poorly attended religious lecture series at University Hall, which appealed to a distinctly middle class audience. The social work at Marchmont Hall was, in fact, closer to Elsmere's efforts among the poor after his crisis of faith:

> the poor pale reformer began to draw out the details of his scheme on its material side. Three floors of rooms brightly furnished, well lit and warmed; a large hall for the Sunday lectures, concerts, entertainments, and story-telling; rooms for the Boy's Club; two rooms for women and girls, reached by a separate entrance; a library and reading-room open to both sexes, well stored with books, and made beautiful by pictures; three or four smaller rooms to serve as committee rooms and for the purposes of the Naturalist Club . . . and, if possible, a gymnasium.[37]

It was this aspect of the Settlement that grew. By the time the Settlement had a permanent home, the religious aspect of Mrs Ward's program had been eliminated.

For a site for a permanent home for the institution it was to the ground landlord, the Duke of Bedford, that the organisers turned for assistance. Although the first location chosen did not in the end work out, the Duke of Bedford was supportive of the venture and contributed £800, later increased to £1,500,[38] to the building fund and granted a lease of 999 years.[39] For the capital to build, Mrs Ward turned to the English philanthropist J. Passmore Edwards.

Considering Mrs Ward's powers of visual description and concern for detail in her novels – what has been called her 'camera eye'[40] – and her husband's position as a London art critic and collector, well aware, as he put it, that 'No branch of art has shown greater activity during the reign of Queen Victoria than architecture',[41] it is not surprising that a great deal of attention was lavished on the architectural expression of the new institution.[42] In the novel, though, Robert Elsmere lives only long enough to see the birth of his Elgood Street Brotherhood, and there is no mention of a permanent home which might serve as an architectural model. Mrs Ward turned to the most up to date in architectural fashion.

That the building should be an example of Arts and Crafts architecture seems to have been Mrs Ward's idea from the outset, as the Arts and Crafts architect and designer Arthur Mackmurdo was initially asked to produce a design. His design, now lost, was rejected

Design by Gerald Horsley

Design by Halsey Ricardo   University Hall Settlement Buildings

69] Surviving designs for the Passmore Edwards Settlement by Gerald Horsley and Halsey Ricardo, from *The British Architect*, 12 July 1895

and Norman Shaw was asked to judge a limited competition. The architects who were invited to compete were all associated with Arts and Crafts design. They included A. H. Mackmurdo, who declined, Gerald Horsley, Ernest Newton, Edward Prior, Halsey Ricardo, E. W.

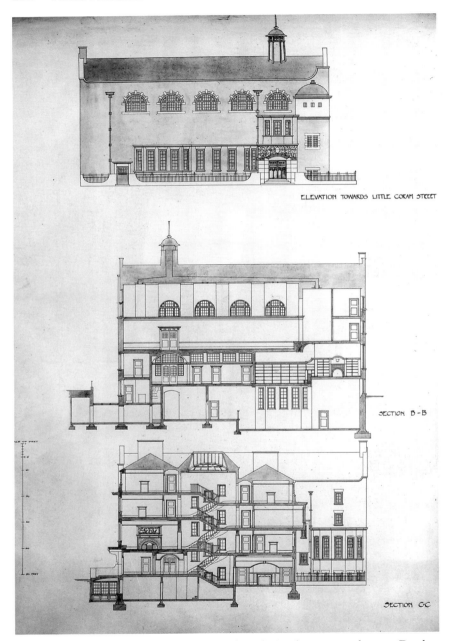

ELEVATION TOWARDS LITTLE CORAM STREET

SECTION B-B

SECTION CC

70] Winning design for the Passmore Edwards Settlement, architects Dunbar Smith and Cecil Brewer

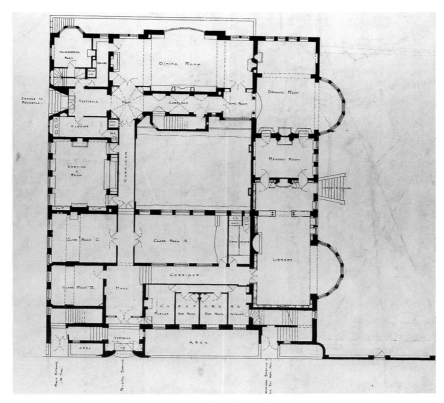

71] Ground plan of the Passmore Edwards Settlement

Mountford, W. Stirling, Francis Troup, Cecil Brewer and Dunbar Smith, who were in partnership, F. Waller, H. Wilson, and M. S. Hack.[43] Two of the losing designs survive, **[69]** one drawing on the Toynbee Hall manorial model of the previous decade, but the other, as in the case of the winning design, was in the style of the Arts and Crafts movement. The manorial language, it would seem, was rejected in favor of the more fashionable alternative.

An examination of the winning design by Smith and Brewer **[70–71]** reveals a self-conscious use of the language of the Arts and Crafts movement to go beyond fashion in order to express their interpretation of the nature of the institution itself, that is, about co-operation, about transformed social relationships as lived within this social experiment. It would seem, in fact, to have been a rejection of the explicit paternalism of the revival architectures of previous institutions of reform and philanthropy: Toynbee Hall, Oxford House, Bermondsey Settlement, and the Board Schools.[44]

As young architects, Dunbar Smith, twenty-nine years old, and Cecil Claude Brewer, twenty-four, were both concerned with the social questions of the day. They were residents themselves at University Hall, engaged in current artistic debate, seeking to express their social ideals through design. Smith and Brewer knew C. R. Ashbee,[45] who had bitterly satirised the Barnetts' paternalistic attitude toward the East End poor at Toynbee Hall.[46] Brewer was an early visitor to Ashbee's Guild experiment in the Cotswolds where Ashbee had founded a Guild of East End craftsmen in the medieval town of Chipping Campden.[47] The mission that Smith and Brewer saw for themselves as architects is best understood within the context of the debates and practices regarding the role of art in philanthropy and social reform.

Imbued with the social ideals of Ruskin and Morris, many Arts and Crafts designers tried to define a role for art in the social experiments of the day. The ambitions of social reformers like the Barnetts or Mrs Humphry Ward intersected with the desire of these socially motivated artists and designers – including committed socialists such as William Morris himself – even when the definition of social service was a far cry from their more revolutionary demands. There were contradictions, and leftist artists assumed a variety of positions in relation to the movements of reform and philanthropy: Morris railed that perhaps art simply could not exist under the current social system, 'that art must go under, where or how ever it may come up again',[48] yet one finds him among the guests at Toynbee Hall or lecturing on 'Art and Socialism' at the Barnetts' annual picture exhibition;[49] Philip Webb worked indefatigably for the socialist cause, donating substantial sums of money, but did not lend his artistic talents to the piecemeal efforts of philanthropists;[50] C. R. Ashbee joined the Barnetts at Toynbee Hall but ultimately broke with them; Walter Crane, while working actively for the socialist cause, lent his talents to countless philanthropic efforts in a self-conscious effort to bring art to the people [72].

That art and design could and ought to play a central role in bringing the 'grace and civilisation' of the West End to the East End, as already noted, had been an important theme in the Settlement movement. The Barnetts, for example, began what became annual picture exhibitions in Whitechapel in 1881. The exhibitions were enthusiastically supported by many leading artists and patrons, including Burne-Jones, Walter Crane, D. G. Rossetti, J. W. Waterhouse, H. Herkomer, W. Holman Hunt, L. Alma-Tadema, G. F. Watts, J. E. Millais, F. Leighton, and F. D. Millet. The Barnetts were fervent believers in the edifying effect of art: 'Well would it be,' wrote Samuel

Barnett, 'if pictures were recognised as preachers, as voices of God, passing His lessons from age to age.'⁵¹ An admirer of the allegorical paintings of G. F. Watts, Barnett likened the paintings to sermons.⁵² And Henrietta Barnett, writing about the success of the picture exhibitions, argued that pictures were, in fact, more powerful than words:

> Words, mere words, fall flat on the ears of those whose imaginations are withered and dead; but art, in itself beautiful, in ideas rich, they cannot choose but understand, if it be brought within their reach.
>   Art may do much to keep alive a nation's fading higher life when other influences fail adequately to nourish it;⁵³

The success of the exhibitions at Whitechapel was commemorated by a gift in 1884 of a mosaic copy of an allegorical painting by G. F. Watts, *Time, Death, and Judgment* on the façade of St Jude's, Whitechapel, unveiled for the occasion by Matthew Arnold.⁵⁴ The picture exhibitions were then emulated by a number of London Settlements.

An art gallery was built between 1899 and 1901 to house the annual exhibitions, funded primarily by Passmore Edwards, and designed by architect Charles Harrison Townsend. An examination of Townsend's work suggests the context in which Smith and Brewer, like Townsend members of the Art Workers' Guild, were working in Bloomsbury. The design of the Whitechapel Gallery [73–74], the earliest version dating to 1898, was a self-conscious attempt to produce in architecture something of the narrative symbolism of the allegorical paintings so proudly exhibited within. The message which the architect sought to convey in built form was that of social transformation as rebirth: the façade of the Whitechapel Art Gallery carries a lavish vegetal motif which appears to grow and stretch upward.

Though never carried out due to financial constraints, the façade of the Whitechapel Art Gallery was to have had a mosaic by Walter Crane depicting 'The Sphere and Message of Art' [75]. Enthroned in the center was Pictorial Art with the mirror of nature in one hand, in the other a sceptre, and at her feet the globe. From the left figures move toward her: first a workman with his wife and children, then a figure ready to crown the workman with the rewards of labor, then a woman carrying a distaff and another bearing produce. From the right figures move toward Art: Time, History, Poesie, Truth and Beauty. At the base of the frieze are four peacocks: the immortality of Art.

Townsend designed bold decorative symbolism of rebirth and social transformation at two other cultural institutions for the poor: the Bishopsgate Institute, designed in 1892, and the Horniman Museum,

72] Drawing by Walter Crane, cover of *St Jude's*

designed in 1896. The Bishopsgate Institute was comprised of a hall, two reading rooms and a lending library for the local populace; its façade was the scene of organic flowering, and the doors were emblazened with the sun [**76–77**]. The Horniman Museum, opened in 1901, was a private collection for the local population of south London. Townsend extended the flowering motif into the building itself. As with the unexecuted design for the Whitechapel Gallery, he incorporated a large allegorical mosaic as the central focus for the exterior of the Museum [**78–80**].

73, 74] Elevation and plan of Whitechapel Art Gallery, 1898–1901, architect
Charles Harrison Townsend

The mosaic, 32 ft (9.7 m) high and 10 ft (3.04 m) long, by Robert Anning Bell depicts an allegory of the course of human life: the central figure is Humanity in the House of Circumstance, which represents the personal limitations of birth, education, and surroundings, while beyond the wall, behind all of the figures, are seen glimpses of sky, fruits, and flowering trees, symbols of things yearned for beyond knowledge. The walls at the ends of the mosaic depict the Gates of Life and Death. Beside the figure of Humanity stand Fine Arts, Poetry, and Music. Endurance, an armed figure, holds a shield and sword, with which to equip Humanity; Love and Hope clothe Humanity with their qualities. Charity is near by, bearing figs and wine, as are white-haired but virile Wisdom, Meditation, in her sad-hued garments, and finally Resignation, with sombre look, resting on his staff in front of the Gates of Death.[55]

Writing in 1897 Walter Crane, the well-known illustrator, designer of the Whitechapel mosaic and bookmarks for the Bishopsgate Library, described the role which the decoration of public buildings should play 'through the vivid language of design':

> The decoration of public buildings should be the highest form of popular art, as it was in the Middle Ages, when a town-hall, or church, was not bad equivalent for a public library storied with legends and symbols – histories, as they were, which impressed themselves upon the unlettered, through the vivid language of design.[56]

The modern era, according to Crane, had not yet expressed its most important themes:

> The modern vision of the evolution of nature, of the stream of human progress flowing ever onwards from its dim prehistoric sources; the great social ideal of a common and interdependent life, involving an unbroken chain of co-operative human labour necessary to the maintenance of life and the creation of collective wealth with its splendid possibilities; the true relationship of the human family on the earth; the conception of the service of humanity as directing and centralising the life and giving it purpose – such themes have yet to be expressed or symbolised in the places where the highest thoughts and aspirations of a people are most fittingly and enduringly expressed – in the design and decoration of noble public buildings.[57]

An important influence in Crane's call for 'legends and symbols' was the publication in 1891 of *Architecture, Mysticism and Myth* by the architect William R. Lethaby, who, like Walter Crane, Robert Anning Bell, William Morris, C. R. Ashbee, C. H. Townsend and Cecil Brewer, was a member of the Art Workers' Guild. Lethaby entreated

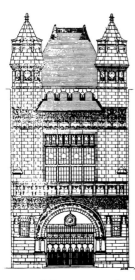

75] Drawing of the
mosaic (which was not
executed) designed by
Walter Crane for the
façade of the
Whitechapel Art
Gallery, from *Studio*,
1901

76, 77] Drawing and
elevation of the
Bishopsgate Institute,
architect C. H.
Townsend. Note sun
symbolism at entrance

78] Horniman Museum, 1898–1901, architect C. H. Townsend

architects to design 'universal' symbols. Architecture, according to Lethaby, was thought embodied in form,[58] and his book was a plea to put *meaning* back into architecture through symbolism:

> Old architecture lived because it had a purpose. Modern architecture, to be real, must not be a mere envelope without contents. As M. Cesar Daly says in his *Hautes Etudes*, if we would have architecture excite an interest, real and general, we must have a symbolism, immediately comprehensible by the great majority of spectators . . .
> What, then, will this art of the future be? The message will still be of nature and man, of order and beauty, but all will be sweetness, simplicity, freedom, confidence, and light[59]

In a lecture of 1895 Lethaby called the quality he was seeking 'Expressionism' and insisted that 'building could only be interesting

79] Horniman Museum, interior

when there existed a widespread ability to read its expressional results.'[60] One architect recalled the impact of Lethaby's ideas:

80] Drawing of the mosaic, by Robert Anning Bell, main elevation, Horniman Museum

This book opened up to us younger men a hitherto undreamt of romance in architecture. The labyrinth, the golden gate of the sun, pavements like the sea, ceilings like the sky, the windows of heaven, and three hundred and sixty five days[61]

Dunbar Smith and Cecil Brewer, the designers of Mrs Ward's center, like many other young architects had also been deeply impressed by the previous generation, by John Ruskin, William Morris and Philip Webb. The architect Owen Fleming, who had been with Smith and Brewer at the Settlement, wrote of their frame of mind at the time:

What a happy band of young architects we were, gathered together in University Hall Settlement . . . those were the days when we believed that earnest and true thought expressed in buildings would awaken some response in the popular mind – Smith and Brewer had an office flat in Gray's Inn, and often we used to go round from the Settlement in the evenings to find them there in their shirt-sleeves. . . . Sometimes we stayed on and pooled our thoughts. . . . At others we all adjourned to Lethaby's rooms and talked things over with him. . . . It was not only architecture which moved us. The economic forces lying behind architecture became the frequent subject of discussion.[62]

The Passmore Edwards Settlement, as Mrs Ward's institution was called, though renamed after her death for its founder, stood apart from the public buildings of the day, as did the work of Townsend, in that Arts and Crafts design had been reserved for domestic buildings.[63] The design of Smith and Brewer for Mrs Ward can best be understood as an attempt to realise Lethaby's ideas – the commitment to put meaning back into building – through the Arts and Crafts ideals of simplicity, honesty in construction, and the use of national or vernacular styles mixed with originality.

Explicit reference to historical styles which spoke of hierarchy and a nostalgia for a past, in which obligation and deference defined class relationships, was rejected in favor of a narrative architecture which would 'speak' of creation, rebirth and the possibilities of new social relationships as cast within this new institution. The social ideals which were the underpinning of the Arts and Crafts movement here found expression in the agenda of Smith and Brewer to wed their social and artistic ideals.

The architects made every effort to make their building readable, expressive of its function and purpose. Although the winning design was thoroughly reworked when it was found necessary to change the intended site of the building, the division between the two functions of the building – private for residents and public for the neighborhood

— was made clear in both schemes. In the original scheme the division between public and private was apparent from the street front: the residents' quarters were signified on the street front by domestic detailing such as sash windows, deep cornices, white friezes and dormered garret, while a large Palladian window signified the public domain [81]. In the final plan the public spaces, which included a large lecture hall, two smaller lecture rooms, a gymnasium, craft workshops, and the private spaces, which included the dining room, bedsitting rooms for residents and a flat for the warden, were reworked for the narrow site so that the street façade indicated the public nature of the institution while the living space for residents was at the back of the site, overlooking the garden. The distinctive feature of the street façade was its massive doorway, which welcomed the public with two smaller entrances on either side, the London County Council having required two separate entrances for the large Hall and one for the rest of the building.[64] Here as in the original design, the vocabulary suggested a combination of public and private functions within the building: while the large Palladian window on the side street elevation, the large blank wall and staircase towers suggested that a Hall lay behind, the wide cornice and white frieze were suggestive of a domestic scale and function.

In contrast to the oriel window surmounting a massive doorway at Bermondsey Settlement [53], here the scale is more intimate; though surrounded by a massive stone porch, the main oak doorway is low and welcoming, only 6 ft 3 in. (1.92 m). At the Passmore Edwards Settlement the simplicity and modesty of the exterior is carried throughout the building: all the doorways inside the building, whether for the public or for residential private spaces, are the same height, 6 ft $1\frac{1}{2}$ in. (1.85 m), their lowness emphasised by their mutin-less top panel and high center rail.[65] [82] The fittings and furnishings, in Arts and Crafts fashion, were also designed by the architects, simple and rustic: a sideboard of painted deal in the dining room, dining tables of oak planks with small heart-shaped frets [83–84].

No two rooms of the residents' quarters were alike, but they all contained the same detailing and joinery as found in the rest of the building, all signs of hierarchy having been thus excluded, an idea reminiscent of the system of 'associates' whereby Marchmont Hall had been run without any system of hierarchy [85].

Central to Arts and Crafts ideals was the Ruskinian commitment to 'joy in labour'. The architects were faced with a limited budget which required the employment of a general contractor, Higgs and Hill, selected through competitive tender. Yet the architects paid enormous

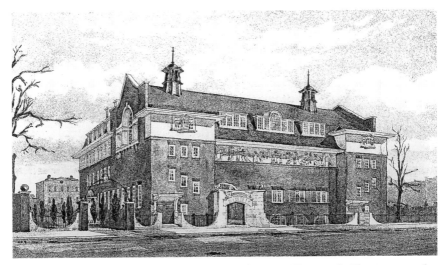

81] Drawing of the Passmore Edwards Settlement, Tavistock Place, opened in 1898, architects D. Smith and C. Brewer

82] Drawing room, fireplace and connecting door to library, Passmore Edwards Settlement. Note the extreme simplicity, the absence of joinery mouldings with the exception of the frieze rail

attention to the detailing, and ensured that wherever possible standard contractors' conventions were *not* followed. In the masonry, for example, Flemish bond, rather than the usual English bond, was used; in the joinery standard sections were avoided whenever possible. The architects developed a system of simple joinery details so the building could be constructed without a high degree of craft skill, at the same time emphasising the virtues of simplicity and humility.[66] The building in its production was a co-operative effort: while the architects designed all of the metalwork themselves, other architects were invited to contribute to the building; the fireplaces in the public rooms were designed by Voysey, Newton, Troup, Lethaby and Dawber.[67]

There is yet another level on which the design of the building can be understood as an endeavor by its architects to express the elimination of hierarchy. This was done through their response to contemporary debates on style, Gothic versus Classical. Looking, it would seem, at the work of Philip Webb, Smith and Brewer mixed late seventeenth century details with craft traditions.[68] Wide cornices, narrow sashes and tile sills had been used by Webb in his country houses and were taken up here by Smith and Brewer. But in Lethaby's writings they would have found a further justification for this highly original mixture of styles, and that was the rejection of any hierarchy between the styles encountered throughout the building. Lethaby, who explored the origins of architecture, began his study as follows:

> Behind every style of architecture there is an earlier style, in which the germ of every form is to be found . . . all is the slow change of growth, and it is almost impossible to point to the time of invention of any custom or feature.

In spite of the

> habit of historians of architecture to lay stress on the differences of the several styles and schools of successive ages . . . in the far larger sense, all architecture is one, when traced through the stream of civilisations, as they followed or influenced one another.[69]

The architects disregarded the differences between styles – and any notion of a hierarchy of style – freely mixing Classical and Gothic features: the front elevation, for example, is symmetrical with a Palladian window and yet the small windows which echo the stairway are staggered in the manner of Gothic architecture. Further, the apparently Classical detailing does not refer to any known Classical order [**86–87**].

As suggested by Lethaby's text, the architects explored the 'origins of architecture' without regard for traditional hierarchies in

83] Dining room, west end, Passmore Edwards Settlement

their application, in keeping with the message interwoven throughout the design of the building, traditional notions of hierarchy are abandoned. Indeed, in their random use of historical motifs they appear to have rejected the myths of the past and, with it, the allegiance to social

84] Dining room, east end, Passmore Edwards Settlement

85] Resident's apartment, Passmore Edwards Settlement

authority. As such it contrasted dramatically with the work of E. R. Robson or Elijah Hoole.

That the building should be expressive of the ideals of the institution is seen in the use of explicit symbolism suggested in

86] Drawing room, Passmore Edwards Settlement. Note the doorway columns

Lethaby's writings: a tree of life motif is displayed on the façade [88], and over the central portal are two egg motifs [89] which, according to Lethaby, were 'firmly and widely accepted as a symbol of life and creation'.[70] These symbols suggested the notion of a new social beginning – even transformation – within Mrs Ward's institution.

Whereas the architects created symbolic meanings which might be conveyed through decoration and the mixing of styles, how in fact *was* the building understood by public and patron? How did the message encoded in the design fit with the intentions and ambitions of its founder? Contemporary criticism of the building from the architectural press suggests that its novel quality, if nothing else, was recognised: it was 'a striking object of interest even if the originality of the design is a little aggressive',[71] according to *The British Architect*. The *Studio*

87] Entrance lobby to drawing room, Passmore Edwards Settlement

acknowledged the work as 'one of the happiest examples of the influence of the "Arts and Crafts" movement upon architecture', and was impressed with its 'sincere and thoughtful architecture', its 'simplicity of manner, this treatment of architecture as construction made beautiful'.[72] But nothing suggests that the meanings which the architects had carefully woven throughout were read as they had intended.

Mrs Ward herself seemed to have missed the point. She described the new building as a 'House Beautiful',[73] 'the most attractive and commodious Settlement building in London',[74] but made no reference to the symbolism of the building. Her own intellectual debt was made explicit in her dedications of the library to T. H. Green [90] and a lecture series to Benjamin Jowett. Though pleased with the smart

88] Tree of Life motif in brickwork, Passmore Edwards Settlement

89] Main entrance, with egg motif over doorway, Passmore Edwards Settlement

90] Library, Passmore Edwards Settlement, Tavistock Place

new building, she neither shared the social vision of her architects nor recognised their message in her building. In fact, there is nothing to suggest that Mrs Ward was ever concerned with the elimination of hierarchy within the Settlement, or with the virtues of simplicity, or with social change or rebirth. Her new institution, as she understood it, was not 'committed to a party or a school of economic affairs'.[75]

Mrs Ward was distinctly ill at ease dealing face to face with the poor; her vision of the institution suggests something far more conservative than that of her idealistic young architects. Indeed, Mrs Ward found Toynbee Hall, as it had evolved by the late 1880s – openly supportive of the Dock Strike – too far to the left for her liking. And in the 1890s Toynbee Hall had grown increasingly involved in such issues as women's suffrage, Home Rule and support for the Boers, positions totally at odds with Mrs Ward's.[76] But the Passmore Edwards Settlement differed in other significant ways as well from Toynbee Hall: while the Barnetts were themselves residents at the Settlement, Mrs Ward had moved from Russell Square in November of 1890 to Grosvenor Place, remarking that the distance was a good thing as her family and literary work came first.[77] Barnett himself confided doubts in a letter after Mrs Ward had visited him on the subject of founding a Settlement. 'I don't think it will go. Why should it? It has neither the force of a sectarian movement nor the charm of a free movement. A few people are caught by the phantom beauty of Elsmere's character, but it cannot be grasped.' And he went on to describe Mrs Ward as an anxious but 'sweet tender woman'.[78]

In the end the institution did not follow either the dreams of the idealistic Robert Elsmere or those of Mrs Ward's utopian architects. As originally planned the Passmore Edwards Settlement was to have been a mixture of adult education classes and recreational activities for the working class residents of the immediate neighborhood. And the Settlement was involved in a variety of activities in its early years: there were classes ranging from French to carpentry, a factory girls' club, a cricket club, a chess club, the Denison club devoted to debate, legal aid for the poor, domestic economy classes, and a re-training center for the unemployed.[79]

The focus of the work, however, the real achievement of the Settlement, lay in its work with children. As a promoter of 'Play-time reform', 'The Fairy Godmother',[80] as Mrs Ward was called, focused on organising programs for children after school hours and during summer holidays, what became known as 'Vacation School'. The Settlement pioneered work with physically handicapped children, and, using her considerable powers of persuasion, Mrs Ward secured the support of the London School Board, opening the first fully equipped school for handicapped children in 1899; the Settlement provided the building, a nurse and an ambulance, while support was sought elsewhere for special furnishings, equipment and a qualified teacher. Both the play center and the invalid school proved to be models emulated elsewhere in the city. Work with children represented an area for which widespread support was readily available at the end of the century, and it provided Mrs Ward with a focus which would, by and large, avoid debate which was either religious or political.[81] Accommodation was extended for the special needs of children in 1903 with the addition of a conventional neo-Georgian building.

Robert Elsmere's Christian Brotherhood amidst the poor, a commitment to Christianity through social service, evolved into a program which fulfilled Mrs Ward's own ambitions within the philanthropic world of late nineteenth century London. The work of the Settlement proved to be an important example for the later work of the London County Council, but, like Besant's dream of a People's Palace, the vision of Robert Elsmere and the utopian ideals of Mrs Ward's architects were transformed by the very immediate realities of social reform and philanthropy. The neo-Byzantine pleasure palace of E. R. Robson, the feudal 'theatre' of the Barnetts, and the elegant essay in utopian planning by Cecil Brewer and Dunbar Smith spoke of desperate solutions to the ills of London. Ultimately the dreams of novelists, architects, and, in piecemeal efforts, philanthropists, would be virtually replaced by State intervention.

Epilogue

The most obvious realm in which progressive London architects found expression for their ambitions was council housing. Under the Artisans' and Labourers' Dwellings and Improvement Act of 1875 (the Cross Act), local authorities had the power to clear slums but were required to provide new accommodation in their place. This could mean, as it often did in London, the construction of housing by philanthropic housing trusts or companies. Whereas slum clearance and housing improvements were made in the 1860s and 1870s, the London County Council, established in 1889, soon entered the field of housing provision.[82] The Council's first housing scheme was the Boundary Street Estate in Bethnal Green and Shoreditch, which was underway in 1890, replacing one of the most notorious slums, the 'Old Nichol', the setting for Arthur Morrison's vivid novel of slum life and the advent of council housing, *The Child of the Jago* of 1896. Boundary Street was soon followed by the Millbank Estate in Pimlico [**91**]. In spite of budgetary restraints which inevitably ensued in creating housing which would be both built to a high standard and affordable to the poor, the direct intervention of government in housing for the poor marked a significant break with reliance on philanthropy.

Young, socially committed architects worked for the London County Council.[83] Owen Fleming, for example, who had been associated with Smith and Brewer at University Hall, led the Housing Branch of the LCC. Like them he had been influenced by Lethaby. In recalling a colleague, a private secretary to the Council, Fleming wrote of their time together in the East End:

> He and I were on the same quest. We were oppressed by the chain of circumstances that had compelled so many of the poor to live in insanitary dwellings. We were trying to get to the bottom of things, and had each of us felt that settlement life hardly afforded those opportunities for intimate contact with the question that we were seeking.[84]

The early experiments at Boundary Street and Millbank left many problems unresolved, particularly the need to supply adequate housing

91] Millbank Estate, Pimlico, showing central garden, 1900, architects London County Council

for the very neediest, as the Council clung to the hope of improving housing standards without raising the rates. Yet both estates were built to a high standard and in a manner which contrasted sympathetically to the grim barrack-like housing of philanthropic trusts.[85] On an extremely tight budget and under the watchful eye of the ratepayer, the architects produced buildings inspired again by Philip Webb, drawing on vernacular traditions of red brick with sculptural chimneys and picturesque gables, restricted to four storeys in height. At Boundary Street there was a circular garden from which the streets radiated. At Millbank, too, there was a picturesque central garden. The vast majority of flats at Millbank were self-contained, departing from the 'associated' plan of shared WC and scullery usually provided in working class housing schemes.

The architectural staff of the Housing Branch was actively involved in the Society for the Protection of Ancient Buildings,[86] which was associated above all with William Morris and John Ruskin. Its membership included Philip Webb, Lethaby, J. J. Stevenson, George Jack, Ernst Gimson, Walter Crane, Emery Walker, Ernest Newton, and Arthur Liberty, all associated with Arts and Crafts design. A sympathy with Arts and Crafts ideals comes through in Owen Fleming's admiration for the workers who actually built the buildings. In speaking before the RIBA he told his audience, 'If any members of this Institute are ever tempted to visit Boundary Street, and find the workmanship worthy of admiration, will they think of the silent unnamed workers, by whose patient labour this great structure has been built?'[87]

Even fictional characters came to reject the piecemeal largesse of philanthropists. When, in the novel *Lord of Latimer Street* by Jane Wardle (Oliver Madox Heuffer) of 1907, young Lord Latimer comes to south London, disguised as a common lodger to reside in the tenements he himself owns in order to discover the real life of the district and its needs, the local residents dissuade him from his plans to transform their world by means of philanthropic schemes:

> 'Openin' a Free Library? Its the game they're all at nowadays. Be more Free Libraries than books to put in 'em soon. Seem to think it'll make a man forget his belly's empty so long as 'e can cram 'is 'ead with the bettin' news in a Free Library'[88]

When the hero proposes to pull down four streets of tenements for a recreation ground, he is told that the housing is sorely needed so that local residents can live near their employment. Worse, he is asked

> 'If I want to live by my work, 'oos this bloomin lord that 'e can say I shan't? Tell-you-what-it-is, mate, there's those that grumbles at these

rich blokes for not doin' what they ought. I say it's a bloomin' good thing when they don't. I don't go round a-worryin' them about where they oughter live, an' 'ow they oughter bring up their children, do I? . . .

What's it got to do with this 'ere lord, 'ow we lives? Whey carn't 'e spend 'is money in 'aving a good time?'[89]

And young Lord Latimer ruefully reflects that

He had come down full of the knowledge of his own powers, as was but natural to one of his age and sex, feeling certain that he had but to interest himself to find out what – if anything – was wrong, in order to put all things right. He had come to realise already – and this may pass for some tribute to his understanding – that the Walls of Jericho will no longer fall before the mere sounding of the trumpet.[90]

Whereas in the first half of the twentieth century there was a growing commitment by government to the provision of education and welfare, recent experience in both Britain and the United States revealed how vulnerable such commitments could be. Again, conservative leadership enjoined private philanthropy to play a larger role in dealing with urban poverty, as government support was withdrawn. In Britain the public was presented, once again, with a revival architecture rooted in nostalgia, which spoke of paternalism and social deference.

Notes

1 Rosemary Aston in the Introduction, to Mrs Humphry (Mary) Ward, *Robert Elsmere* (1888; rpt. Oxford: Oxford University Press, 1987), p. vi.
2 W. E. Gladstone, '"Robert Elsmere" and the Battle of Belief', *The Nineteenth Century* (May 1888), pp. 766–88.
3 W. Besant, 'On University Settlements', in W. Reason (ed.), *University and Social Settlements* (London: Methuen, 1898), p. 7.
4 W. S. Peterson, 'Gladstone's review of Robert Elsmere: some unpublished correspondence', in *The Review of English Studies* 21 (1970), p. 448.
5 B. Willey, 'How "Robert Elsmere" struck some contemporaries', *Essays and Studies*, 10 (1957), p. 55.
6 L. Trilling, *Matthew Arnold* (1939; rpt. New York and London: Harcourt Brace Jovanovich, 1954), p. 316.
7 From a letter to Lord Acton of 13 January 1887 in J. Morley, *The Life of William Ewart Gladstone*, 2 (New York: Macmillan, 2nd edn, 1911), p. 357.
8 Mrs Humphrey Ward, *A Writer's Recollections* (New York and London: Harper and Brothers, 1918) 1, pp. 220–1.
9 Ward, *Robert Elsmere*, p. 400.
10 *Ibid.*, p. 473.
11 Ward acknowledged the relationship between her character and T. H. Green: *A Writer's Recollections*, 1, p. 132.
12 *Ibid.*

13 Ward, *Robert Elsmere*, pp. 512–13.
14 Mrs G. M. Trevelyan, *The Life of Mrs Humphry Ward by her Daughter, Janet Penrose Trevelyan* (London: Constable, 1923), p. 25.
15 According to G. Sutherland, *Policy-Making in Elementary Education 1870–1895* p. 316, fn. 18, Acland recognised himself as the model for the character and quarrelled with the author; they never spoke again.
16 V. Colby, *The Singular Anomaly: Women Novelists of the Nineteenth Century* (New York: New York University Press, 1970), p. 169, fn. 11.
17 R. L. Wolff, *Gains and Losses: Novels of Faith and Doubt in Victorian England* (New York: Garland Publishing, 1977), p. 455.
18 *Ibid.*, p. 459.
19 J. Sutherland, *Mrs Humphry Ward: Eminent Victorian, Pre-Eminent Edwardian* (Oxford: Clarendon Press: 1990), pp. 114–15.
20 Colby, *Singular Anomaly*, p. 115.
21 Willey, 'How "Robert Elsmere" struck some contemporaries', p. 56.
22 The book found a wide audience in the United States as well, prompting one reviewer to assert that 'No book since *Uncle Tom's Cabin* has had so sudden and wide a diffusion among all classes of readers . . . and perhaps the best sign of all, it has been preached against by the foremost clergymen of all denominations.' W. R. Thayer as quoted by Willey, 'How "Robert Elsmere" struck some contemporaries', p. 57.
23 Trevelyan, *The Life of Mrs Humphry Ward*, p. 79. Henrietta Barnett includes Mrs Ward as one of the people who lent their country homes for visits from students at Toynbee Hall as well as for poor children. Mrs Ward was also a lecturer at Toynbee Hall.
24 Trevelyan, *The Life of Mrs Humphrey Ward*, p. 79.
25 Ward, *A Writers Recollections*, 2, p. 146.
26 C. H. Herford, *Philip Henry Wicksteed* (London and Toronto: J. M. Dent, 1931), p. 99.
27 Trevelyan, *The Life of Mrs Humphry Ward*, p. 85.
28 Herford, *Philip Henry Wickstead*, pp. 96–7.
29 Revd P. H. Wicksteed, 'Early memories of University Hall by its first Warden', *In Memoriam: Mrs Humphry Ward and the Passmore Edwards Settlement*: Mary Ward Settlement, 1921, pp. 22–3.
30 Ward, *A Writer's Recollections*, 2, p. 147.
31 As quoted by E. P. Hennock, 'Poverty and social theory in England: the experience of the 1880s', *Journal of Social History* (1 January 1976), p. 71.
32 Ward, *A Writer's Recollections*, 2, p. 146.
33 *Ibid.*, p. 147.
34 *Ibid.*
35 As quoted by Trevelyan, *The Life of Mrs Humphry Ward*, p. 84.
36 J. Sutherland, *Mrs Humphry Ward*, p. 220.
37 Ward, *Robert Elsmere*, p. 548.
38 'New Social Settlement for Central London', *London* (7 October 1897), p. 803.
39 J. Rodgers, *Mary Ward Settlement (Late Passmore Edwards Settlement): A History 1891–1931*, Passmore Edwards Series, No. 1, Horace Fleming (ed.), p. 6.
40 Colby, *Singular Anomaly* p. 121.
41 T. H. Ward, *The Reign of Queen Victoria*, 2, (London: 1887), p. 546.
42 In her *Recollections* Mrs Ward recalled how she and her husband had decorated their first home together with 'the fashion of the movement which sprang from Morris and Burne-Jones' and how in their circle the women 'donned . . .

Liberty gowns', p. 160. When the Wards moved to London, chimney pieces by Norman Shaw were fitted in the drawing room: J. Sutherland, *Mrs Humphry Ward*, p. 83.

43 M. Richardson, *Architects of the Arts and Crafts Movement* (London: Trefoil Books, 1983), p. 140. Hack and Waller did not submit designs. Only the entries by Ricardo and Horsley survive, *The British Architect*, 44.

44 The two surviving unsuccessful entry designs published in *The British Architect* would appear to suggest the alternatives deemed possible in this competition: whereas the design by Ricardo is reminiscent of Toynbee Hall or Oxford House, the entry by Horsley, with its mural designs, is closer to the work of Townsend or Smith and Brewer.

45 Alan Crawford notes their involvement in Ashbee's project to survey London for buildings which should be safeguarded for preservation; Smith and Brewer took on Whitechapel, *C. R. Ashbee: Architect, Designer and Romantic Socialist* (New Haven and London: Yale University Press, 1986), p. 60.

46 See C. R. Ashbee, 'A tea-party', in *The Building of Thelema* (London: J. M. Dent and Sons, 1910), pp. 168–82.

47 F. MacCarthy, *The Simple Life: C. R. Ashbee in the Cotswolds* (Berkeley: University of California Press, 1981), pp. 55–6.

48 William Morris in a letter of 1882 to Mrs Burne-Jones, in P. Henderson (ed.), *The Letters of William Morris to His Family and Friends* (London: Longmans, Green and Co., 1979), p. 157.

49 *The Builder* of 12 April 1884, p. 504, notes that Morris spoke on the subject of Art and Socialism at the fourth annual picture exhibition arranged by the Barnetts in Whitechapel. Henrietta Barnett includes Morris's name in the list of interesting dinner party guests that they entertained at Toynbee Hall, in *Canon Barnett*, 1, p. 216.

50 See M. Swenarton, *Artisans and Architects: the Ruskinian Tradition in Architectural Thought* (London: Macmillan, 1989), pp. 48–60 for a discussion of Webb's relationship to the socialist cause.

51 As quoted, 1886, in H. Barnett, *Canon Barnett*, 2, p. 152.

52 *Ibid.*, p. 172.

53 H. Barnett, 'Pictures for the Poor', S. and H. Barnett (eds), *Practicable Socialism: Essays on Social Reform* (London: Longmans, Green & Co., 1888; rpt. New York: Books for Libraries Press, 1972), pp. 124–5.

54 H. Barnett, *Canon Barnett: His Life, Work and Friends* (London: John Murrey, 1918), 2, p. 179.

55 From a summary report held at the Horniman Museum and Library.

56 W. Crane, *Of the Decoration of Public Buildings* (1897), p. 138.

57 *Ibid.*, pp. 164–6. The desire to find ways in which art could convey a meaningful social message as the expression of a co-operative effort can be seen in the masque produced by the Art Workers' Guild in 1899 before the Lord Mayor of London; participants included Crane, Lethaby, Townsend, Ashbee and May Morris (daughter of William Morris) among others. See the special Summer Number (1899), *Studio*.

58 Godfrey Rubens in the Introduction to the 1974 edition of W. R. Lethaby, *Architecture, Mysticism and Myth* (1891; rpt. London: Architectural Press, 1974), p. viii.

59 Lethaby, *Architecture, Mysticism and Myth*, pp. 7–8.

60 W. R. Lethaby addressing the Technical Education Board at the Central Art Department on the subject of 'Modern Building Design' as quoted in *The Builder* (2 November 1895), pp. 311–12.

61 R. Weir, 'William Richard Lethaby', *Architectural Association Journal*, 73 (June 1957), p. 10.

62 Owen Fleming in the *Journal of the Royal Institute of British Architects* (27 April 1935), p. 738.

63 I am particularly indebted to Adrian Forty, both in conversation and in his written analysis of the Mary Ward Settlement to be found in *The Architects' Journal* (2 August 1989), pp. 28–49.

   It is important to note that the architects of the Passmore Edwards Settlement left no written records; their intentions must be gleaned largely from an examination of the building itself.

64 Forty, p. 37.

65 *Ibid.*, p. 38.

66 *Ibid.*, pp. 46–7.

67 *Ibid.*, p. 48.

68 *Ibid.*, p. 41.

69 Lethaby, *Architecture, Mysticism and Myth*. pp. 2–3.

70 *Ibid.*, p. 266.

71 'The Passmore Edwards Settlement', *The British Architect*, (25 February 1889), p. 124.

72 G. L. Morris and E. Wood, 'The architecture of the Passmore Edwards Settlement', *Studio: an Illustrated Magazine of Fine and Applied Arts*, 16 (1899), pp. 11–18.

73 Mrs Humphry Ward, 'Social Ideal', *Manchester Guardian*, 11 October 1897.

74 Mrs Humphry Ward in an open letter soliciting funds, February 1918, Mary Ward Centre Archives.

75 J. Sutherland, *Mrs Humphry Ward*. p. 224.

76 *Ibid.*, p. 217.

77 *Ibid.*, p. 221.

78 H. Barnett, *Canon Barnett*, 1, p. 389.

79 Rodgers, *Mary Ward Settlement*, pp. 9–14.

80 According to Miss Milligan, Head Teacher of the Invalid School, in the *Memoriam* of June 1921 on the death of Mrs Humphry Ward.

81 J. Sutherland, *Mrs Humphry Ward*, pp. 227–9.

82 A hindrance to what ultimately was Council ownership and management of housing estates was the legal requirement for councils to sell housing within one year of its completion unless special consent was granted. This was not changed until the Housing Act of 1909. See G. Gibbon and R. Bell, *History of the London County Council 1889–1939* (London: Macmillan, 1939), p. 370.

83 For an account of the LCC architects see S. Beattie, *A Revolution in London Housing: LCC Architects and Their Work 1893–1914* (London: Greater London Council and Architectural Press, 1980); or A. Service, 'The Architect's Department of the London County Council 1888–1914', in A. Service (ed.), *Edwardian Architecture and Its Origins* (London: Architectural Press, 1975), pp. 406–11.

84 Quoted by Beattie, *A Revolution in London Housing*, p. 21, for the LCC *Staff Gazette* (June 1901), pp. 71–2.

85 In documenting the English architectural scene in 1904 for a German audience, Hermann Muthesius included the achievements at Boundary Street and Millbank: *The English House* (Berlin, 1904; rpt. London: Granada Publishing, 1979), p. 60.

86 Beattie, *A Revolution in London Housing*, p. 17.

87 O. Fleming, 'The rebuilding of the Boundary Street Estate'. *Journal of the Royal Institute of British Architects* (7 April 1900), p. 273.

88 Jane Wardle, *The Lord of Latimer Street* (London: Alston Rivers, 1907), p. 225. In assessing the attitude of the 'multitude' in *The Condition of England* (1909; rpt. London: Methuen 1960), p. 92, C. F. G. Masterman cites the attitudes toward philanthropy in this novel.

89 Wardle, *The Lord of Latimer Street*, p. 227.

90 *Ibid.*, p. 256.

INDEX

Note: all page references to figures are in *italics*